Look Before Leaping

Look Before Leaping

Risks, Liabilities, and Repair of Study Abroad in Higher Education

Gregory F. Malveaux

ROWMAN & LITTLEFIELD
Lanham • Boulder • New York • London

Published by Rowman & Littlefield
A wholly owned subsidiary of The Rowman & Littlefield Publishing Group, Inc.
4501 Forbes Boulevard, Suite 200, Lanham, Maryland 20706
www.rowman.com

Unit A, Whitacre Mews, 26-34 Stannary Street, London SE11 4AB

Interior illustrations created by Lisa Malveaux

British Library Cataloguing in Publication Information Available

Library of Congress Cataloging-in-Publication Data

Library of Congress Cataloging-in-Publication Data Available
ISBN 978-1-4758-2555-8 (cloth : alk. paper) -- ISBN 978-1-4758-2556-5 (pbk. : alk. paper) -- ISBN 978-1-4758-2557-2 (electronic)

∞ ™ The paper used in this publication meets the minimum requirements of American National Standard for Information Sciences Permanence of Paper for Printed Library Materials, ANSI/NISO Z39.48-1992.

Printed in the United States of America

Contents

Foreword

Look Before Leaping: Risks, Liabilities, and Repair of Study Abroad in Higher Education is an important and praiseworthy work about many subjects. Yet, I would like to focus on a subject that I know particularly well that this work focuses on—leadership. I have stressed in numerous talks in the country and around the world, as well as through published work, that real leadership takes the courage to tell people what they don't want to hear. It requires investment, honesty, and personal accountability. Dr. Malveaux does not mince words in this work; leaders of study abroad, international education, and global studies are put on notice about the potential risks with study abroad, how program leaders can improve in their delivery, and needed solutions to enhance safety with international travel. His investment, honesty, and call for accountability are expertly communicated.

It takes a lot of work and a certain amount of wisdom to lead. Leaders have to accept that they may step into a bear trap or fall off a cliff. My years in the military gave me the tools to become a great leader through having to act—whether months spent abroad training the Egyptian Army, or years committed to completing military missions in Korea; or at home to secure and repair a devastated New Orleans after one of the worst national disasters ever with the aftermath of Hurricane Katrina. Dr. Malveaux uses his experience and that of other experts to fulfill a mission that shows leaders in the field how to fully know the risks involved, understand methods for navigating through those risks, be aware of past legal issues, understand techniques to ensure student safety, and know when to apply those techniques.

Dr. Malveaux's work is pivotal in its purpose of guiding program leaders in the right path to avoid going over the cliff, and in turn, not having the group follow. He has outlined careful planning, rigorous work, and proper utilization of resources (this is also what we do in the military) that needs to happen to effectively lead study abroad in higher education.

In the military, if we don't view our job as a mission, with a specific task to be completed in a specific time frame tied to a specific purpose, we put our organization and the organization of others at risk. In the worst-case scenario, we put other's lives at risk. With *Look Before Leaping,* Dr. Malveaux also connects the importance of having a mission. He reveals that it is essential for study abroad program leaders and student participants to realize their own mission, and properly prepare for it. Dr. Malveaux shows that outlining roles and responsibilities, giving strong pre-departure orientation sessions, introducing risk-averting documents, utilizing institutional mission and conduct standards, and other means bring clarity to the mission of safe study abroad. We share the belief that people are essential Ambassadors of the world. We share our mission to our people so that they know the significance of what they do and its impact on others.

Through *Look Before Leaping,* Dr. Malveaux shows that high stakes are involved with leading study abroad in higher education. Dr. Malveaux makes clear that uninformed study abroad participants, and poor decision-making or neglect by program leaders, can bring forth a worst-case scenario, even death, as a result. Dr. Malveaux brings enlightenment with risk assessment, guidance, and leadership approaches for program supervisors and students. Dr. Malveaux's well-selected, carefully described court cases with study abroad tragedies show the major stakes with proper delivery of study abroad programs, and suitable duty of care for participants.

With the trials we face today with terrorism, kidnapping, identity theft, cyber security, and other issues that can occur overseas, the desire to isolate ourselves is an easy temptation, but is limiting. Dr. Malveaux also recognizes that our future and our safety are not in becoming more isolated. Our future is in becoming more global. *Look Before Leaping* shows our need to work through overseas threats to continue to be a presence throughout the world. Now more than ever, American students are needed around the world to bring goodwill, and return home to give our nation a global perspective we greatly need. Dr. Malveaux's work confirms that he sees American students as a major defense to dispel foreign misconceptions of US citizens. Like Dr. Malveaux, I agree that we as Americans should understand the global environment and willingly take part in it. *Look Before Leaping* is a call to do so.

At the same time, Dr. Malveaux uncovers the more common threats that students are likely to encounter overseas. For example, you're a lot more likely to be killed by a mosquito than a terrorist. Dr. Malveaux discloses cases of study abroad students stricken by disease from insect bites, yet also gives precautionary and emergency response measures to combat this threat, just as he does for other common threats overseas. A sudden hurricane, earthquake, or tsunami can strike with little warning. I know from my own efforts to rebuild the communities in New Orleans after the wake of Hurricane Katrina that when trouble hits, an organization has to adjust immediately, and the leader's first job is to work through the chaos and confusion. Dr. Malveaux provides three very important chapters that contain 23 well-detailed "Best Practices" to avoid risks and liabilities with study abroad.

Look Before Leaping is an important work. Whether your work is in the military, business, education, or another field, this book speaks to anyone who faces potential crises, and ways to prevent them. This book addresses the need for leadership necessary in our global society, and for gaining improved cultural competency, as Dr. Malveaux describes, with our overseas neighbors. Our author shows us the turmoil that can come with leaping haphazardly into study abroad and overseas travel. He uncovers the havoc that program leaders bring when they are ill equipped for the task. *Look Before Leaping* can serve as a guide for practically all subjects related to risk assessment and leadership, and gives lessons that can be applied to life as a whole.

—**LTG Russel L. Honoré**, US Army, Retired, www.generalhonore.com

Preface

My Encounter with Nelson Mandela and My Life's Journey

A chance meeting with civil rights activist Nelson Mandela, who had only been recently released from prison, set the course for my life's journey. It occurred during my first travel experience abroad as a high school student, exploring Africa through Cairo, Luxor, and Aswan, Egypt; as well as Harare, Lupane, Victoria Falls, and Beitbridge, Zimbabwe. I gained acculturation of ancient civilizations, but no lessons eclipsed the impact of meeting a living, historical icon.

On an aircraft headed to Zimbabwe, a few half-hearted murmurs passed from passengers as the flight attendant announced a few dignitaries aboard. But then the plane erupted (figuratively speaking, of course) when her voice rose, punctuating: "Newly-freed prisoner Nelson Mandela is on our flight!" A mix of gasps and excited exclamations were followed by a stampede toward the first-class section of the plane.

Now, her voice came back in earnest: "Everyone, please take your seat! The craft cannot properly function with such a poor distribution of weight! Mr. Mandela will come and greet each and every one of you at your seat." And that is exactly what this gracious man did, walking down the aisle of coach seating receiving each and every passenger as if acknowledging an old acquaintance.

That day, I realized that only by leaving the familiarly safe environment of home could I experience such a thing. I made the decision to give myself every opportunity to take in the world and become a global citizen.

Look Before Leaping: Risks, Liabilities, and Repair of Study Abroad in Higher Education is the result of a lifetime of exposure, research, and leadership in study abroad—as a student who studied abroad, an instructor and director of the English and U.S. Business Department at Yonok College in Thailand, producer of a doctoral dissertation on overseas risks and liabilities, and as a professor and coordinator of Study Abroad at Montgomery College for over a decade and a half. This book is a culminating result of my passion as a global citizen.

As the book title implies, too often students *and* program leaders jump into study abroad without properly researching the risks involved. Sometimes the results are tragic, even deadly. Students need to be fully aware of the potential risks and weigh their own responsibilities as participants. Unfortunately, faculty leaders with too little training or leaders who are negligent on the job have contributed to mishaps abroad. Fittingly, students and their parents are leveling study abroad programs with more and more lawsuits. Study abroad programs, and institutions' reputations, may be decimated in the aftermath.

This book is produced for both the coordinator who creates study abroad and the participant who desires to engage in it. Each must be scrupulous and *look before leaping.*

Acknowledgments

First I want to thank you, Lisa, my loving wife. Thank you for providing daily wisdom and grace for me, and extra care for our spirited son, Gabriel, while I worked on this book. Dad, big brother Courtney, Suzanne, and Suzette, thank you for your support and highly constructive feedback. General Honoré, you are one of the great leaders of our time with crisis management, and I feel so honored to have your written Foreword to the book. It is truly appreciated. Rebecca, Malissa, and Randal, your assistance was such an asset. Thank you. I also want to express my gratitude to all of the experts who were interviewed for this book. Your instructive insights were so essential to this work. And I thank God for blessing this work. In these ways, and so many more that remain unstated, I thank you all.

Introduction

The reality is that study abroad leaders, students, and institutions have been quite fortunate considering the degree of risks involved and rather limited number of resources available for study abroad implementation. With current court trends, study abroad programs and their institutions are being held far more accountable for damages than in previous years.

Even with the risks involved, study abroad is the most highly impactful, cutting-edge form of education available. Don't most worthwhile endeavors have a certain degree of risks attached? Study abroad is no exception.

To say that study abroad is worth pursuing is an understatement. As a high school student, my first overseas experience brought a fortunate chance encounter with Nelson Mandela. Even now as an old hand with study abroad, with every new program that I lead, a rush of excitement fills me as I anticipate the new chance encounters my students will face.

I stand by my premise that truly transformative events take hold when you are willing to leave the familiar safe haven of your own backyard. Of course, that *backyard* is figurative for the *United States*. Mark Twain expressed it best: "Travel is fatal to prejudice, bigotry, and narrow-mindedness, and many of our people need it sorely on these accounts. Broad, wholesome, charitable views of men and things cannot be acquired by vegetating in one little corner of the earth all one's lifetime" (Twain, 1869, p. LXII).

One should not deny themselves the opportunities that come with study abroad due to its inherent risks, especially when you consider that those risks may be averted or resolved. This is what the book sets out to do.

The reality is that not everyone wants to hear, or have publicized, the fact that intrinsic risks come with study abroad. As coordinators, we cannot be concerned that this fact, or this book, may be used as fodder for opponents of study abroad who view it as too risky to support. Many of you work within institutional frameworks where supervisors hold such limited views. I encourage you to remain dauntless in your tasks. You understand the value of your work.

My passion, shared by my counterparts, to bring life-altering study abroad experiences to students demand there be forthright communication on the risks and liabilities with overseas studies. Exposing shortcomings will set us on the right path to improving its overall quality. It is a major motivating factor for writing this book, along with an overwhelming desire to honor the voices of study abroad sufferers, whose accounts are shared in lawsuits and court cases. These cases are not presented to sensationalize the mishaps, but to draw them out so that we can closely scrutinize what could have been done to prevent them. And hopefully, we can do better in the future.

The devotion that coordinators have with leading study abroad is without question (table 2.1, Key Demographic Characteristics of Coordinators in chapter 2, provides key demographic data about the contributing coordinators for the book.) For example, when asked "What are the major highlights of working in your profession?" consider the selfless reflection of Coordinator Trevor, who has led study abroad for twenty-five years—"There's no real enjoyment for me in seeing these places, but the real enjoyment for me is seeing the look on these kids' faces. We don't live in one county, we don't live in the State, we don't live just in the United States; we live in the world . . . we're in a global society. We're not in a national or state or county society."

My counterparts make up a group of professionals who are as passionate and dedicated in what they do as any person in their respective field. Yet they are human, and in this book I "call them out" for errors with program approaches, just as quickly as I give them praise. Many lessons can be learned from their experiences. There is a shortage in literature with scrutinizing the risks, liabilities, and repair of study abroad in higher education, and it needs to be filled.

Again, the reality is a degree of risk accompanies study abroad—those hazards, which may consequently lead to liabilities, continue to increase, just as steadily as study abroad participation with its record numbers coming each subsequent year. This book unearths, through court documents, the risks and liabilities plaguing study abroad. The truth is that incidents are numerous enough that no book can fully present every peril. The good news is that if practical safeguards and solutions are put into place, as this book proposes to do, even the undiscovered can be averted through understanding the broad landscape of hazards to avoid.

To clarify, I am not an attorney and am not attempting to impart legal advice. I describe legal cases to show trends in litigation that I believe significantly impact study abroad. I attempt to inform the reader of hazards that led to lawsuits and ways to avoid them. As a coordinator, I provide potential resolutions for combating risks and liabilities.

College and university officials are becoming more vigilant about providing a "duty of care" to study abroad students by increasing focus and measures to ensure their well-being. The expectation is that by providing best practices, taking close scrutiny of impractical elements in risk-averting documents, and using the generous advice from interviewed experts (coordinators, directors, and/or administrators of study abroad, international education, and global studies), additional safeguards for study abroad students, coordinators, and institutions will result.

ORGANIZATION OF THE BOOK

The audience that the book predominantly addresses is experts (coordinators, directors, and administrators) of study abroad, international education, global studies, and analogous departments. A secondary, yet equally important, audience that motivated the book is students of study abroad and their supportive parents.

Chapter 1, The Growth, Evolution, and Aspects of Study Abroad, addresses the issues of study abroad growth; its evolution, enrichment, and lucky streak; a new litigious culture; 9-11; gender disparity; the umbrella of study abroad; a conceptual framework; and research elements for the book. It delivers recent statistical data to show that students are presently pursuing study abroad more than in any other period in American higher education, even with new and increasing reports in the media about tragedy abroad. The chapter also reveals that study abroad is a highly impactful, cutting-edge form of education that makes it well worth pursuing, despite the inherent risks that accompany it. At the same time, the reality is that study abroad leaders, students, and institutions have been quite fortunate considering the degree of risks involved and the minimal guidance offered, at times, to students when study abroad programs are implemented.

The chapter establishes that current court trends are holding study abroad programs and their institutions increasingly accountable for damages than in previous years, and college and university officials need to become more vigilant about providing a "duty of care" to study abroad students by increasing the focus and measures to ensure their safety and well-being while overseas.

The vast majority of study abroad participation by females is pointed out to explain a natural disparity in cases involving women, including in this book. The chapter provides a Conceptual Framework for Averting Risks in Study Abroad and key terms used in the text. It closes with noting that important findings from juridical texts, interviewed experts, and currently used institutional waivers of liability shape the book.

Chapter 2, The "LARGEST 3" Areas of Risks and Liabilities with Study Abroad, starts to explore separate lawsuits and cases brought against study abroad programs, their institutions, and the partnering agencies. The purpose is to show that three predominate issues have led to student tragedies overseas. I name this the "LARGEST 3": Liabilities And Risks in Global Education and Study-Travel tend to be most often linked to (1) medical risks; (2) sexual assault; and (3) supervisory neglect. Awareness of the LARGEST 3, along with steps that may be taken to avoid them, may dramatically reduce a student's potential to be at risk and institutions' exposure to lawsuits.

Also introduced is the fact that sample waivers and risk-advertising documents, including the Malveaux Sample Recommended Waiver, are examined throughout the book in order to give additional safeguards to coordinators and students of study abroad. These documents have served as a main line of defense with mixed results of protection provided; therefore, tips on bolstering these documents will be given.

This chapter clarifies that future chapters will present an array of tragic incidents and cases that consistently fall within the LARGEST 3 in an effort to expand reader awareness of such risks. This is often followed with recommended measures to avoid these hazards. Painful mistakes from the past must not be repeated!

Chapter 3, The Prevalence of Medical Risks and Resulting Lawsuits in Study Abroad, scrutinizes medical risks with study abroad, a main component of the LARGEST 3.

Related lawsuits and cases, such as one with Westmont College (a student was disfigured after contracting leishmaniasis from a mosquito bite while in Costa Rica), the University of Pittsburgh Semester at Sea Program (four U.S students were killed and three injured in a crash of a chartered bus in India), the University of Florida (a student in Bolivia was severely burned while studying when a kerosene lamp exploded), and *Paneno v. Centres for Academic Programmes* (a student of Pasadena Community College sustained paralysis, while in Florence, as a result of a fall from a sixth-floor balcony giving way), are examined.

These and other cases bring important insights on medical issues abroad. For example, study abroad participants often do not have proper medical coverage in place prior to departure or administrators frequently furnish participants with ineffective risk-averting documents and waivers with stock language containing inefficient details, which fail to adequately inform students or protect institutions from medical issues. Potential solutions for avoiding medical risks abroad come from the perspective of experts. Also, suggestions are given for designing more effective waivers and risk-averting documents.

The chapter also considers how to best serve students with disabilities, and deliberates on extraterritorial application of Section 504 (of the Rehabilitation Act) and the Americans with

Disabilities Act. To give coordinators awareness on ways to advise and serve students with disabilities, Resources for Coordinators to Aid Students with Disabilities and Top 10 List of Best Practices for Coordinators to Serve the Needs of Students with Disabilities sections are provided.

Chapter 4, Sexual Assault Risks and Liabilities with Study Abroad, closely considers the reoccurring issue of sexual assault abroad, which also makes up one of the "LARGEST 3."

Deep investigation of associated lawsuits shows that courts expect universities to remain conscientious of activities that may endanger students and bring forth lawsuits relative to sexual assault. Some closely surveyed suits and cases involve St. Mary's College (five female students in a study abroad group were ambushed and raped in Guatemala), *Earlham College v. Eisenberg* (a student alleged she was sexually harassed and raped by her host father while participating in the college's study abroad program in Japan), and *Bloss v. Univ. of Minnesota Board of Regents* (a student studying abroad in Mexico, en route to meet friends for a social evening, was raped at knifepoint by a taxi driver).

On a whole, this chapter explores the major issue of sexual assault with study abroad, as revealed by the courts and through experts. In addition, recommended protective measures come to help students evade this inherent risk, and coordinators are given advice on how to properly orient participants, both verbally and through written form, on this common danger.

Chapter 5, The Tragedy of Supervisory Neglect in Study Abroad, explores the frequency of supervisory neglect, a third of the most common risk types in the "LARGEST 3."

Some illustrative cases include *King v. Board of Control of Eastern Michigan University* (a supervisor fails to address a hostile environment in which female students are subjected to sexual harassment by male students while in South Africa), Radford University (a faculty member's poor decision to drive a truck with students results in an accident and death), and *Fay v. Thiel College* (supervisors leave a student for days with a minor illness in a Peruvian health clinic where she is subjected to unnecessary surgical removal of her appendix and is sexually assaulted by the surgeon and anesthesiologist).

Overall, this chapter emphasizes the major problem of supervisory neglect, its impacts on study abroad participants and programs, and considers what must be done to improve the ongoing problem.

Chapter 6, Increasing Concerns with Cyberthreats, Identity Theft, and Terrorist Acts, delves into growing issues that threaten study abroad (this may be through overseas internships, workforce development, service learning, or general study abroad) that are not new, but are increasingly worrisome for Americans: cybersecurity threats, identity theft, and terrorism. One section in the chapter considers how improved technology is being used overseas to steal information, hijack individuals' identities, and cause overall havoc.

A separate section considers a changing world landscape. This includes a current global refugee movement in which people are fleeing their homelands (Afghanistan, Eritrea, Libya, Pakistan, Somalia, Syria, and so forth) in pursuit of a better life. In addition, American travelers need to be aware of countries that are unsafe for travel, as terrorist attacks increasingly spread to areas that were once considered safe.

Terrorism is well defined in the chapter to help participants understand its outreach extends far beyond extremists in the Middle East. Study abroad participants need to be wary of their potential kidnapping. Human trafficking, whether it is labor trafficking or sex trafficking, is a serious threat. In addition, Americans are often seen as wealthy and may be kidnapped for ransom.

The chapter provides expert analysis and potential safeguards to combat mounting issues involving cybersecurity issues, identity theft, and terrorism abroad.

Chapter 7, The Experts' Advice on Best Practices #1-6, highlights essential insights gathered from personal interviews of higher-education coordinators and administrators of study abroad, global studies, and international education, who tackled such questions: "How can risks and liabilities be minimized in study abroad?" "What inspired you to provide career service to students?" "What influence do legal issues have upon your work approach?" "How do you explain/understand the major risks involved with conducting a study abroad program for students and their institutions?" "How can risks and liabilities be affected through the use of a waiver and other forms?"

The immense amount of information resulting from the experts' experiences and advice are organized into twenty-three of the most essential steps or best practices needed for reducing study abroad risks and legal repercussions. The first six out of twenty-three are detailed in this chapter and include:

- predeparture orientation
- parental/guardian involvement
- faculty leaders
- foreign institution partnerships
- reputable travel companies/agencies
- professional organizations/conferences

Each of the twenty-three steps, over the course of three chapters, is backed by analysis from coordinators who believe that each and every step must be heeded by colleagues to avoid risks for the student and liability for the institution. Overall, the raw analysis that comes with the voices of study abroad administrators provides great energy, authenticity, and personalization for each of the first six of twenty-three best practices described in the chapter. In addition, court cases and risk-averting documents are explored to further assist with securing safe practices in study abroad.

Chapter 8, The Experts' Advice: Best Practices #7–15 continues where chapter 7 left off, and chapter 9 ensues. This chapter also presents information from twenty-three of the most essential, best practices to reduce risks and liabilities, stemming from experts' encounters and advice. Additional support comes from legal trends and current risk-averting documents. The best practices are:

- foreign laws and cultural awareness
- participant selection process
- consultation with the institution's legal office
- reentry orientation
- program procedures
- participant medical history
- institutional administrators/committees
- passport, cash, and protection of other valuables
- U.S. State Department warnings

Just as it was the case in the previous chapter, the transparent discourse from coordinators is illuminating, honest, and passionate.

Chapter 9, The Experts' Advice: Best Practices #16–23 completes the twenty-three most critical and best practices to reduce hazards and legal issues with study abroad. These are also the outcomes of expert opinions, are supported by legal trends, and are punctuated by current risk-averting documents. These include:

- coordinator-to-student ratio
- emergency response plan
- participants with disabilities and the Americans with Disabilities Act
- waivers and their construction
- code of conduct and policy
- foreign housing assignments
- empowerment of program leaders
- trial and error

Chapter 10: Final Thoughts and Encouragement, closes with final advice for study abroad participants, coordinators, and administrators to avoid risks and liabilities in study abroad. I encourage my colleagues to continue with their strong work ethic and the duty of care that they have provided students.

In addition, with this chapter I comment that there is a bit of reticence among coordinators to disclose information about their programs, or to openly share risk-management documents. Yet this was not "across the board." This lack of transparency serves to weaken study abroad. I fear that unnecessary concerns about judgment could limit the effectiveness of study abroad program delivery and put people at unnecessary risk.

I reflect that as study abroad evolves so does its potential for serving the greater good of our students in higher education, as well as our neighbors around the world. To bring this book to full circle, I reiterate its overall purpose—*to ultimately protect students (and put their loved ones at ease), programs, and institutions*. I am optimistic about the continuing growth and evolution of the best educational approach (study abroad) available being done in a safe manner. I end the book the way I began it, acknowledging that similar to my own experience, a first study abroad endeavor has the potential to alter the course of one's life. But never jump into it blindly. Always "look before leaping."

Chapter One

The Growth, Evolution, and Aspects of Study Abroad

Among other things, this chapter provides recent statistical data to show that students are presently pursuing study abroad more than at any period in American higher education, even with new and increasing reports in the media about tragedy abroad. One reason for this is that amid today's unstable environment with institutions of higher education, study abroad has easily evolved to meet the professional and educational goals of contemporary American students.

Research and literature leaves no doubt that study abroad is a very educationally enriching experience. Even more so, what truly distinguishes study abroad from other higher education offerings are opportunities with workforce development, service learning, and practical internship work often not attainable on campus and in the local community.

Yet the truth is that inherent risks come with study abroad, and many issues remain unreported or are settled out of court. By considering common risks and ways to avert them, coordinators can increase safety for students and protect their institutions from liability issues.

The chapter explores other topics, including an unexpected outcome left by the September 11, 2001, attacks, and a unique gender disparity with study abroad participation. This gender difference serves to explain the reason for more cases of hardship endured by females with study abroad.

Both a conceptual framework for risk avoidance and a list of key terms give important insight for readers. Last, the chapter details how court documents, experts' analysis, and institutional waivers of liability serve to be essential forces that determine risks, liabilities, and best practices for study abroad.

STUDY ABROAD ON THE RISE

Study abroad is on the rise. Study abroad by U.S. students has more than doubled in the past fifteen years.[1] In fact, the total number of current American students studying abroad is at an all-time high, and close to three hundred thousand American students studied abroad in the 2012 to 2013 academic year.[2] To be precise, 289,408 U.S. students studied abroad during the 2012 to 2013 academic year, with 66,408 more students enrolled than the previous year.[3]

STUDY ABROAD EVOLVING WITH THE GOALS OF CONTEMPORARY STUDENTS

The reasons that students are leaving in droves to take advantage of study abroad are numerous. These are not your Baby Boomers or Generation Xers whose reason to study abroad was almost exclusively to learn a new language and culture. According to those American students, they participated in these programs due to a desire to travel, to experience a new culture, and to improve their skills in a foreign language. [4]

Today's Millennials (born between 1980 and 2000) and Boomlets (born after 2001) continue to study abroad for these valuable reasons, *and* have brought expanded objectives to overseas education and training. This is the reason for immense study abroad expansion in the last decade, and why it will continue to exponentially grow in the future.

For these career-minded students, workforce development opportunities in their academic discipline serve as a driving force for overseas program choices. Often these are STEM (science, technology, engineering, and mathematics) students. These are students of nursing and health sciences working in state-of-the-art medical facilities in Gondar, Ethiopia; of chemistry and the environmental sciences interning at the Geothermal Power Plant of Hellisheid in Reykjavik, Iceland; of computer science and cybersecurity being sent abroad by Homeland Security to improve encoding and decoding methods.

American students majoring in STEM fields showed the largest increase in study abroad, up 9 percent from the prior year, outnumbering study abroad students in the social sciences, the second largest field. [5] In fact, study abroad increased among students majoring in all STEM fields, with the largest growth occurring in the health sciences, which increased by 15 percent. [6]

This increase in study abroad interest comes at a good time. There is a pressing need for a U.S. workforce that is more globally aware, more competent in foreign languages and intercultural skills, and more familiar with international business norms and behaviors. [7] Skills acquired through study abroad help to fill the void.

RESEARCH AND LITERATURE CONFIRM THAT STUDY ABROAD IS AN EDUCATIONALLY ENRICHING EXPERIENCE

There has not been a great degree of scholarly literature dedicated to considering risks and liabilities in study abroad, yet the literature has been quite constructive with addressing the positive outcomes of study abroad in the face of involved risks. In spite of the risks involved in study abroad, the professional development and educational outcomes that result from these programs far outweigh the sporadic issues that have risen. Unique to other curriculum programs, study abroad creates a far greater bond between student and coordinator than most courses. [8]

With this close bond, often a special relationship forms between university officials and students. [9] With living conditions, travel, meals, and student learning taking place abroad, the student and coordinator become far more dependent upon one another, and in order for student growth to take place, students need to actively engage in their environment. [10]

Overall, study abroad, with its nontraditional approach, has an advantage over traditional pedagogical approaches. As Astin et al. (2002) purports in his theory of student involvement, instructors have a major impact by encouraging a learning technique that promotes active learning for students beyond the walls of the classroom, and even beyond the campus itself. [11]

Well-developed, out-of-class experiences are a significant learning approach that provides engaged postsecondary undergraduates valuable educational development and shapes desirable student outcomes. [12] Out-of-class experiences allow students to learn more because they are actively involved in their education and have opportunities to apply what they are learning in different settings. [13] This is a main objective with study abroad.

As a result, the student is not a passive participant but a proactive contributor to activities while studying abroad. [14] Students who proactively participate in study abroad programs derive certain growth and development, as well as educational outcomes. [15]

Again, strong student development and desired educational outcomes have been derived from participation in study abroad. [16] Students involved in study abroad develop a sense of intercultural awareness, cultural pluralism, multicultural awareness, increased success in college, and "world-mindedness." [17]

This methodology to study abroad is not only supported by the literature but also is mirrored by experts in the field. Consider the work ethic of Coordinator Felix:

> We have a lot of work we put in [programs]: immersion projects, visits, and working with directors to make sure this remains one, an academic experience, and two, a cultural immersion experience in terms of community service. We want all of our students to do community service while abroad. And that gets them away from the university culture. We don't want them coming home just knowing the university culture [abroad either]. [We expose them to] the culture of the people— most people don't go to university anywhere in the world [and] do community service to see another aspect.

Within the same discussion, he deliberates on the impacts left upon participants:

> When [a student] says "this was the best semester or year of my life," we know exactly what it means. It does not mean they had just a great, fun time. No, we know what they mean. We know what the grades are, we know the service they did, [and] we know how the director immersed them in the culture through study trips, cultural tours, and things like that. So I think knowing that they've gotten this experience, and that has provided growth, that is most important.

Research supports the high-impact learning that accompanies study abroad and makes it a top option. Students are realizing this, and that is why study abroad enrollment has reached record numbers. But this is not the only reason. The various components that fall under the umbrella of study abroad make it matchless when compared to other higher education offerings.

INTERNSHIPS AND WORK ABROAD AS A PART OF THE "STUDY ABROAD" UMBRELLA

Internships and workforce development are major pieces to study abroad that provide students with essential vocational training, making them immediately marketable in today's global workforce. In other words, within the umbrella of *study abroad* are various opportunities including *work abroad*. Overseas internships make up a valuable part of work abroad. *Work abroad* is a broad term that describes an immersive experience in an international work environment where the primary purpose is educational, whether for academic credit or not. [18] By design, work abroad programs are temporary, lasting anywhere from a few weeks to two or three years, and they may or may not be related to specific career goals. [19] The key is that they are out-of-classroom experiences that are immersive and experiential. [20]

Students are cognizant that we live in a global workforce. Internships and work abroad prepare them to be necessary global specialists in the interweaving world economies that make up the twenty-first century. The ability to negotiate in a culturally sensitive manner with business people in India, speak Chinese with foreign ambassadors, or host a global web conference to train overseas faculty on a satellite campus will give students a distinct advantage in our global economy.

For this reason, foreign internships are highly sought after by students. In its annual Open Doors survey, the Institute of International Education (IIE) has collected data over the past decade on participation by U.S. students in credit-bearing internships abroad. There has been substantial growth in this sector, with close to seven hundred U.S. campuses reporting that twenty thousand of their students received credit for internships, volunteering, or work abroad in 2009 and 2010.[21] This represented a 7 percent increase over the prior year's total, and almost triple the number reported a decade ago.[22]

Just as safeguards are placed with traditional study abroad, so should protections be in place for students participating in internships abroad. As a guide for study abroad coordinators, a sample Internship Agreement form is provided (Appendix J).

The Internship Agreement is similar to other waivers of study abroad; the coordinator is the orchestrator of a solid academic and work plan. However, instead of having a partnering travel agency, the university coordinates with a work agency, simply referred to as an *AGENCY*. Responsibilities for both the university and agency should be outlined, as done in the sample form. Here is one of seven responsibilities outlined for the university:

I.02 <u>Placement Plan</u>: Provide the **AGENCY** with its overall plan for the placement of students at the **AGENCY** at least four weeks prior to the commencement of the academic term. The plan shall include, as a minimum, the objectives of the academic plan, the number of students to be assigned, the dates and times of assignment, and the level of each student's academic preparation. The **UNIVERSITY** shall consider any modification necessary to accomplish the reasonable requirements of the **AGENCY**.

Additionally, the Internship Agreement aptly provides a clear list of responsibilities that the partnering agency must abide by; this element actually makes it more instructive than many study abroad waivers that are currently utilized. Here is one of six conditions listed for the Agency:

II.01 <u>Primary Responsibility</u>: Plan and administer all aspects of internship responsibilities at facilities. The **AGENCY** has primary and ultimate responsibility for the quality of care, service, or operations, and as such, **AGENCY** staff have final responsibility, authority, and supervision over all aspects of quality of care, service, operations, and administrative operations. **UNIVERSITY** students shall at all times abide by such supervision.

The agreement goes so far as to outline fourteen "mutual responsibilities" between the University and Agency. This extensiveness also differentiates it from numerous waivers of study abroad currently in use. Hopefully, study abroad officials will find this risk-averting document, along with the others detailed in the book (and provided in the appendices), to be useful.

THE IMPORTANCE OF SERVICE LEARNING IN STUDY ABROAD

Not every study abroad official will agree that service learning is an important component of overseas study. However, this one certainly does. Service learning is work. If you speak to any of the students who have participated in one of my service-learning programs, they will concur. Recall, *work abroad* is a broad term that describes an immersive experience in an international work environment where the primary purpose is educational, *whether for academic credit or not.*[23] Students who are initially intimidated by a service-learning objective often go on to identify it as the most fulfilling component of a study abroad program.

INTERNATIONAL GOODWILL WITH SERVICE LEARNING

There is no greater activity than service learning to spread international goodwill. This has been my experience with leading study abroad. For example, with a program to Germany, a main objective was for students to conduct service learning at a farm for disabled youth. To give proper background, hippotherapy is a form of physical, occupational, and speech therapy that uses the characteristic movements of a horse to provide carefully graded motor and sensory input.[24] A few horses grazed on this small farm in Germany, but there was no horse track for the youth to use.

The service objective was for students to build a horse track so that the techniques of hippotherapy could be applied with disabled youth. The horse track needed to be a quarter mile in diameter, and dug out by shovel and pick ax. The clumsy plow was not able to cut out the necessary streamlined trenches. Then, the dirt needed to be loaded into wheelbarrows to be meticulously distributed among crop-bearing fields. After, the trenches needed to be filled with sod, a suitable surface for the horses to trek on.

As we worked on our task, alongside German volunteers and farm staff members, we were intermittently asked questions from them, including, "So you say that you are Americans?" Followed by, "We really appreciate your help, but why you are doing this? Don't you have some wealth?" Or they would inquire, "Aren't you going to spend time visiting the museums and such?" They could not fathom why, if we had the means to do "comfortable" activities in Germany, we would choose to be knee deep in dirt, shedding blood (minor injuries fortunately), sweat, and tears with them. This was something that they *had* to do and were flummoxed that this was something we *chose* to do.

News of the Americans' goodwill spread. A local newspaper was notified and a reporter came to do a story on this improbable *event*—Americans, out of sheer goodness, laboring shoulder to shoulder with German farmers. Students were given breaks to conduct interviews and reflect on the importance of this service, only adding to the educational value of the experience. Figure 1.1 shows the group picture, which appeared with the article in the local paper.

Figure 1.1.   Service Learning Group in Local German Newspaper

Other high-impact service-learning objectives from past programs served to be valuable experiences: building smokeless stoves in a rural community in South India, leading initiatives to build a water well and irrigation system in a drought-ridden Senegalese village, or postprogram sponsorships put toward the educational endeavors of Gambian students, to name a few. The point is that the educational and professional growth for students, and the global, political, economic, and social impacts resulting from service learning, are simply immeasurable.

RISK-AVERTING SERVICE-LEARNING FORMS

Analogous to any facet of study abroad, service-learning components must safeguard students from injury. In turn, risk-averting documents and predeparture orientation classes are essential for overseas service-learning participants. A sample Service Learning Agreement document has been provided for this purpose (see Appendix K).

Similar to the previously detailed sample Internship Agreement, the Service Learning Agreement suitably provides a section on Responsibilities of the University (six in total), and another section on Responsibilities of the Agency (five in total).

OVERALL, STUDY ABROAD HAS BEEN FORTUNATE

Although this book is comprehensive, in all honestly, it cannot possibly showcase the full extent of suits filed against study abroad programs and their institutions, and that is okay. This is why the book, in part, also takes great strides to provide problem-solving steps and sample documents to address risks and liabilities. You do not need to know about every suit that has been filed against study abroad in order to comprehend its major risks; in turn, necessary precautions can be taken to avoid past pitfalls.

Vincent R. Johnson, of St. Mary's University School of Law in Texas, rightly points out in *The Journal of College and University Law* that a majority of cases related to study abroad have probably been settled, rather than fully tried, which is common for tort claims.[25] For that reason, he says, "The number of unreported cases based on harm to students participating in study-abroad programs may be considerably larger than what appears in legal-research data-bases."[26]

Issues with study abroad are underreported, and the full scale of risks and liabilities in study abroad is not fully known. Even well-documented cases are often unfamiliar to coordinators and officials of higher education. An objective of this book is to bring to light the major risks involved with study abroad, court cases that have surrounded them, and lessons that may be learned to avoid them.

Overall, study abroad leaders and institutions have been rather fortunate, yet this climate has been steadily changing. As far as a couple of decades ago, courts began to hold study abroad programs and their institutions more accountable for damages than in previous years.[27] This tendency has only intensified in recent years.

Pearson and Beckham (2005) understand this developing mentality within the U.S. courts concerning proper duty of care for participants in study abroad: "Legal liability can arise if a duty of reasonable, prudent care was owed to the injured party, the duty was breached by one who owed that duty of care, and the breach may be said to have proximately caused an injury actionable in damages. While colleges and universities are not normally regarded as the insurers of a student's well-being, judges have imposed institutional liability for breach of a duty of care."[28]

The rise of study abroad participation and prevailing legal trends underscore the importance for providing reasonable and prudent care for students, improved safeguards for participants, and better defenses for colleges against liability.

THE UNEXPECTED IMPACT OF SEPTEMBER 11

The terrorist attacks of September 11, 2001, not only failed to discourage American students from studying overseas but also stoked new interest in students to gain improved familiarity with the world. Despite September 11, there seems to be opportunities for students to better understand the world, and that has translated into increased interest in studying abroad.[29]

But let's be honest. This new interest and growth in study abroad has not brought an expanded world landscape for American students to traverse. The international landscape continues to shrink for American students due to issues of safety. For example, the risk of terrorist acts perpetrated against Americans, including U.S. students, has become an ever-increasing concern. It was appropriate to have a chapter (chapter 6) recognize and scrutinize this serious issue with study abroad.

GENDER DISPARITY IN STUDY ABROAD

Among students studying abroad, the overwhelming majority has been female. This has been a consistent trend. So why bring this point forth? The main reason in identifying the gender disparity is to inform that it contributes to the disproportionate number of female-to-male court cases and lawsuits explored in the book. With more females taking part in study abroad, they have encountered a greater likelihood of injury.

In addition, one of the major hazards with study abroad is sexual assault. Females have a greater likelihood of being victims of this kind of peril than males. In turn, this also contributes to the greater number of cases and suits that involve females.

To further understand the phenomenon of this gender discrepancy, let's consider it more closely. Sixty-five percent of all American postsecondary students abroad during the 2012 to 2013 academic year were female, while only 35 percent of participants were male.[30]

The 2012 to 2013 academic year is not unique; studies conducted every year over the past decade by the Institute of International Education indicate a consistent gender participation imbalance.[31]

Hoffa and Pearson (1997) give three primary explanations for the long-standing gender imbalance: (1) study abroad participants have primarily come from female-dominated majors such as languages and the liberal arts; (2) cultural values in the United States encourage men to pursue more "serious" curricular matters while in college; and (3) women are expected to excel in social relations, and those can be enhanced by studying abroad.[32]

This is certainly an archaic view of study abroad and its participants. As noted in the earlier section, Study Abroad Evolving with the Goals of Contemporary Students, study abroad numbers have dramatically risen as contemporary students pursue overseas study for discipline-driven objectives (many being outside of the liberal arts field), workforce development, and purposeful service-learning endeavors to improve their employment marketability.

In fact, according to Open Doors 2010, the leading fields of study for Americans studying abroad are the social sciences (21 percent of those studying abroad) and business and management (20 percent).[33] Study abroad students can no longer be labeled liberal arts majors who hope to gain added cultural and social experiences. This is only a microcosm of study abroad today. There is an evolution taking place *and* notice that the gender disparity remains in place. We can safely conclude that women are helping to lead the shift.

This is consistent with the program experiences of coordinators. Female students still principally attend nonliberal arts study abroad programs. Female students predominately joined one of my science-heavy programs to Iceland with a focus on geology, chemistry, and environmental sciences that took place in the summer 2015. The same can be said for a program to Germany, Luxembourg, and Belgium that took place in the summer of 2013, with a focus on business and economics.

There was, admittedly, a slight increase of male student participation in these STEM-based programs, but again, the majority of interested participants were female students. At the same time, student engagement in study abroad within the liberal arts, for increased language proficiency or improved cultural competency, should not be devalued. These also make for valuable learning experiences. But to cast study abroad students, who happen to be a majority female, in such a limited light is inaccurate and outdated.

A CONCEPTUAL FRAMEWORK FOR AVERTING RISKS IN STUDY ABROAD

To further assist study abroad administrators, A Conceptual Framework for Risk Avoidance for Student Study Abroad is provided.

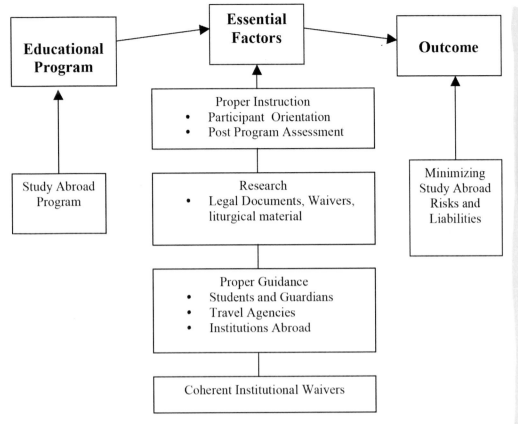

Figure 1.2.

The conceptual framework contains three main parts: educational program, essential factors, and outcome. The educational program influences the essential factors, which in turn leads to outcome. The educational program portion has only one subsection, study abroad program; similarly, the outcome portion has a single subsection, minimizing study abroad risks and liabilities.

Between educational program and outcome come the various essential factors that are: proper instruction, research, proper guidance, and coherent institutional waivers. With proper instruction, coordinators are expected to educate by means of participant orientation and postprogram assessment, as listed in the conceptual framework. Research, by institution officials, comes with that of legal documents, waivers, and liturgical materials.

Proper guidance or voiced expectations, by the coordinator, is addressed to students and guardians, travel agencies, and institutions abroad. Coherent waivers are the final essential factor, as noted in the conceptual framework.

KEY TERMS IN THE TEXT

Here are some key terms to know that appear throughout the book. There will be additional terms and phrases as well, but this is a good starting point prior to moving forward.

Americans with Disabilities Act—Protects individuals with disabilities. This Act prohibits discrimination against people with disabilities in employment, transportation, public accommodation, communications, and governmental activities.[34]

Coordinator—An expert in the field of study abroad, international education, global studies, and/or any similar department in which the person advises, designs, and leads study abroad and individual programs. This book uses the term interchangeably with *expert*. In addition, interviews with these individuals bring essential findings and best practices for the book.

Cultural competence—Sometimes referred to as cultural competency, it is an ability to interact effectively with people of different cultures. It comprises four components: (1) awareness of one's own cultural worldview, (2) attitude toward cultural differences, (3) knowledge of different cultural practices and worldviews, and (4) cross-cultural skills. Developing cultural competence results in an ability to understand, communicate with, and effectively interact with people across cultures.

Duty of care—An obligation to protect individuals from dangers and injury. In this study the term refers to properly protecting participants engaged in study abroad. Coordinators with programs that take this approach may be considered as not being negligent or liable for participants' injuries.[35]

ESOL—English for Speakers of Other Languages.

Exculpatory clause—Part of an agreement that relieves one party from liability. It is a provision in a contract that is intended to protect one party from being sued for their wrongdoing or negligence.[36]

Foreign institutions—Colleges, universities, or institutions with instructional facilities and grounds that are located abroad. Study abroad coordinators and their institutions often arrange for students to use these campuses and facilities that are abroad.

Homestay—Optional housing arrangements made for long-term study abroad students in which they live in the home of a family native to the region while overseas. An advantage with this type of housing arrangement is increased cultural acclimatization for participants who share meals, discussion, and activities with the host family.

Human trafficking—Labor trafficking and sex trafficking. Labor trafficking occurs in contexts that can include all forms of labor and services, including domestic servitude, sweat shops, and farm laborers forced to work without pay. Sex trafficking occurs in contexts that encompass the commercial sexual exploitation of children, as well as all adults who engage in a commercial sex act because of force, fraud, or coercion. Kidnapping is a threat to study abroad participants who may become victims of labor and sex trafficking.

In loco parentis —A concept derived from a common law doctrine that enabled institutions, presidents, faculty, and educational staff to act in place of the parents of students. It was primarily faculty members that enforced discipline to students in a draconian manner. Generally, students were not permitted to refer to each other by nicknames, swear in public, play cards publicly or privately, engage in offensive language, or pander in or around local inns.[37]

International education—A variety of activities and programs designed to encourage the flow of ideas and people across cultural and geographic boundaries.[38]

International terrorism—Activities with the following three characteristics: 1) involve violent acts or acts dangerous to human life that violate federal or state law; 2) appear to be intended (i) to intimidate or coerce a civilian population; (ii) to influence the policy of a government by intimidation or coercion; or (iii) to affect the conduct of a government by mass destruction, assassination, or kidnapping; and 3) occur primarily outside the territorial jurisdiction of the United States, or transcend national boundaries in terms of the means by which they are accomplished, the persons they appear intended to intimidate or coerce.[39]

Liability—Legal action taken against a study abroad program, program supervisor(s), foreign agencies, and/or the college/university. This often stems from risks that are not avoided, leading to injury, death, or negative program results.[40]

Long-term study abroad—Full time, credit-bearing programs that are a semester or year in length.

Program leader—Refers to faculty members, in particular, who lead study abroad programs. Proper training and orientation of these individuals has proven to be paramount for well-conducted study abroad programs.

Reverse culture shock—A common reaction or feeling felt when returning home from studying abroad. It is a psychological and emotional stage of readjustment, similar to the initial adjustment to living abroad.

Risks—Activity, behavior, and factors that may lead to injury, death, or negative program results left upon participants, faculty, tour leaders, the program, the institution, and/or all parties linked to the study abroad program. Legal action and liability issues may follow as a result.[41]

Section 504 of the Rehabilitation Act—Guarantees certain rights to people with disabilities. It was the first U.S. federal civil rights protection for people with disabilities.[42]

Short-term study abroad—A program shared with a group of people lasting typically from ten days to a month in length. Such programs tend to be all-inclusive with travel, accommodations, venues, and meals included in the cost of the program.

Special relationship—This concept exists between an institution of higher education and a student, particularly to an institution's "invitees" to the campus.[43] In this case, invitees are construed as students and special guests for events held on campus, while trespassers are typically excluded from this definition. In addition, the institution has a responsibility to provide medical treatment reasonably.[44]

Study abroad—An educational approach for students to study outside of the traditional university classroom setting. It consists of programs and curriculum for students that combine travel with a recognized, legitimate form of study likely to count toward a degree. These programs tend to be a part of the broader pedagogy at most universities and colleges known as international education.[45]

Study abroad coordinators—Leaders of study abroad programs, including coordinators of international education and study abroad, often at colleges and universities, who provide study abroad services and programs for interested participants.

Title IX—Of the Education Amendments of 1972 ("Title IX"), 20 U.S.C. §1681 et seq., is a federal civil rights law that prohibits discrimination on the basis of sex in education programs and activities. All public and private elementary and secondary schools, school districts, colleges, and universities receiving any federal funds must comply with Title IX. Under Title IX, discrimination on the basis of sex can include sexual harassment or sexual violence, such as rape, sexual assault, sexual battery, and sexual coercion.[46]

Tort law—A Latin phrase for "twisted relationship" and more specifically a "civil wrong."[47]

Waiver—Formal document that identifies the responsibilities of participants and liabilities of the college or university hosting a study abroad program. Other names for this document include Student Agreement form, Release and Indemnification form, Acceptance, Release and Waiver form, and Statement of Responsibility and Assumption of Risk form.[48]

Work abroad—A broad term that describes an immersive experience in an international work environment where the primary purpose is educational, whether for academic credit or not.[49]

FINDINGS FOR THE BOOK TAKEN FROM COURT DOCUMENTS, EXPERTS' ANALYSIS, AND INSTITUTIONAL WAIVERS OF LIABILITY

Juridical Texts

By implementing in the book best practices based on lessons learned from court documents, risks and liabilities may be minimized. Findings from lawsuits reveal a pattern of risks, and consequent liabilities, which I coin the "LARGEST 3" (Liabilities And Risks in Global Education and Study-Travel); nearly all study abroad tragedies and lawsuits tend to be linked to three common risk types—(1) medical risks, (2) sexual assault, and (3) supervisory neglect.

The LARGEST 3 brings awareness of past pitfalls, providing guidance to study abroad leaders and protective armor for participants to map out strategies for engaging in the most prudent and best practices. The result is risk reduction for participants, and curtailed liability issues for organizers and institutions.

Chapters 2 through 5 closely scrutinize various court cases that underscore the LARGEST 3. Expert opinions from coordinators and current risk-averting documents are brought forth to provide further awareness of risks, liabilities, and necessary protections with study abroad.

Expert Opinions from Coordinators

Risk avoidance may also be understood by consulting experts—interviewed coordinators and directors of study abroad, international education, and global studies in higher education—who share valuable experiences with conducting study abroad programs. Experts agree that risk reduction and overall success of study abroad result from sustaining high educational standards, fully training faculty members, and carefully scrutinizing partnering agencies. These are just a few of the overall recommendations made in the book by coordinators. These individuals hold in-depth awareness for how to conduct successful programs. Their voices will be heard throughout the book.

Institutional Waivers of Liability

In addition, risk avoidance may result from better utilization of institutional waivers to reduce threats for participants and legal issues for institutions of higher education. The language in a waiver should clearly outline expectations for program participants, as well as the factors for which the institution should be held accountable.

Experts concur that both the students and institutions must work together to ensure that participants have a clear understanding of their role, of potential dangers, and of situations that may arise while abroad. In addition, study abroad leaders need to be fully aware of their own role in providing a safe, educationally enriching experience for students. The waiver is a tool to assist both participant and program leader.

You will see through numerous sample cases that risk-averting documents, including waivers, may be used in a court of law. These documents have both protected *and* decimated study abroad programs in a court of law. There is a lot at stake with providing language that gives proper safeguards to students. Together, legal documents, expert opinion from coordinators, and institutional waivers are key resources for evaluating risks, liabilities, and resolutions of study abroad in higher education. They served to be the necessary resources that brought essential findings for this work.

NOTES

1. Institute of International Education. (2014). Press release Open Doors 2014: International students in the United States and study abroad by American students are at all-time high. Retrieved from http://www.iie.org/Who-We-Are/News-and-Events/Press-Center/Press-Releases/2014/2014-11-17-Open-Doors-Data.

2. *Id.*

3. *Id.*

4. Carlson, J. S., Burn, B., Useem, J., & Yachimowicz, D. (1990). *Study abroad: The experience of American undergraduates in Western Europe and the United States.* New York: Greenwood Press.

5. Institute of International Education. (2014).

6. *Id.*

7. Donohue, D., & Altaf, S. (2012, May). Learn by doing: Expanding international internships/work abroad opportunities for U.S. STEM students—A briefing paper

    from IIE's Center for Academic Mobility Research. Retrieved from
    http://www.iie.org/Research-and-Publications/Publications-and-Reports/IIE-Bookstore/Learn-by-Doing.

8. Kast, R. (1997). In loco parentis and the "reasonable person." *International Educator 7*, 1. Kuh, G. D., Kinzie, J., Schuh, J. H., & Whitt, E. J., & Associates. (2005). *Student success in college: Creating conditions that matter.* San Francisco: Jossey-Bass.

9. Kast, R. (1997).

10. Astin, A. W. et al. (2002). *The American freshman: Thirty-five year trends.* Los Angeles: Higher Education Research Institute, University of California, Los Angeles. Kuh, G. D., Schuh, J. C., Whitt, E. J., Andreas, R. E., Lyons, J. W., Strange, C. C., Krehbiel, L. E., & MacKay, K. A. (1991). *Involving colleges: Successful approaches to fostering student learning and development outside the classroom.* San Francisco: Jossey-Bass. Kuh, G. D., Kinzie, J., Schuh, J. H., & Whitt, E. J., & Associates. (2005).

11. Astin, A. W. et al. (2002).

12. Chickering, A., & Reisser, L. (1993). *Education and identity.* San Francisco: Jossey-Bass.Kuh, G. D., Schuh, J. C., Whitt, E. J., Andreas, R. E., Lyons, J. W., Strange, C. C., Krehbiel, L. E., & MacKay, K. A. (1991). Kuh, G. D., Kinzie, J., Schuh, J. H., & Whitt, E. J., & Associates. (2005). Pascarella, E. T., & Terenzini, P. T. (2005). *How college affects students: Volume 2, a third decade of research.* San Francisco: Jossey-Bass.

13. Medina-Lopez-Portillo, A. (2004). *College students' intercultural sensitivity development as a result of their studying abroad: A comparative description of two types of study abroad programs.* Doctoral dissertation, University of Maryland, College Park, 2004. Retrieved from ProQuest Digital Dissertations. (AAT 3137038)

14. McClenney, K. M. (2004). Redefining quality in community colleges: Focusing on good educational practice. *Change 36*, 16–21.

15. Pickert, S. M. (1992). *Preparing for a global community: Achieving an international perspective in higher education.* Washington, DC: Clearinghouse on Higher Education.

16. Pascarella, E. T., & Terenzini, P. T. (2005).

17. Bates, J. (1997). The effects of study abroad on undergraduates in an honors international program. *Dissertation Abstracts International 58*, 8, 4162A. (UMI No. 2637042). Retrieved from Dissertations & Theses database. Kuh, G. D., Kinzie, J., Schuh, J. H., & Whitt, E. J., & Associates. (2005). McCabe, L. (1994). The development of a global perspective during participation in semester at sea: A comparative global education program. *Educational Review 46*, 275–86.

18. Donohue, D., & Altaf, S. (2012, May).

19. Nolting, J., Johnson, M., & Matherly, C. (2005). WIVA: Work abroad and international careers. In Joseph L. Brockington, William W. Hoffa, Patricia C. Martin (Eds.),

    NAFSA's guide to education abroad for advisers and administrators (3rd Ed.).
    Washington, DC: NAFSA: Association of International Educators.

20. Donohue, D., & Altaf, S. (2012, May).

21. *Id.*

22. *Id.*

23. *Id.*

24. Children's TherAplay. (2010–2013). Hippotherapy. The Children's TherAplay Foundation, Inc. Retrieved from http://www.childrenstheraplay.org/hippotherapy.

25. Van Der Werf, M. (2007, June 6). A wide world of risk. *Chronicle of Higher Education 53*, 30, p. A1.

26. Van Der Werf (2007, June 6).

27. Gehring, D. (1993). Understanding legal constraints on practice. In M. J. Barr & Associates (Eds.), *The handbook of student affairs administration* (pp. 274–99). San Francisco: Jossey-Bass.

28. Pearson, D. R., & Beckham, J. C. (2005). Negligent liability issues involving colleges and students: Balancing the risks and benefits of expanded programs and heightened supervision. *Student Affairs Administrators in Higher Education (NAPSA) Journal 42*, 4, p. 461.

29. LaFranchi, H. (2003, August 19). Why more students are studying abroad. *Christian Science Monitor*, p. 3.

30. Institute of International Education. (2000–2013). Open Doors data U.S. study abroad: Studentprofile. Retrieved from http://www.iie.org/Research-and-Publications/Open-Doors/Data/US-Study-Abroad/Student-Profile/2000-13.

31. Id.

32. Hoffa, W., & Pearson, J. (1997). *NAFSA's guide to education abroad for advisors andadministrators* (2nd ed.). Washington, D.C. NAFSA: Association of International Educators.

33. Institute of International Education. (2015). Press release: Study abroad by U.S. studentsslowed in 2008/09 with more students going to less traditional destinations. Retrieved from http://www.iie.org/Who-We-Are/News-and-Events/Press-Center/Press-Releases/2010/2010-11-15-Open-Doors-US-Study-Abroad.

34. U.S. Department of Labor. (2015). Disability resources: Americans with Disabilities Act. Washington, DC: U.S. Department of Labor. Retrieved from http://www.dol.gov/dol/topic/disability/ada.htm.

35. Gehring, D. (1993). Pearson, D. R., & Beckham, J. C. (2005).

36. LegalMatch Law Library. (2014). Exculpatory Clauses. Retrieved from http://www.legalmatch.com/law-library/article/exculpatory-clauses.html.

37. Dannells, M. (1997). From discipline to development: Rethinking student conduct in higher education. *ASHE-ERIC Higher Ed. Report 25*, 2.

38. Mitzel, H. (1982). International education. In *encyclopedia of educational research* (Vol. 2, pp. 945–58). New York: McGraw-Hill.

39. Federal Bureau of Investigation. (2015). Definitions of terrorism in the U.S. Code. Retrieved from https://www.fbi.gov/about-us/investigate/terrorism/terrorism-definition.

40. Guernsey, L. (1997, April 11). A lawsuit raises difficult questions about liability and study-abroad programs. *Chronicle of Higher Education 43*, 31, pp. A37, A39.

41. Kaplin, W. A., & Lee, B. A. (1997). *A legal guide for student affairs professionals*. San Francisco: Jossey-Bass.

42. U.S. Department of Health and Human Services: Office for Civil Rights. (2006). Fact sheet:Your rights under Section 504 of the Rehabilitation Act. Washington, DC: U.S. Department of Health and Human Services. Retrieved from http://www.hhs.gov/ocr/civilrights/resources/factsheets/504.pdf.

43. Kaplin & Lee, 1997. Kaplin, W. A., & Lee, B. A. (2011). *The law of higher education*. San Francisco: Jossey-Bass.

44. Id.

45. Kuh, G. D., Kinzie, J., Schuh, J. H., & Whitt, E. J., & Associates. (2005). *Student success in college: Creating conditions that matter*. San Francisco: Jossey-Bass. Pickert, S. M. (1992). *Preparing for a global community: Achieving an international perspective in higher education*. Washington, DC: Clearinghouse on Higher Education.

46. U.S. Department of Education. (2015). Know your rights: Title IX prohibits sexualharassment and sexual violence where you go to school. Washington, DC: U.S. Department of Education Office for Civil Rights. Retrieved from http://www2.ed.gov/about/offices/list/ocr/docs/title-ix-rights-201104.pdf.

47. Kaplin & Lee, 1997.

48. Carr, J. W., & Summerfield, E. (1995). *Forms of travel: Essential documents, letters and flyers for study abroad advisors*. Pennsylvania: NAFSA Publishers.

49. Donohue, D., & Altaf, S. (2012, May).

Chapter Two

The "LARGEST 3" Areas of Risks and Liabilities with Study Abroad

LAWSUITS LEADING TO THE LARGEST 3

Various types of tort-related litigation have been brought against study abroad programs, their institutions, and the agencies associated with the programs and institutions. [1] In fact, "lawyers, rarities in the past, are cranking up lawsuits in state and federal courts, forcing [university officials] to determine who is responsible for taking care of students thousands of miles from home." [2]

Protecting student participants and programs is paramount. As noted in chapter 1, multitudes of study abroad tragedies described in lawsuits indicate a pattern of risks and consequent liabilities, which I label the "LARGEST 3." To reiterate, this is an acronym for Liabilities And Risks in Global Education and Study-Travel. More specifically, the LARGEST 3 are (1) medical risks; (2) sexual assault; and (3) supervisory neglect.

The LARGEST 3 reveal past pitfalls, and in turn give the opportunity for study abroad participants to map out strategies for engaging in the most prudent and best practices. The result is major risk reduction for participants and curtailed liability issues for organizers and their institutions.

The next three chapters include a multitude of cases and lawsuits that substantiate the LARGEST 3. They are brought forth to fully detail calamities abroad, dissect errors in judgment and/or ill preparedness by program leaders, and give preventative measures to avoid the overseas mishaps. Chapter 3 is dedicated solely to medical risk issues, chapter 4 to sexual assaults, and chapter 5 to gross supervisory neglect.

As noted in chapter 1, this book includes expert opinions from interviewed coordinators and directors of study abroad, international education, and global studies in higher education. For simplicity's sake, they are referenced as *coordinators*, or at times, *experts*. Table 2.1 presents key demographic characteristics of coordinators in this book. In particular, these data include institutional type (i.e., two-year or four-year colleges and universities), number of years working in the study abroad field, at the institution, gender, and geographic locations where they have led study abroad. These variables give a snapshot into the experience and background of the coordinators. The coordinators are identified anonymously, using pseudonyms.

Table 2.1.   Key Demographic Characteristics of Coordinators

Coordinator	Institution Type	No. of Years	Gender	Selected Study
Coordinator Arianna	Four-Year	3	Female	England France
Coordinator Baron	Four-Year	2	Male	Argentina East Africa England Jordan
Coordinator Braxton	Four-Year	37	Male	Barbados Canada Central America Europe India South America Turkey
Coordinator Desiree	Two-Year	4	Female	Central America Europe South America
Coordinator Eve	Four-Year	11	Female	Africa Asia Australia Central America Europe New Zealand South America
Coordinator Felix	Four-Year	23	Male	Africa Asia Central America Europe South America
Coordinator Levi	Two-Year	15	Male	Asia Australia Central America South America
Coordinator Lonna	Four-Year	3	Female	Africa Asia
Coordinator Pearl	Two-Year	9	Female	England Italy Russia Spain
Coordinator Poppy	Four-Year	1	Female	Africa Russia
Coordinator Tabitha	Two-Year	3	Female	China
Coordinator Trevor	Two-Year	25	Male	England Germany Italy Portugal Spain

Note: The locales where coordinators led study abroad represented a "selected" listing of recent sites. For the purposes of this study, not all locations were presented.

Waivers of liability are used by coordinators to better protect students; however, this measure has had mixed results.[3] With an increase in suits being filed against study abroad programs, their coordinators, and their institutions, protection has become a top priority.[4] The waiver has been central to court cases.

To further assist coordinators, this book provides sample risk-averting documents that may be used as models. But the forms should be amended as needed to reflect the academic standards and philosophy of your own institution. *It is important to consult legal counsel and other appropriate departments during this process.*

In addition, with the coming chapters I provide analysis of strengths and weaknesses with the sample waivers of liability (among the risk-averting documents) presently used by experts within higher education in an effort to apprise students of potential risks and to protect coordinators from liability. Coordinators are predominantly addressed throughout the book.

Let's start to consider what constitutes the LARGEST 3: (1) medical risks; (2) sexual assault; and (3) supervisory neglect. The cases of *Paneno v. Centres* (2004),[5] *Bloss v. The University of Minnesota Board of Regents* (1999),[6] and *Fay v. Thiel College* (2001)[7] in this chapter give opening insight into issues, impacts of risk-averting documents, and measures to avoid study abroad mishaps.

MEDICAL RISKS

Paneno v. Centres

Medical risks have been a prevailing theme in lawsuits such as *Paneno v. Centres*. The case exposed an ineffective arrangement made between Pasadena Community College (PCC) and the partnering travel agency, Centres for Academic Programmes Abroad (CAPA). CAPA-USA and CAPA-UK are distinct but affiliated companies that make up CAPA.[8] The significance of this detail will be explained soon.

A critical injury to a student and a major lawsuit against both the college and its foreign partnering agency resulted.[9] The case also exposed the limitations of a signed waiver as a method for protecting an institution from liability.

Through Pasadena Community College (PCC), a student, Rocky Paneno, enrolled in a study abroad program called the Florence Program.[10] Here is a timeline of events that took place. In April 2000, prior to departure, Paneno signed a release purporting to discharge CAPA-USA and its employees, directors, officers, agents, and affiliates for any loss or damage.[11]

In September 2000, Paneno traveled to Italy and commenced the academic program.[12] He lived in an apartment in Florence with roommates who were also participating in the program.[13] PCC provided the accommodations for Paneno through CAPA.[14]

On October 21, 2000, Paneno and a friend were on the apartment balcony; Paneno leaned against the balcony railing and a portion of it gave way.[15] He fell six stories and sustained serious injuries, including paralysis, as a result.[16]

Although Paneno had signed a release discharging CAPA-USA, its directors, officers, employees, agents, and affiliates for all losses or damages, Paneno sued the agency, which made the housing arrangements, as well as PCC.[17]

It would appear that CAPA was attempting to use generic trade names, CAPA-USA and CAPA-UK, to evade liability. The court specifically concluded with:

> This conclusion is particularly compelling herein given CAPA-UK and CAPA-USA's confusing use of the same generic trade name and the game "CAPA" appears to be playing.[18]

The court continued:

> According to CAPA-USA's motion for summary judgment, CAPA-USA had nothing to do with the arrangements made for the student accommodations abroad: "CAPA-UK . . . [is] the entity which actually organized the various elements of the PCC Florence program, which included, *inter alia*, student accommodations in Florence, air and ground transportation, and various sightseeing excursions," thereby relieving it of any liability to Paneno for injuries he suffered. [19]

The court followed with:

> On the flip side, according to CAPA-UK, CAPA-UK cannot be sued in California for any of its alleged negligence because it has no ties to California. Basically, by setting up two related corporate entities—one to recruit and enter into contracts with students and one to provide all necessary accommodations for them—"CAPA" is attempting to avoid answering to any claim for negligence in California. We will not allow such trickery to be used to deny Paneno his day in court. [20]

The decision shown in the court disposition was "Paneno is entitled to his costs on appeal." [21]

What Can Be Learned from *Paneno v. Centres*?

Writer Boorstein conjectures "courts have held that colleges are legally responsible for some injuries that befall students on campus, but whether that applies overseas—and to what sorts of injuries—is unknown." [22] *Paneno v. Centres* provides an answer. Colleges *can* be held legally responsible for injuries sustained by students that occur overseas, including cases in which the hired agency was responsible for mishaps.

Even though chapter 3 goes into the subject with greater depth—with numerous scenarios, cases, and resolutions for avoiding medical liability issues—it is important to immediately reflect upon some lessons learned from *Paneno v. Centres*.

Carefully Vet Foreign Partnering Agencies

Coordinators and college officials need to carefully consider selected foreign agencies that reserve accommodations for students. The ethical practices of CAPA came into question with *Paneno*. PCC study abroad officials need to consider if CAPA places the well-being of students front and center, and may need to reexamine their relationship. Coordinators need to closely research the history of potential partners. They need to consider if agencies have had past student complaints or lawsuits, and the manner in which those suits were handled.

Scrutinize Foreign Accommodations for Students

Paneno v. Centres exposed an ineffective arrangement made by the foreign partner, CAPA, which left PCC liable and a student maimed for life. Coordinators should closely scrutinize accommodations provided by foreign partnering agencies prior to entrusting them with the care of their students. Interviewed experts agree.

Coordinator Levi admits that "when past students had expressed dissatisfaction with a foreign institute, describing it as an anemic educational experience abroad . . . I took a hands-on approach by attempting to visit the foreign site [and develop] a close working relationship with the officials, particularly the teaching staff, to ensure [that] students receive a quality education."

This approach is ideal, as most coordinators tend to agree. Coordinator Poppy avows, "I refuse to work with a foreign institution unless it allows programs to be closely scrutinized.

This means a college representative is able to frequent the foreign institute and negotiate terms."

When a student goes to a foreign institute, you need to have consistent communication with not only the student but also the assigned foreign advisor. Also, make it mandatory for the student to regularly meet with the advisor. Coordinator Poppy correctly affirms, "I expect foreign institutions to provide on-site counselors and advisors for study abroad participants." She goes so far as to have "a residence administrator from their home institution work in the housing unit [abroad]."

The luxury of having a home institution member serving as a residence administrator abroad is quite advantageous. The reality is that coordinators tend not to have the resources to visit all of the foreign sites prior to sending students, and are even less likely to have a satellite campus where they can have a personal presence at the partnering institute. So you have to make concessions. Become an active member of the partnering consortium and serve on its board. This will give you increased access to and familiarity with the foreign institute's officials. In turn, they can provide updates on any happenings that occur with student dormitories, homestay families, and off-campus apartments.

Prior to sending a student to a location where you have never been, have numerous conversations with foreign faculty and staff members who will be assisting. Of course, nothing compares with seeing the facilities firsthand and meeting foreign partners in person, but this is a good alternative.

In addition, reentry orientation and postprogram evaluations are helpful tools to gain additional information from students about foreign accommodations.

Chapters 7–9 provide twenty-three best practices for avoiding risks and liabilities with study abroad. Best practice #21, Foreign Housing Assignments, provides added information on the subject.

Avoid Nonspecific Language in Risk-Averting Documents

What may be also learned from *Paneno v. Centres* is that regardless of having a waiver in place, if the document fails to address dangers specific to the program region and its accommodations, it leaves the student and institution at risk. Congruently, many coordinators question the effectiveness of waivers with protecting students and study abroad programs due to the often vague language in these forms.

Coordinator Pearl cynically relays that "anything or anyone that coordinators hire or use . . . is mentioned in the waiver stating they are not responsible. So it's expanded to include almost everything but the grandmother that they are not going to be accountable for . . . a judge may throw out a waiver in a case if it were to say too much, deeming it ineffective." True point.

Coordinator Trevor conveys a similar lack of faith: "A waiver is not going to eliminate liability. . . . When it gets down to it, it won't stand up in court . . . My brother in law [who] is an attorney . . . traveled with me many times. And he signed those perfunctory statements. He said 'this is not worth the paper it's written on.'"

Frustrated, concerned (and rightly so with the high-stakes involved) coordinators should scrupulously review the model waiver titled, Malveaux Sample Recommended Waiver for Minimizing Risks and Liability in Study Abroad, from the fictitious school, Perilpure College (see Appendix I).

The Malveaux Sample Recommended Waiver is constructed to show how to best thwart risks and liabilities in study abroad; it results from examined court documents, personal experience, the expertise of interviewed experts, risk-averting documents, and scholarly literature. It is a *recommended* waiver. I make no claims that it is faultless, or will protect everyone from every calamity. Just like any waiver, it would need to be presented to legal counsel and college officials to reconstruct it in a way that best fits individual program and institutional needs.

In addition, the appendices to this book contain twelve risk-averting documents used by coordinators. Both faulty and sound sections within these documents are discussed in book chapters; advice is provided to assist with the assembly of these essential forms used in study abroad.

Coordinator Levi notes, "Since the world is changing so much, [coordinators] need to do some changing with the waiver form to address problems we have no control over." This is the change that I am trying to lead—to address problems that we *do* have control over.

Swift Action to Amend Unsafe Accommodations

Another instructive point from *Paneno v. Centres* is that protective action must be swift if a potential hazard arises with a student's housing. It is better to overreact than underreact in such cases. An overreaction means you may have avoided a risk, but an underreaction that leads to a risk realized can never be fixed.

Experts affirm that foreign institutions have failed to provide their students secured accommodations at times. Again, there should be immediate action to thwart potentially dangerous situations.

For example, Coordinator Eve recounts, "One of the students [studying in Mexico] claimed that the son of the host family in which she was living invited her to the top of the roof to look at the sunset . . . [and] made an advance on her. She called home all upset, and her mother called me. So we called the foreign school . . . and the student [was immediately] taken from that family and put with a different family. But she was freaked out and decided she was coming home. So [our] college made arrangements, and paid the supplemental difference in the airfare to exchange her ticket."

No litigation ensued. The rapid response from Coordinator Eve properly protected the student and safeguarded her institution.

This noted situation, in fact, segues into a chief problem within study abroad, and another category of the LARGEST 3—sexual assault.

SEXUAL ASSAULT

Bloss v. The University of Minnesota Board of Regents

Sexual assault litigation is a leading class of suits aimed at study abroad programs. Kast (1997) backs that university and study abroad programs are susceptible to risks and liabilities in relation to sexual assault. One sample court case, *Bloss v. University of Minnesota Board of Regents*, shows that university officials must remain conscientious of activities that may expose participants to sexual assault crimes and bring unwanted lawsuits. [23]

While participating in the University of Minnesota's cultural immersion program in Cuernavaca, Mexico, student Adrienne Bloss was traveling to meet friends for a social evening and was raped at knifepoint by a taxi driver. [24]

Bloss was partaking in the University's Spanish in Cuernavaca Program at the Cemanahuac Educational Community. [25] The university contracted with Cemanahuac to instruct the students and administer the program. [26] She was housed with a host family that lived approximately 2.5 miles from Cemanahuac, which is thirty minutes by bus or ten minutes by car. [27]

Bloss took the bus to and from school, as well as to attend social and cultural events.[28] On the night of the assault, Bloss left her host family home, on her own, and hailed a taxi about one-half block down the street.[29]

She was planning to meet friends at the host home of several fellow students and then to go to a bar or restaurant.[30] The taxi driver told her the back door was broken and that she could sit in the front of the cab; Bloss relocated and sat in the front with the driver.[31]

Court documents cite that while traveling to her friends' home, the driver pulled over to the side of the road and raped her.[32] Bloss sued the university due to negligence in failing to secure housing closer to the Cemanahuac campus, imprudence in not providing transportation to and from the campus, and inattention to impart warnings about various serious risks, including the use of taxicabs in Cuernavaca.[33]

Cuernavaca, through mandatory student orientation sessions, an Acceptance, Release, and Waiver document, and orientation materials, provided students with safety warnings and information concerning dangers of the city.[34] University officials believed the institution was not responsible for Bloss's injuries due to her signing the waiver form and due to the fact that she was given specific warnings, which, had she heeded them, would have prevented the attack.[35]

"The University demonstrated that at its orientation session it provides information about academic, health, travel, financial, safety, and social issues," according to the court opinion.[36]

In addition, the court opinion conveys:

> The undisputed evidence shows that the program materials, the release form and program orienta-tion, and Cemanahuac's orientation materials all warn students about their safety. The student testified that she received explicit oral and written warnings relating to safety in Cuernavaca at mandatory orientation sessions prior to the start of the program.[37] The warnings included specific admonitions that it was dangerous for women to go out alone at night, that [women] should call for a taxi at night rather than hail a taxi on the street, and that women should never sit in the front seat of taxis. These warnings specifically addressed the circumstances under which the student sus-tained her injuries.[38]

What Can Be Learned from *Bloss v. The University of Minnesota Board of Regents*?

What happened to Adrienne Bloss while studying abroad in Mexico was tragic, and she should not be blamed for the assault. Yet the incident brings to light a major concern among coordina-tors for their students—unread or misunderstood safety warnings in risk-averting documents.

There was a major disconnect that occurred. Bloss testified that she received explicit oral and written warnings relating to safety in Cuernavaca at mandatory orientation sessions prior to the start of the program.[39] Yet she sued the university for the inattention to impart warnings about various serious risks, including the use of taxicabs in Cuernavaca.[40] Among the warn-ings given on safety, how did she miss key ones concerning taking taxicabs?

One plausible explanation is that Bloss may not have fully read or understood the Accep-tance, Release, and Waiver document and orientation materials provided on safety warnings in Cuernavaca. Unread or missed information in risk-averting documents is an ongoing problem with study abroad participation and presents serious concerns for student safety.

The Issue of Risk-Averting Documents Not Being Understood or Read

A vexed Coordinator Pearl retorts, "If a student signed a waiver, but did not read it, than the waiver was pointless." Bluntly speaking, Coordinator Felix declares a function of the waiver is that it "allows us to say 'I told you that' . . . So you want to cover your rear end a bit."

However, most coordinators view the waiver as more than a means for deflecting liability; it is an essential tool for safeguarding participants.

Quite simply, a coordinator needs to be sure that participants read and understand the potential risks of a program noted in risk-averting documents. This may mean dedicating time during orientation to read such forms aloud, and then field questions to the best of your ability. Having a member of legal counsel present would greatly assist.

Chapter 4 takes an in-depth look at other sexual assault cases, provides viable solutions to improve student safety, and guides the proper construction of risk-averting documents.

NEGLIGENT SUPERVISION

Fay v. Thiel College

The issue of negligent supervision and/or inaction by program leaders has impacted study abroad immensely. As a result, negligent supervision has surfaced as a major topic in the courts and makes up another area of the LARGEST 3. "Parents are demanding schools shoulder blame for death and injury and beef up training for program leaders."[41] These parents, along with students, are increasingly filing lawsuits due to negligence.[42] A worst-case scenario resulting from supervisory neglect involved Amy Fay, a student at Thiel College in Pennsylvania.

Three faculty members supervised the program—two professors of religion and one professor of language.[43] Prior to departing on the trip to Peru, Fay was required by Thiel College to sign a Waiver of Liability form and a Thiel College Consent form; she signed them both.[44] In fact, if a student refuses to sign the documents, Thiel College will not permit that student to go on the trip.[45]

During the trip, Fay became ill. She was taken to a medical clinic located in the city of Cuzco, where she was eventually admitted.[46] After she was admitted to the medical clinic, all of the faculty supervisors and all of the other students left on a prescheduled trip that was to last several days, leaving Fay alone at the clinic with only a Lutheran missionary by the name of Karen Helikson to act as Fay's translator.[47] The primary language in Peru is Spanish, and Fay spoke little of it.[48]

Fay had only met Helikson while in Peru; Helikson was not in any way related to Thiel College nor was acting as an agent and/or representative of Thiel College.[49]

While at the medical clinic, Fay was subjected to unnecessary surgical removal of her appendix; after the appendectomy was complete, she was sexually assaulted by the same surgeon who had performed the surgery and the same anesthesiologist who had administered the anesthesia.[50] The plaintiff knows that she was sexually assaulted because she was fully conscious during and after her surgery.[51]

This resulted in Fay filing suit against Thiel College.[52] The waiver of liability form and the consent form became key areas of focus by the court to determine responsibility of the university for Fay's injuries.[53] Again, Thiel College required the students taking part in the study abroad program to sign these forms.[54]

The language in the Waiver of Liability form stated that as a condition for participation in the study or project, the participant agrees and understands that they waive any and all claims arising out of or in connection with the program; also, the waiver held the condition that the individual, family, heirs, or others connected with the participant had to give up their right to hold Thiel College and/or its personnel accountable for liability.[55] This part of the waiver is referred to as an exculpatory clause, or a part of an agreement that relieves one party from liability.

The waiver served as a standardized contract form offered to consumers of goods and services on a take-it-or-leave-it basis without allowing the individual a realistic opportunity to bargain except by acquiescing to the form contract.[56]

Both the plaintiff and defendant agreed the Waiver of Liability form was presented to the plaintiff on a take-it-or-leave-it basis; the plaintiff either signed the form or she did not go on the Thiel-sponsored trip to Peru.[57]

Because rejecting the transaction entirely was the plaintiff's only option other than accepting the contract, the court concluded that the exculpatory clause contained in the Waiver of Liability form was not valid.[58]

With concern to the separate Thiel College Consent Form, it included the statement: "In the event of sickness or injury of my/our/daughter/son/ward/spouse/myself, Amy L. Fay (name of student), who is 22 years of age, birthday November 5, 1973, I/we hereby authorize the representative abroad of Thiel College to secure whatever treatment is deemed necessary, including the administration of an anesthetic and surgery."[59] Defendants contend that the consent form that Fay was required by Thiel College to sign is . . . another Waiver of Liability form.[60]

Defendants argued that they had no special relationship with the plaintiff beyond the fact that the plaintiff was a student at Thiel College.[61] Defendants also maintained that since there was no special relationship between the parties, the college owed Fay no special duty beyond that of a reasonable standard of care, and that the college did not violate that reasonable standard of care in leaving Fay alone at the Peruvian medical clinic while the rest of the group continued on with the prearranged travel itinerary.[62]

On the other hand, the plaintiff contended that (1) the consent form created a special relationship between Fay and the college, and (2) pursuant to that special relationship, the college owed a duty to the plaintiff to secure, in the event of her sickness or injury, "whatever treatment is deemed necessary, including the administration of an anesthetic and surgery."[63]

The plaintiff also argued that (1) pursuant to that duty, one or more of the faculty supervisors should have stayed with her during her stay at the Peruvian medical clinic, and (2) defendants breached that duty by "abandoning" her in the Peruvian medical clinic.[64]

The court, after carefully reviewing all of the evidence of record, concluded as a matter of law that Thiel College did owe Fay a special duty of care as a result of the special relationship that arose between Thiel College and the plaintiff pursuant to the consent form that she was required to execute prior to participating in the Thiel-sponsored trip to Peru.[65]

In addition, the defendants' assertion that the "intention of the defendants in having the plaintiff and the other students sign the medical consent form before leaving on the trip was to be free from liability if the defendants needed to make medical decisions for the students while in Peru" was dismissed by the court.[66]

The court concluded "the consent form does not spell out, with the greatest of particularity and by express stipulation, the intention of the parties to release Thiel College from any liability stemming from any medical decisions that one or more of the faculty supervisors made on behalf of, or in conjunction with, a student while participating in the Thiel-sponsored study abroad trip to Peru . . . [and] is *not* . . . a waiver of liability."[67]

What Can Be Learned from *Fay v. Thiel College*?

When supervisory neglect is blatant, no risk-averting document or orientation will protect that supervisor and institution from being held liable—and they *should* be held accountable. A well-trained, adept program leader is the best defense against risks abroad.

A Competent Program Leader Is Always Your Best Defense

Coordinator Poppy aptly recognizes "a good university will make sure the faculty member is given the proper information and training so that they understand what [he or she's] responsibilities are before going abroad . . . you need to have university faculty workshops about liability issues and about safety issues." Amen.

With so much emphasis on predeparture orientation for students, study abroad coordinators may overlook the importance of fully apprising faculty program leaders of their responsibilities, of the potential hazards native to the program, and their day-to-day duties while abroad. In addition, coordinators may falsely assume that because their colleagues excel in the classroom, this translates to being strong study abroad leaders. This is not an automatic.

Leaving No Participant Alone for an Extended Period and a Proper Student/Leader Ratio

Participant illness, as was the case for Amy Fay, is a common part of study abroad. When a student becomes ill, more supervision, not less, is the appropriate response. There needs to be a leader available to remain with the sick or injured student while an additional program leader, or leaders, continue the program with the group. A 10 to 1 ratio of students to program leader is recommended, and a program should never run with less than two leaders. The fact that three faculty leaders were on hand during Amy Fay's program and not one felt an obligation to remain behind with her in the Peruvian clinic is not only a huge lapse in judgment but also is inexcusable.

Coordinator Trevor weighed in on students/program leader ratios: "Well, actually I only take twenty [participants on a program] . . . Two [supervisors], [sometimes] my wife and I, have done very well. And my wife who is a mother [serves the students well when they] are away from home. Again, [students] are away for two weeks. They are fending for themselves—food, shelter, and they're doing their laundry. And I've had kids who are homesick, which is natural. I've had kids that have had tummy aches, [and wondered] 'Where is my mommy?' My wife is really good at that."

While a nurturing element in a program can bring a positive presence, this approach is not preferable. A spouse can join a coordinator on a program, but should not serve as a co-leader. Coordinator Trevor is leaving his program and institution at risk because a spouse, family member, or friend does not make for an official program leader. How well has the person been trained to lead study abroad? Is the person a faculty member or even an employee of the college? If not, aside from risk factors, academic merits for the program could come into question.

Fay v. Thiel College also reveals that risk-averting documents (the medical consent form in this case) should be concise in spelling out with the greatest of particularity from what a college is and is not liable.

CHAPTER SUMMARY

Various types of litigation have been brought against study abroad programs, their institutions, and the agencies associated with the program and institution. The cases commonly fall into three major areas—medical issues, sexual assault, and supervisory neglect—or the LARGEST 3.

With an increase in suits being filed against study abroad programs, coordinators, and their institutions, safety has become a main concern,[68] and risk-averting documents have been a focal presence in case law.

Later chapters will more thoroughly examine additional court cases that substantiate the LARGEST 3 and closely scrutinize issues with current risk-averting documents used by coordinators. Also, recommended strategies to improve program methods and current risk-averting document construction are provided so that students will receive better protection from perils and institutions from legal wrangling.

In addition, future chapters provide rich feedback from interviews with experts who recount firsthand experiences, give advice, and provide best practices for avoiding risks and liabilities in study abroad.

NOTES

1.　Marklein, M. B. (2009, May 28). Students studying abroad face dangers with little oversight. *USA Today*. Retrieved from
　　http://usatoday30.usatoday.com/news/education/2009-05-27-study-abroad-main_N.htm.

2.　Buckley, T. J. (1997, September 12). India crash wake up call for schools and parents. *USA Today*, p. A1.

3.　Carr, J. W., & Summerfield, E. (1995). *Forms of travel: Essential documents, letters and flyers for study abroad advisors*. Pennsylvania: NAFSA Publishers.

4.　Gehring, D. (1993). Understanding legal constraints on practice. In M. J. Barr & Associates (Eds.), *The handbook of student affairs administration* (pp. 274–99). San Francisco: Jossey-Bass.

5.　*Paneno v. Centres for Acad. Programmes Abroad, Ltd.*, 13 Cal. Rptr. 3d 759 (Cal. Ct. App. 2004).

6.　590 N.W.2d 661 (Minn. Ct. App. 1999).

7.　55 Pa. D. & C.4th 353 (Com. Pl. 2001).

8.　*Paneno*, 13 Cal. Rptr. 3d at 761.

9.　*Id.*

10.　*Id.*

11.　*Id.* at 762.

12.　*Id.*

13.　*Id.*

14.　*Id.*

15.　*Id.* at 763.

16.　*Id.*

17.　*Id.*

18.　*Id.* at 766.

19.　*Id.*

20.　*Id.*

21.　*Id.*

22.　Boorstein, M., & Wright, S. W. (1998). Fears about safety—and lawsuits—plague study abroad programs. *Community College Week 10*, 12.

23.　590 N.W.2d 661, 662 (Minn. Ct. App. 1999).

24.　*Id.* at 662.

25.　*Id.*

26.　*Id.* at 663.

27.　*Id.* at 662.

28.　*Id.*

29.　*Id.* at 663.

30.　*Id.*

31.　*Id.*

32.　*Id.*

33. *Id.*
34. *Id.*
35. *Id.*
36. *Id.* at 666.
37. *Id.*
38. *Id.*
39. *Id.*
40. *Id.* at 632-33.
41. Buckley, T. J. (1997, September 12).
42. Buckley, T. J. (1997, September 12).
43. *Fay v. Thiel Coll.*, 55 Pa. D. & C.4th 353, 354-55 (Com. Pl. 2001).
44. *Id.* at 355.
45. *Id.*
46. *Id.*
47. *Id.*
48. *Id.*
49. *Id.* at 355–56.
50. *Id.* at 356.
51. *Id.*
52. *Id.*
53. *Id.*
54. *Id.* at 355.
55. *Id.* at 357–58.
56. *Id.* at 359.
57. *Id.* at 360.
58. *Id.* at 360–61.
59. *Id.* at 358.
60. *Id.* at 368.
61. *Id.* at 361.
62. *Id.*
63. *Id.* at 361–62.
64. *Id.* at 362.
65. *Id.* at 363.
66. *Id.* at 368–69.
67. *Id.* at 369.
68. Gehring, D. (1993).

Chapter Three

The Prevalence of Medical Risks and Resulting Lawsuits in Study Abroad

This chapter explores the medical risk phenomena within the LARGEST 3. Among the lawsuits and cases examined are Westmont College (a student disfigured after contracting leishmaniasis from a mosquito bite while in Costa Rica), University of Pittsburgh Semester at Sea Program (four U.S students killed and three injured in a crash of a chartered bus in India), and the University of Florida (a student in Bolivia severely burned while studying when a kerosene lamp exploded) to enlighten study abroad participants and coordinators about common trends with risks and liabilities.

Due to the fact that *Paneno v. Centres* was amply considered in the previous chapter, only a brief reexamination of the case and its impacts are included in this chapter.

Some of the cases unveil improper medical coverage in place for overseas participants; others uncover inept risk-averting documents and unsatisfactory orientation given by program leaders that left students ill informed about program dangers and opened institutions to potential lawsuits. Interviewed coordinators provide expert advice for preventing study abroad risks and liabilities. Critical analysis of risk-averting documents is also provided.

In addition, the lawsuit involving Westmont College and the India Iguana case was brought to the forefront to examine the major threat of potential disease transmission while overseas. Also, accidental death makes up another component of medical liability; it periodically occurs and its easy acceptance in some foreign locations is a point of concern. The University of Pittsburgh Semester at Sea Program lawsuit punctuates this concern. Coordinators claim that parental involvement during the program orientation stage may offset this risk and increasingly protect colleges from suits.

A substantial part of the chapter is also dedicated to considering an often overlooked population in study abroad: students with disabilities. Proper advising and services to these students remains a difficult task for coordinators. At the same time, with increased popularity of study abroad participation over the past decade, the number of students with physical and mental disabilities has likewise increased in recent years.[1]

The cases involving study abroad students with disabilities, which include *Furrh v. Arizona Board of Regents* (1983),[2] *Bird v. Lewis & Clark College* (2002),[3] and Arizona State University (2001)[4] are provided to investigate how well Section 504 and the Americans with Disabilities Act (ADA) are enforced with overseas programs.

The chapter closes with a section on Resources for Coordinators to Aid Students with Disabilities and a Top 10 List of Best Practices for Coordinators to Serve the Needs of Students with Disabilities to further assist program leaders' efforts to counsel and accommodate an expanding population of study abroad students with disabilities.

MEDICAL RISKS WITH STUDY ABROAD AS REVEALED BY THE COURTS

Paneno v. Centres

Court documents reveal that medical risks have been a prevailing study abroad problem addressed in lawsuits.[5] Chapter 2 fully disclosed the case of *Paneno v. Centres* as one such example.

To revisit, an ineffective arrangement made between Pasadena Community College (PCC) members and their partnering travel agency, Centres for Academic Programmes Abroad (CAPA), led to the critical injury of student Rocky Paneno.[6] Paneno was on the balcony of housing provided by CAPA, leaned against the railing where a portion of it gave way, and fell six stories, resulting in his paralysis.[7] Paneno filed a lawsuit against PCC and CAPA as a result.[8]

In Brief, What Does *Paneno v. Centres* Disclose?

The previous chapter's section What Can Be Learned from *Paneno v. Centres*? supports that coordinators must closely evaluate student housing provided by their foreign partnering agencies. Also, *Paneno v. Centres* exposes the limitations of a signed waiver with protecting an institution from liability. It is now helpful to move forward with other medical liability cases of impact.

Westmont College

Medical liability coverage was at the forefront with the small California school, Westmont College, which incurred an economic loss due in part to the school not having a waiver of liability in place.[9] Incidentally, a Westmont College student who participated in a program with the Coalition for Christian Colleges and Universities in Costa Rica was bitten by a mosquito and contracted leishmaniasis, which causes disfigurement.[10]

The student sued the college and the coalition, charging that she had not been adequately warned of potential risks.[11] The suit was settled out of court before trial.[12] Up until that lawsuit, the Coalition for Christian Colleges and Westmont College had never required a signed waiver.[13]

Diseases acquired overseas from an insect bite or through foreign organisms are a very common threat with study abroad. Warnings about this specific threat should be included in risk-averting documents and with predeparture orientation.

India Iguana Case

Another resulting lawsuit due to a student contracting a foreign disease involved a private university in California; the student caught a skin disease while working at a jungle iguana preserve in India.[14] Also named in the suit was the consortium that supported the program that the student was participating in.[15] The defendants alleged to have assured the student that there would be no danger or health risks in that particular country.[16] Clearly this claim was unrealistic and inaccurate. Such guarantees should not be made.

Additional Health Risks May Come with Programs in More Exotic Regions of the World

Study abroad participants are pursuing more exotic regions. In fact, there were 4 percent fewer American students studying in Europe in 2008 and 2009, while the number of students to Asia increased by 2 percent, those to South America increased by 13 percent, and those to Africa increased by 16 percent.[17]

Student participants and study abroad program leaders need to be aware of native risks and take distinctive precautions with overseas studies in these regions. Naturally, proper immunizations should be emphasized with any study abroad program, but with programs that have more rural, warm climates, additional emphasis needs to be stressed.

Participants Must Have Updated Immunizations

The Westmont College and India Iguana lawsuits confirm what coordinators already know— the contraction of disease is prevalent with study abroad, and coordinators must furnish participants with a list of mandatory immunizations in advance of study abroad to the region. This list should be presented early in the orientation process, preferably during the first orientation session. It may take a good deal of time to acquire an appointment with a personal physician to administer the vaccinations.

If a participant is unable to obtain the necessary inoculations through a personal physician, the company Passport Health provides reliable preventative health care services, including immunizations. The company has 230 clinics in the United States,[18] so finding a clinic near your home is quite possible.

Individuals' reactions to inoculations vary. After receiving a vaccination, a person may have a brief period of illness; therefore, getting vaccinations early allows suitable recovery time prior to departing overseas.

Disease Risks Must Be Related during Orientation Sessions

Well before departure, a separate list should be provided to program participants specifying names of required immunizations to obtain and the diseases that they thwart. In addition, any other medical concerns native to the region need to be related.

The U.S. Centers for Disease Control and Prevention (CDC) is a top resource to consult. It recommends immunizations to acquire before going overseas. For example, in order to study abroad in Ethiopia, here is such a list provided by the CDC, with its format altered to fit this book.

VACCINES AND MEDICINES

Check the vaccines and medicines list and visit your doctor (ideally four to six weeks) before your trip to get vaccines or medicines you may need.

All Travelers

You should be up to date on routine vaccinations while traveling to any destination. Some vaccines may also be required for travel.

- Routine vaccines: Make sure you are up to date on routine vaccines before every trip. These vaccines include measles-mumps-rubella (MMR) vaccine, diphtheria-tetanus-pertussis vaccine, varicella (chickenpox) vaccine, polio vaccine, and your yearly flu shot.

Most Travelers

Get travel vaccines and medicines because there is a risk of disease in the country you are visiting.

- Hepatitis A: CDC recommends this vaccine because you can get hepatitis A through contaminated food or water in Ethiopia, regardless of where you are eating or staying.

It should be noted that not every region of a country has the same disease threats. You should not automatically discount an entire country, or continent, as some would, as unsafe for study abroad due to issues in a separate region.

For example, with the outbreak of the Ebola virus, various college and university officials deemed the continent of Africa unsuitable for overseas study. This alarmist mentality trumped common sense and proper research.

As reported by the CDC, at present there is an outbreak of the Zika virus in South American and U.S. territories. Should outside nations eliminate the continents of North and South America as safe study abroad destinations? Certainly this would be an overreaction.

Disease Threats Need to Be Specified in Risk-Averting Documents

Often, risk-averting documents provide a laundry list of potential risks yet fail to mention the threat of disease. It is not superfluous to directly name the diseases in the risk-averting documents and orientation materials.

Consider the list of dangers in Waiver F (see Appendix F): "I understand and agree that there are certain dangers, hazards, and risks inherent in international travel . . . weather conditions, conditions of equipment used, differing standards of design, safety, and maintenance of buildings, public spaces and transportation, language barriers, strikes, natural disasters, civil unrest or hostilities, terrorists activities or acts of war, varying quality of available medical treatment and differing health, safety, legal, and religious beliefs and conditions." Yet what risk factor is not mentioned?

It is unsettling that such documents, one after the other, can provide a long list of potential dangers abroad yet not warn about one of the greatest overseas hazards—potential disease transmission.

Again, stressing protection against area diseases and the entities that spread them should be included in risk-averting documents and orientation materials. The Malveaux Sample Recommended Waiver has such an insertion (see Appendix I): "In addition, I am aware that transmittable diseases are a risk; I have consulted the U.S. Centers for Disease Control and Prevention (CDC) listing of necessary and recommended immunizations to acquire before going to the planned destination, and will procure the necessary inoculations specified by this list, and through orientation."

Program leaders should also furnish participants with supplemental information on best practices to avoid diseases and health risks specific to the region. As with any waiver, seek advice from legal counsel with its construction. Every institution is different, and one size does not fit all.

The lesson is clear—all institutions with study abroad should have risk-averting documents in place with language specifying clear and accurate risks specific to that individual region, accompanied by instructive orientation sessions. This point of concern was at the forefront with *Bloss v. The University of Minnesota Board of Regents* (chapter 2), *Fay v. Thiel College* (chapters 2 and 5), and *Earlham College v. Eisenberg* (1998)[19] (chapter 4).

Experts' Thoughts on the Matter and the Waivers That They Use

Again, in order to better inform the participant of medical risks inherit to a program region and potentially safeguard the institution from liability, construction of a separate waiver for each study abroad program, detailing the unique risks in the region, is key. Coordinator Felix believes the waiver "should make clear that there are potential dangers and almost highlights it for them." But why stop at *almost* highlighting the dangers? Do so. In addition, after the program is complete, evaluations should be distributed to participants. The coordinator can learn what improvements need to occur to safeguard students for future programs.

Reevaluate the Quality of Programs and Their Dissemination of Foreign Laws and Practices

Constant evaluation and reevaluation of programs is no small part of the job for a coordinator. This practice aids risk reduction, including health hazards, for future programs. Coordinator Desiree knows this: "After each year's program we assess what went well and what could be improved. We identify if there were problems or potential for problems and work through to find solutions that minimize risk and enhance best practices."

Mandatory predeparture orientation sessions serve to augment risk-averting documents by giving participants added alertness to the laws, cultural practices, risks, and other relevant details in an overseas region. The accompanying risk-averting documents, in turn, solidify information (many people need to read something in writing in order for it to stick in their consciousness) from the orientation classes.

How does this relate to medical and health risks? The better you know a region's customs and practices, the better chance you have for avoiding disease-carrying agents. You need to know if the water is potable, and what foods to avoid consuming. What bodies of water should you not enter or even dip your feet into? What cultural activities are better to avoid? Your digestive system may lack certain antibodies that the natives already have that protect them from illness. These are just a few things to consider.

How else does alertness to the laws and cultural practices of a foreign location aid a participant's health? For one, breaking the law and spending time in a foreign jail is not good for one's health. Waiver E (see Appendix E) attempts to provide such insight with: "I understand that each foreign country has its own laws and standards of acceptable conduct, including dress, manners, morals, politics, drug use, and behavior."

This is a decent attempt to address the matter. However, the language could go further in detailing *example* conduct, dress, and behaviors that are considered acceptable or not. The waiver can forewarn participants about foreign practices that they may encounter. Then, additional orientation materials can provide greater specificity. This approach supports the need for individualized program waivers. The participant will start to gain cultural competence for the overseas location, essential for off setting potential health hazards and risks on a whole.

Again, I want to stress that coordinators must make their best attempts to give students increased cultural competence to assist with risk-reduction abroad. The issue of cultural competence was paramount to *Bloss v. The University of Minnesota Board of Regents.*

Certain habits that are safe in much of the United States proved to be disastrous for the student Adrienne Bloss while in Cuernavaca, Mexico—going out alone at night, hailing a taxi on the street, and sitting in the front seat of the taxi.[20] In fairness to the university, it should be reiterated that predeparture materials and orientation had been provided that forewarned the students of these cultural risks.[21]

The point is orientation sessions accompanied by risk-averting documents that specify cultural and legal differences between the United States and the country abroad may help to protect institutions from legal wrangling and aid participants' recognition of potential hazards.

"ACCIDENTAL DEATH" AS A DISTINCT RISK WITH STUDY ABROAD

Lawsuits reveal that *accidental death* is a valid risk factor with study abroad. The fact that student deaths occur abroad is not new. Yet by scrutinizing related cases and courts' reactions, we may gain a better understanding for factors that led to student deaths and apply strategies to help to prevent future incidents.

Accidental death is a realistic concern for study abroad participants that, pardon the cliché, "comes with the territory." Between 2003 and 2009 the U.S. State Department reported a total of 5,903 non-natural death events of Americans overseas.[22]

Americans who that have done significant travel abroad, especially to more remote areas, discover that accidental deaths are more commonplace and readily accepted in other regions of the world. Let me provide a personal example.

Thailand as an Example of Support

While instructing English in Thailand, I learned about a sad circumstance that afforded me the job I acquired at a college. Here are the details. Upon first arrival, I began to settle into my new living quarters. It was a little townhouse a bit off from campus.

As I unpacked, I found it odd that various used items—a half empty bottle of shampoo and a worn-down bar of sandalwood soap in the bathroom, partially consumed food in the refrigerator, a ratty pair of slippers under the bed, and so forth—remained about. Either someone left in a hurry or unexpectedly never returned. With a few inquiries, I discovered that the previous tenant, also a foreign instructor, had recently met an untimely death.

These are the circumstances that led to his unfortunate death. Apparently, one evening, desirous to stretch his legs a bit, the instructor walked a quarter-mile stretch down a dirt path to get to the highway. He then began to jog along the freeway. The highway is modestly constructed with a mix of dirt and gravel. Nonetheless, it still serves as a major interstate where a combination of large trucks, various cars, and motorbikes barrel along.

That part of the freeway had no posted speed limit or streetlights. Three-and-a-half-foot ditches line each side of the interstate, yet are not easily identifiable since a natural covering of weeds and brush fall over them. As a side note, to get to town and back, I would ride along this road on a motorbike provided by the college, and learned the commute was precarious. But traversing the road by foot at night is plain deadly. The next day, the foreign instructor did not report to his classes. By the end of the day, someone from the college thought to knock on his door. No response came. By the second day, local authorities were notified of his missing whereabouts.

Over a week passed before his remains were found. Not to go into unnecessary detail, but a ditch, less than one-mile-and-a-half from the college, had a lot of scavengers. It was determined that he had been struck by a truck, and the driver never stopped. He landed in a ditch, concealed by brush (I pray he instantly died upon impact—with the assortment of wild animals and insects in that region, I hate to think about the hell he would have endured in that hovel otherwise.)

The college officials were troubled by the loss of the foreign instructor but showed no signs of being jarred by it. It seemed to be a common-enough occurrence. They accepted accidental deaths with a certain ease that initially made me feel unsettled. With enough exposure to this rugged, muggy, and wild environment, I came to more readily accept death, illness, and injury as an inherent facet of the place.

To further illustrate this point, within the first few months of my arrival, two other foreign instructors (with a total of six of us) incurred medical issues severe enough to be unable to stay to fulfill a yearlong contract. Perhaps we should have been oriented with the same ominous speech that arriving freshmen undergraduates often receive—"look at the person to your left; now look at the person to your right; one of these people will not be here by the time you finish."

With time, I accepted an administrative position at the college. Part of my job was to hire new foreign instructors, or *Ajahns*, to replace those who continued to depart.

While in this position, I saw a need that other college administrators tended to overlook. Mainly, I wanted to give transparency to new *Ajahns* about inherent risks in the community prior to their arrival and on the job. The tragedy of the *Ajahn* who perished on the side of the freeway always remained in the back of my mind. Did the deceased *Ajahn* know that Thailand had the highest rate of non-natural deaths of U.S. citizens abroad due to road traffic crashes? Apparently at a rate of 16.49 per 1,000,000.[23] I did not realize then, over seventeen years ago, that my journey to uncover and share risks and liabilities with study abroad had begun.

The main point is that accidental deaths, depending on where you go abroad, may be more commonplace than in the United States; it is a significant facet of medical risks within the LARGEST 3. Court cases reveal that the waiver may serve as an important tool in protecting a university from risks and liabilities if an accidental death of a participant transpires while on a program.[24]

Cases May Merge into More Than One Area of the LARGEST 3

Like most things in life, there are gray areas. It is the same for court cases relative to study abroad. Cases have aspects that may naturally merge into more than one area of the LARGEST 3. However, if a case has more dominant traits in one of the three areas (medical risks, sexual assault, or supervisory neglect), it is categorized as such.

University of Virginia Semester at Sea Program in the Caribbean (2012)

The University of Virginia Semester at Sea Program in the Caribbean is an example of a case that merges into more than one area of the LARGEST 3. Both medical risks and supervisory neglect are relevant to the lawsuit. Overall, the more dominant issue of supervisory neglect pervades the lawsuit that resulted from the death of a study abroad student.[25] The lawsuit has been identified as *Schulman v. Institute for Seaboard Education*. The case is more fully discussed in chapter 5, The Tragedy of Supervisory Neglect in Study Abroad, but it is considered here since medical risks also surround it.

The lawsuit filed in federal court in Miami discloses that Casey Schulman, then a fourth-year student of the University of Virginia, was swimming off Mero Beach, near Roseau, Dominica, on December 1, 2012, when a small dive boat struck her.[26] Dominican authorities charged Andrew Armour, the boat's captain, with manslaughter more than six months later.[27]

Unfortunately, as previously noted, accidental death is a potential risk with study abroad, and when participants go to more remote regions of the world, accidental death may be more prevalent. It is the job of the coordinator to research, and as morbid as it may be, fully apprise participants of a high rate of non-natural deaths for foreigners, where it's a factor. Elements that increase the potential for death need to be spelled out. Sure, you may turn some people off from joining your program. But you are professionally obligated to be candid with them. But the first step is for coordinators to give general statements in risk-averting documents that identify death as a potential hazard with study abroad. *Any* location in the world poses this risk, and students need to be apprised of this.

Risk-Averting Documents Should Identify "Death" as a Study Abroad Risk

For the reasons previously communicated, the Malveaux Sample Recommended Waiver (see Appendix I) provides a statement identifying *death* as a potential risk with study abroad: "I understand . . . that there are certain inherent risks associated with any travel abroad. . . . These inherent risks may lead to serious injury, or even death." Waivers A, C, E, F, and G also properly identify *death* as a potential danger with study abroad.

University of Pittsburgh Semester at Sea Program in India

While taking part in the University of Pittsburgh's Semester at Sea program, four U.S students were killed and three injured in a crash of a chartered bus in India in 1996.[28] Anne Schewe, a mother of one of the students who died in the bus crash, expressed, "We [mothers] are madder than hell our daughters were killed."[29] A lawsuit was filed against the program operators and the University of Pittsburgh, which was the trip sponsor.[30]

The accident prompted many colleges to review their own policies.[31] Buckley (1997) adeptly reported: "The outcome of the litigation [surrounding the deaths of the four students] will take years to resolve and will be far-reaching because . . . this case will test the limits of liability as defined by travel law. It will also have courts define more precisely the extent of a school's duty to protect its students on and off campus."[32]

Multiple lawsuits against the University of Pittsburgh and Semester at Sea have been filed, most likely by grieving parents. In fact, the result from one of those separate lawsuits resulted in a Pennsylvania court finding Semester at Sea/ISE Institute for Shipboard Education negligent in a wrongful death claim of Cherese Mari Laulhere in March 2011.[33]

PARENTAL INVOLVEMENT WITH STUDY ABROAD PROGRAMS

The University of Pittsburgh Semester at Sea Program case reminds us that parents are the main orchestrators of lawsuits. This makes sense considering that they also tend to be the chief financers of student participation in study abroad.

To be clear, a parent, guardian, or the like is a person who has at least one son or daughter participating in a study abroad program, yet is not engaged in study abroad themselves. For simplicity's sake, when using the word *parent*, I am also referring to a potential guardian or caretaker. If coordinators and their administrators want to improve safeguards with study abroad programs, I recommend that they aggressively seek out parental involvement.

Coordinators Weigh In

Coordinators agree that it is important to have strong parental involvement to avoid risks and liabilities. For this to occur, coordinators should readily provide parents access to orientation sessions and materials.

For instance, Coordinator Eve, Coordinator Felix, and Coordinator Levi encourage parents to attend orientation sessions; and Coordinator Eve recounts the exact event that moved her to open orientation classes to parents:

> One of the students said, "My mother wanted to come to an orientation. I told her, 'No mom, you'd embarrass me if you come.'" But then some of the others said, "Yea, my parents might like to come." And [a student asked the other students] "Now if they had a [special] session, how many of your parents might come?" And most of [the other students] said their parents would [come].

She continues to relate:

> By the time we got to the end, one said, "Would you consider doing an evening orientation session for our parents?" And I said, "Yea, we could do that . . . Talk to your parents over Thanksgiving and [see] if they'd like it and I could see what works; [having them participate with orientation] could ease some of their concerns."

The result was a large turnout of parents with vested interest in the program. By having parental involvement, according to Coordinator Eve and Coordinator Levi, risks taken by students, and the likelihood of lawsuits, diminish.

As related by Coordinator Levi, "Sometimes it is very necessary for me to contact parents to reassure them of the safety of the area where their children are going and discuss with them the financial arrangements so that we can be aggressive at it. Also to find out if there are any particular medical problems their son or daughter has we can address before leaving."

Similarly, Coordinator Trevor also assures parents that close monitoring occurs with programs abroad: "I'm not going to bring [students] to London and say 'see you in two weeks.' That is one of the things I want to make clear to parents. Every day is regulated."

Risk-Averting Documents and Orientation Should Support Parental Involvement

Nearly all of the waivers provided and used by coordinators correctly give a statement requiring the signature of a parent or legal guardian for a participant under the age of eighteen. Some directly address the parent, as exemplified by Waiver E (see Appendix E):

I: (a) am the parent or legal guardian of the above participant/student; (b) have read the foregoing Release (including such parts as may subject me to personal financial responsibility); (c) am and will be legally responsible for the obligations and acts of the student/participant as described in this Release, and (d) agree for myself and for the student/participant to be bound by its terms.

The language in waivers should strike a healthy balance. The student should recognize that he or she needs to be a self-regulating, independent participant of study abroad. The parent will not, typically, join them abroad. Addressing a parent directly, in a waiver, could have the negative impact of diminishing this perceived self-accountability by the son or daughter.

Therefore, in the Malveaux Sample Recommended Waiver there is a portion that requests that all parties, including parents of participants under 18 to read and agree to the terms; specifically addressing a parent is unnecessary and can occur at orientation sessions. Like any risk-averting document, there should be a signature line and statement for parents requesting their review and acceptance of the terms. The Malveaux Sample Recommended Waiver contains these details (see Appendix I):

I acknowledge that I have read this entire document and that in exchange for the College's agreement to my participation in this program, I agree to its terms.

_____

Full Name of Participant (Print) / Date:

_____

Signature of Participant / Date:

_____

Signature of Parent/Guardian (if participant is under 18)* Date:

At the risk of vacillating, direct address of parents in a waiver is really a personal choice for coordinators to make since the latter understand the needs of their students better than anyone. Therefore, if the strategy used in Waiver E increases safeguards for students, it should not be deterred.

Aiding Parental Involvement for Students Who Are Not Minors and during the Orientation Period

The reality is that if their child is not a minor, the parents may never see a waiver they do not have to sign. In addition, with busy schedules, parents may not have the ability to attend orientation sessions. Scheduling orientation sessions on Saturdays allows for less potential work conflicts. At the same time, to spare all involved from having to sacrifice a large portion of their day off, begin orientation meetings in the morning, but not too early. A 10:00 a.m. start is reasonable so that people can arrive well rested. The sessions should close by early afternoon. You will have helped your program from the start. Who wants the resentment of participants and their parents who had to take off work and/or feel drained prior to going abroad?

In order to keep parents, who may never see the waiver or attend an orientation session, informed, coordinators need to send them orientation materials. The approach of Coordinator Eve and Coordinator Poppy is spot on in this regard. Coordinator Eve mails (email may also be acceptable) "participants' parents brochures from outside agencies, such as the Council on International Educational Exchange (CIEE), that assist in organizing programs." To offset risks and liabilities, Coordinator Poppy furnishes "parents of participants with manuals relative to the program, the expected code of conduct, and the college policy handbook."

ADDITIONAL MEDICAL RISK LAWSUITS WITH STUDY ABROAD

University of Florida

Medical risks and liability with study abroad came to the forefront at the University of Florida when a student doing research in Bolivia was severely burned when a kerosene lamp exploded.[34] Her medical insurance didn't cover her in Bolivia, and she had no coverage for emergency evacuation; the university chartered a plane to bring her back to the United States, at a cost of some $50,000.[35]

Richard Downie, then associate director of the program, stated the institution felt a "responsibility" to take care of her.[36] The incident prompted him to reexamine university policies.[37]

U.S. courts are attempting to clarify what an institution is liable for when accidents occur overseas. The "courts have held colleges are legally responsible for some injuries that befall students on campus. Yet, whether that applies overseas, and to what sorts of injuries, is unknown."[38] Courts are in fact holding colleges and universities legally responsible for injuries that students sustain overseas, similar to the duty of care expected on home campuses.

Court Trends—the Same Policies and Care at the Home Campus Transfer Abroad

Female students in the case of *King v. Board of Control of Eastern Michigan University* (2002)[39] (fully detailed in chapter 5) endured a hostile environment while on an Eastern Michigan University (EMU) program fraught with sexual harassment and verbal threats.[40]

The threats also became physical. A male student named Frame struck a South African student on the head with a cane, causing a gash on the student's head.[41] Frame then chased another South African student down the corridor, where he took refuge in a female EMU student's room. Frame then began to kick and pound at the door, causing bruises to the female student who was attempting to hold the door closed against Frame's onslaught.[42]

King v. Board of Control of Eastern Michigan University supports that courts are holding colleges legally responsible for injuries (verbal and physical) that deny students "equal access to institutional resources" due to an unsafe environment.[43] A U.S. District Court for the Eastern District of Michigan, Southern Division, noted that the same duty of care that a student receives on the institution's home campus transfers to a program abroad.[44]

Students attending [an] American university are persons in the United States protected by Title IX from discrimination (a type of injury) in educational programs receiving federal financial assistance, and the same rights remain in place during their institution's sponsored study abroad program.[45] In this case, the study abroad program was always under the control of Eastern Michigan University in every respect, rather than under the control of any foreign educational facility.[46]

Not only was this idea central to the case but also has far-reaching implications. Study abroad programs should be held to the same educational standards and student duty of care as campus programs.

Potential Threats Come with Lack of Full Health Disclosure by Participants

Coordinators must make a point of acquiring the medical history of participants prior to study abroad. One of the last things that a program leader wants is for a medical issue, unrelated to program activities, to crop up. They are then placed in the precarious position of trying to figure out the root cause of the issue. All the while, they must still try to conduct the study abroad program as planned. Court documents and coordinators' experiences show that undisclosed medical issues serve to be a serious concern with medical risks and liability.

Furrh v. Arizona Board of Regents

Furrh v. Arizona Board of Regents[47] shows that unforeseeable dangers can spring up when a participant fails to disclose important medical background information. A Court of Appeals of Arizona disclosed that University of Arizona student Jonathan Furrh, who had chronic mental disorders, needed to be physically restrained while on a study abroad program in the Baja Peninsula, Mexico.[48] The court notes refer to Jonathan Furrh by his first name. To be consistent with my address of all individuals in court cases and lawsuits, I use his last name.

After the completion of the program, Furrh sued the university with the complaint that program leaders assaulted him, unlawfully restrained him, and caused him to become lost and exposed to [dangerous] elements in Mexico.[49] The case initially went to a trial court that judged in favor of the defendants, or the university,[50] and the higher Court of Appeals affirmed the trial court ruling.[51]

Furrh v. Arizona Board of Regents is instructional for program leaders who may encounter student medical issues that surface that are not triggered by program activities. Therefore, it is worthwhile to examine the program mishap and the lawsuit that ensued.

The program that Furrh enrolled in was an ecology field trip to the Baja Peninsula conducted by the university.[52] Robert Humphrey was employed by the university to conduct the educational aspects of the trip, and Michael Symons was engaged to furnish the necessary transportation, food, and shelter.[53]

Unknown to anyone involved was Furrh's chronic mental and emotional disorder, or the fact that he had been under the care of a psychiatrist for several years.[54] This mental illness was exacerbated by the experience of the trip to the point where Furrh was a threat to the safety of himself and other members of the group.[55]

He had delusions that the other persons were "Mafioso" who were going to kill him; on a boat trip to Ventana Island, he believed he was going to be thrown to the sharks, and on two occasions he wielded a knife.[56] A trial court had found that Furrh's behavior created potentially serious harm.[57]

In addition, on several occasions, including after dark, Furrh ran away from the group at camp, once to the village of Bahia de los Angeles, fifteen miles away.[58] The site where the study group had its permanent camp was in a remote area, and the surrounding desert and mountains were dangerous.[59] Both rattlesnakes and cholla cactus presented serious problems.[60]

Because program leaders believed there was the realistic possibility that Furrh, through various acts, might bring serious injury or death to himself or others, at times he had to be restrained.[61] Furrh's acts of concern were frequent.[62] Here is description of some of the unstable acts committed and the controlled action that program leaders took to stabilize the volatile environment.

On the way from the village to camp, Furrh was taken by a delusion that he was in the custody of the Mafia and that [members of the group] were going to kill him.[63] Furrh thereupon attempted to jump from the moving vehicle and had to be physically restrained.[64]

In the ensuing struggle, Furrh obtained a knife, which the other members of the party present at the time reasonably believed he intended to use or might have used on them.[65] The members of the party acted reasonably and properly in attempting to restrain him.[66]

Following the struggle, Furrh was subdued, and he asked the members of the group to permit him to walk a short distance from the vehicle to urinate.[67] He was permitted to do this, and thereupon again ran off into the desert.[68] This occurred at approximately midnight, and Furrh was totally unfamiliar with the area, putting himself at risk of potential injury or death.[69]

The next day, Symons restrained Furrh by placing him in a pickup truck, binding Furrh's hands and feet.[70] This was done with the reasonable belief that the student would otherwise run off into the desert or the mountains and run a significant risk of serious injury or death.[71] The confinement was reasonable under the circumstances, and no undue force or restraint was used.[72]

While he was so restrained, Furrh was in the company of Dr. Keith Pierce, who attempted to make sure that Furrh was not unduly uncomfortable, that he was fed, and that his needs were attended to.[73] During this period Furrh showed no fear or irrational belief that he was in the custody of anyone wishing him harm.[74]

Humphrey and Symons took [an] inflatable boat across Bahia de los Angeles to the village, contacted an American pilot who was flying back to the United States, and requested that the pilot get word to Furrh's parents and to the University of Arizona that the student was having mental and emotional problems and should be returned to the United States.[75] This was a reasonable manner of communicating with responsible persons in the United States given the remoteness of the area and the nature of communications from the village.[76]

Humphrey attempted to assure Furrh that his father was on his way to the village in an airplane and that he had talked with Furrh's mother, who gave her love and assurances.[77] Humphrey gave his own assurances that there was no cause for fear or alarm.[78] Nevertheless, Furrh again fled from the area and ran into the mountains where he became lost.[79] He was only found after a substantial search involving both members of the study group, including Humphrey, and residents of the village.[80] Furrh sustained physical injuries during the period of time he was lost.[81]

The faculty program leaders should be commended for their efforts to protect the student Furrh, and other participants, from serious injury during the program. It seems unjust that program leaders were hit with a lawsuit in response to their efforts to assist Furrh, especially when considering they were given no foreknowledge of the chronic mental and emotional disorders with which he suffered. The program leaders should feel some vindication that their actions were seen as warranted by the court.[82]

Further, all of the protective measures taken by the program leaders were without animosity to Furrh; no harm was intended.[83] The leaders reasonably believed Furrh was mentally incompetent and a threat to himself and other members of the group; no one was responsible for creating his delusions.[84]

Program leaders acted promptly and reasonably after having reason to know of Furrh's serious mental disorders.[85] Furrh's temporary detainment (and the means taken to effect it) was reasonably necessary and justified and in the best interests of the student and other members of the group.[86]

All program leaders should know that if faced with a similar problem, they need to act. Had program leaders in *Furrh v. Arizona Board of Regents* done nothing, they would have been negligent.[87] Ironically, inaction from the leaders would have more fittingly warranted a lawsuit; potentially, multiple suits from various program participants could have resulted. Then, this would have then been a case of supervisory neglect (and appropriately placed in chapter 5).

Perhaps it should give solace to all study abroad coordinators and program leaders to know that the court gives them authority to take action against this kind of issue. The basic common-law rule is that a person who is so insane as to be dangerous to himself/herself or others may be arrested and detained without judicial or quasi-judicial proceedings, when there is an urgent necessity to prevent immediate injury to such person or to others.[88] For study abroad coordinators, participants, program leaders, and the like, this rule should bring relief.

Seek Parental Input with Participant Health Disclosure

Furrh v. Arizona Board of Regents underscores how important it is for program leaders to obtain full medical disclosure from students. This case also affirms an earlier point made in the chapter—it is extremely helpful to get parents involved in the predeparture orientation process. Coordinator Levi considers parents to be helpful with "find[ing] out if there are any particular medical problems their son or daughter has [that leaders] can address before leaving."

It is without question that the program leaders in *Furrh v. Arizona Board of Regents* would have benefited from knowing Jonathan Furrh's medical history in advance of the program. Consider his parents' ordeal with events surrounding the program. One imagines that the parents would be quite willing (yes, hindsight is 20/20) to disclose their son's cognitive issues as opposed to receiving jolting news from college officials about his mental breakdown while abroad; hastening to get on a plane and fly to Mexico; becoming part of a search party to recover him in a remote, rattlesnake-infested, mountainous region; and discovering him riddled with physical injuries.

Why Jonathan Furrh, or any study abroad participant for that matter, would not choose to disclose their medical history can only be speculated. A lack of openness by some students likely comes from needless feelings of shame with having a disability. Often, parents are able to look beyond potential discomfort, knowing the greater good that comes with fully disclosing a son's or daughter's medical history in order to secure their safety.

Parents are often more aware, and willing than their children, to disclose the latters medical history to coordinators. Therefore, for the good of the ailing student, other program participants, and the college, program leaders should diplomatically solicit parental involvement with completing health disclosure forms. To assist coordinators, I have provided a sample Health Disclosure Form (Appendix L).

A Health Disclosure should effectively draw out potential medical concerns with students, but clearly not discriminate. The sample Health Disclosure Form uses such tact with a statement in bold that maintains: "This information does not affect your admission to the study abroad program" (Appendix L).

This standard must apply for students with disabilities. They should not be judged by their disability, nor should the disability impact their study abroad admission. It will be up to the coordinator and the student to determine if accommodations bring a secure enough environment for the student to take part in study abroad. As with any risk-averting document, perusal of this form should occur with legal counsel at the institution.

With that said, it is imperative with the case of *Furrh v. Arizona Board of Regents* to not overlook a third party (aside from the program leaders and parents) who deserves a sympathetic ear—Jonathan Furrh. He went through a very difficult ordeal. Furrh should not be ridiculed, nor should his tribulation in Mexico be trivialized.

For those who simply proclaim that Jonathan Furrh should have disclosed his disability and view his lawsuit as a mere *teachable moment* for coordinators who do not require students to complete a mandatory health disclosure form, realize that this does not equate to "problem solved." On a whole, coordinators need to expand their awareness and improve available resources to students with disabilities.

DISABILITY SUPPORT AND ITS IMPLICATIONS WITH MEDICAL RISKS

The care of students with disabilities studying abroad, and its impact in U.S. courts, warrants serious review in this chapter on medical risks and liability. One immediate concern is failed marketing for this group of students.

A Limiting Image of Study Abroad and the Need for a Makeover

You have probably seen the sleek, colorful study abroad brochures with exuberant young students posing before some of the world's most renowned, foreign fixtures and prehistoric sites. The students appear youthful, physically fit, and confident. Yet how often do you see a gray-haired, obese individual in a wheelchair featured on the cover? How about with just a single one of those traits?

Print advertising for study abroad is narrow, and the overall image limits, among others, students with disabilities. Unfortunately, the message being sent to would-be participants is "if you do not look like this, you need not apply." This archetypal image necessitates updating, and study abroad needs to expand opportunities for nontraditional students, such as the middle-aged, stout, disabled veteran who attends my college.

For those who believe that disabled students are a group that can be overlooked, you had better reconsider. This group makes up a significant number of U.S. students in higher education. According to the U.S. Department of Education's National Center for Education Statistics (2006), in 2003 to 2004, approximately 11 percent of U.S. undergraduates reported having a disability.[89] This figure has sustained. A "Profile of Undergraduate Students: 2011–2012" put forth by the U.S. Department of Education reported 11.1 percent.[90]

Court Trends That Impact Students with Disabilities Abroad

When considering court cases that relate to students with disabilities studying abroad, it is essential to know two key pieces of U.S. legislation. First, Section 504 of the Rehabilitation Act (1973) guarantees certain rights to people with disabilities.[91] It was the first U.S. federal civil rights protection for people with disabilities.[92]

In addition, the Americans with Disabilities Act (ADA) protects individuals with disabilities. This Act prohibits discrimination against people with disabilities in employment, transportation, public accommodation, communications, and governmental activities.[93] The Department of Education's Office for Civil Rights (OCR) enforces Section 504 and the ADA as they relate to disability accommodations for college and university students.[94]

Legal officials have sent mixed messages with regard to allowing the same duty of care for individuals with disabilities abroad as provided at home. In other words, extraterritorial application of Section 504 and the ADA remains unsettled in U.S. courts. What is meant by extraterritorial application is whether federal disability discrimination laws are applicable to study abroad programs.

Bird v. Lewis & Clark College

In *Bird v. Lewis & Clark College*, a federal district court in Oregon analyzed the actions of a college study abroad program under the ADA and Title III of the Rehabilitation Act to uphold the lower court's finding that the program had not discriminated against the student.[95] Arwen Bird was an undergraduate student who used a wheelchair to participate in Lewis & Clark

College's own sponsored study abroad program in Australia.[96] For the majority of the activities, the college accommodated her disability; at times she had to be carried.[97]

Bird sued the college for being in violation of Section 504 and ADA claims.[98] All of the claims essentially share one premise: during Bird's stay in Australia, the College discriminated against her on the basis of disability by failing to provide her with wheelchair access.[99] In ruling on the extraterritoriality issue, the district court emphasized that the plaintiff was an American student participating in an American university's overseas program, taught by American faculty.[100]

The court cautioned that if Section 504 and the ADA did not apply to study abroad programs, "students in overseas programs would become the proverbial 'floating sanctuaries from authority' not unlike stateless vessels on the high seas."[101]

To follow, on appeal, the Ninth Circuit did not address the district court's ruling on extraterritoriality, yet nonetheless denied the plaintiff's Section 504 and ADA claims, finding that Lewis & Clark's program, "when viewed in its entirety, [was] readily accessible to and usable by individuals with disabilities."[102]

Significant was the fact that while the court denied the student's federal discrimination claims, the court determined that the college had a fiduciary relationship with the student under state law because the college assured the student that it would accommodate her disability and indicated that adequate facilities would be available for most of the outdoor trips.[103] In addition, the court found that the student had reason to trust the college's guarantees since the college had accommodated the student on the home campus.[104]

Rulings in *Bird v. Lewis & Clark College* imply that the same duty of care and rights afforded to students with disabilities under U.S. law may be expected with study abroad, and that those rights are protected in a court of law.

Arizona State University Case

However, law officials are inconsistent with granting the same protections for students with disabilities overseas as they would on the home campus. At least one of the Department of Education's Office for Civil Rights (OCR) has openly made its position known that the ADA and Section 504 *do not* apply to overseas programs.[105]

In a case with *Arizona State University*, a deaf student asked university officials to provide a sign language interpreter for him while he studied abroad at an Irish university.[106] The University rejected the request, and the student filed a complaint with OCR.[107]

In response, OCR determined that "Section 504 and Title III protections *do not* extend extraterritorially . . . [n]or does either statute otherwise prohibit discrimination on the basis of disability in overseas programs."[108]

In contrast, in three other matters, OCR area offices concluded—without explicitly discussing extraterritoriality—that under certain factual scenarios, Section 504 and the ADA *do* apply to study abroad programs;[109] those matters involved Husson College (2005), College of St. Scholastica (1992), and St. Louis University (1990).[110]

Even though it remains unsettled whether students with disabilities will receive extraterritorial application of Section 504 and the Americans with Disabilities Act by law officials, coordinators of study abroad must continue to make every effort to provide suitable accommodations for these students.

Courts Remain Inconclusive on the Rights of Students with Disabilities Who Study Abroad

Again, it is apparent that courts and regional offices that make up the Department of Education's Office for Civil Rights (OCR) have been indecisive concerning the degree of rights to afford students with disabilities while abroad. As shown, some decisions relate that Section 504 and ADA apply to study abroad; others have determined they do not. College and university officials will need to continue to remain attentive to future decisions as the courts and OCR work this out.

Coordinators Weigh in on the Subject of Students with Disabilities Studying Abroad

Overall, coordinators greatly yearn to serve the needs of students with disabilities who desire study abroad. In her desire to remain responsible to these students' needs, Coordinator Poppy maintains awareness for the varied approaches and resources available to serve students with disabilities abroad: "[Coordinators] have to be looking at how the university itself actually addresses disability issues . . . universities take very different approaches. Some universities in terms of [being] American Disability Act (ADA) compliant adhere to beyond a compliance philosophy, which means that not only are they actively encouraging students with disabilities to participate in things, but they are actually making it possible for them to do it beyond the letter of the law."

She rightly maintains, "Mobility International is an advocacy group that has spent a lot of time looking at the issues of ADA compliance. And they've put together a handbook that is almost two hundred and fifty pages long which basically looks at study abroad issues. So it's an excellent resource." Mobility International is featured in this chapter's coming section, Resources for Coordinators to Aid Students with Disabilities. Additional resources are also named in this section.

However, due to concerns about program affordability, coordinators voiced difficulty with making accommodations to include these students. Coordinator Levi relates that "many countries do not have disability support services, and even if they are provided by the host college, it becomes enormously expensive to send someone abroad. If someone is deaf, what if a school doesn't have signers? Then you have to send a signer abroad and it becomes extraordinarily expensive for the college involved."

He continues:

> So [coordinators] have to find a way to make things available for disability students, and there are some countries that do provide services. But you need to know which ones they are. When students [come] to me with disabilities, I [have] to ask our host organizations what schools provide for deaf or blind or disability support. Then that way I can send the disability student abroad.

To help resolve this matter, coordinators may need to go no further than their own campus. They should consult their campus Disability Service Office, Accessible Education Office members, or similar groups. These offices tend to meet requests for sign language interpreters on campus, among other things. Its employees may be able to assign, or at least direct the coordinator, to organizations that have reliable, affordable sign language interpreters who are available in the desired overseas region.

Also, a helpful resource that would directly assist Coordinator Levi is Mobility International USA (MIUSA)'s "Resource Library." If you put in "interpreters abroad" as a keyword search, the first three (out of forty-eight) informative items found are "Hiring Sign Language

Interpreters," "10 Tips for Reducing Sign Language Interpreter Costs," and "Locating Sign Language Interpreters in Non-U.S. Countries." In addition, the webpage has instructive tip sheets, provides helpful links, and points to other useful resources.

DisabledTravlers.com is extremely useful for individuals with disabilities who desire assistance while traveling. The web source has a page, "Travel Companions," which emphasizes that a travel companion is needed for some travelers due to their disability. This is certainly true. DisabledTravelers.com also provides links to companies that provide travel companions for disabled travelers. Coordinator Levi could directly inquire about travel companies that assign sign language interpreters.

If unanswered questions still remain, access Ability Info. This resource provides free help, information, and advice for people, and their advocates, who are disabled.

A Growing Number of Students with Disabilities Who Need to Be Served

As the study abroad population has grown, it has also diversified, and students with disabilities are increasingly pursuing opportunities overseas. According to Open Doors, more than one thousand students with disabilities studied abroad in 2006 to 2007; of these students, half reported a learning disability, 25 percent reported a mental health condition, and the remaining 25 percent were students with physical, sensory, or other disabilities.[111] These are merely the reported cases. A far greater number of students with disabilities study abroad each year.

Increased resources need to be made available to serve students with disabilities who desire overseas study. Coordinators must continue to research new opportunities, accommodations, and practical equipment available to students with disabilities so that the latter can take full advantage of this highly impactful educational approach.

Resources for Coordinators to Aid Students with Disabilities

In order to give coordinators greater awareness for ways to advise and serve students with disabilities, here are a few key resources to consider:

- Ability Info at http://www.abilityinfo.com provides people who are disabled with free help, information and advice.
- DisabledTravelers.com at http://www.disabledtravelers.com/airlines.htm is dedicated to accessible travel information for individuals with disabilities; the resource also provides information about businesses from around the world that specialize in disability travel.
- Emerging Horizons at http://emerginghorizons.com gives travel information for wheelchair users and slow walkers.
- Mobility International USA at http://www.miusa.org is a disability-led nonprofit organization that fulfills its mission to empower people with disabilities to achieve their human rights through international exchange and international development. This organization also provides the "National Clearinghouse on Disability and Exchange," a project to increase the participation of people with disabilities in all types of travel with a purpose.
- NACUANOTES's "Federal Disability Laws: Do They Translate to Study Abroad Programs?" may be retrieved via http://www.calstate.edu/gc/documents/NACUANOTES10. pdf; it is produced by Josh Whitlock and Allison Charney, and it reports on the current state of federal disability discrimination law with respect to college and university study abroad programs for students, suggests best practices (with many adopted in the coming top 10 list section in this chapter), and gives additional resources for college and university counselors and administrators.

- NAFSA: Association of International Educator's "Education Abroad Advising to Students with Disabilities," provided by Heidi M. Soneson, is a guide that furnishes study abroad advisers with procedures and resources to support students with disabilities who plan to go overseas; it considers student disability-related accommodation needs, gives predeparture preparation materials, and provides Web links to additional resources, among other things.
- NAFSA: Association of International Educator's "Students with Disabilities Studying Abroad," offered by Eve Katz, is an article that encourages students with disabilities to study abroad, provides instructive tips for advising students with disabilities, and gives helpful resources.

Top 10 List of Best Practices for Coordinators to Serve the Needs of Students with Disabilities

This top 10 list aims to give coordinators increased insight for advising and furnishing students with disabilities additional study abroad opportunities; many of the recommendations are adopted from NACUANOTES's (2012) best practices:

1. Include comprehensive information for students with disabilities in your orientation materials and institutional website. Clearly describe the process students should follow to request reasonable accommodations abroad and strongly encourage students who plan to seek accommodations to contact the disability services office as early as possible in the process. This will show students you are open to accommodating their needs and will enable you to start as early as possible to help them find the most appropriate programs and accommodations.
2. Do not make any direct preadmission inquiries regarding whether students have disabilities (including mental health disabilities), but do clearly inform students of essential program requirements and make narrowly tailored and disability-neutral inquiries aimed at determining whether students are "otherwise qualified" for a specific program. Indicate that all program participants must meet the essential program requirements (such as GPA, letters of recommendation, and language fluency requirements), with or without reasonable accommodations.
3. If, in the preadmission context, you choose to require students to submit forms from physicians certifying that the students are able to fully and safely participate in a particular study abroad program, ensure that such forms do not ask about disabilities, but rather focus on the essential program requirements. Also, ensure that such forms are required of all program applicants.
4. Consider making confidential disability-related inquiries (perhaps as part of a mandatory health disclosure form) after students have been admitted to a given program, and consider having the disability services office handle all such inquiries.
   Critical points: All determinations as to whether a student meets the definition of a student "with a disability" must be made by the disability services office in accordance with its typical protocol for such determinations. Also, while the study abroad office and others can certainly be part of discussions regarding whether a student is "otherwise qualified" for a program and regarding the reasonableness of requested accommodations, the ultimate determinations must be made by the disability services office in accordance with its typical protocol for such determinations.
5. Make sure your study abroad office, disability services office, and relevant individuals in other countries, such as employees and program administrators, have open lines of communication and work collaboratively. For example, many schools have the study

abroad office or the disability services office serve as a liaison between the overseas program staff and the disability service provider to ensure that information is communicated clearly and effectively. Include the student in all "what if" discussions and accessibility planning.

6. Use technology to your advantage. For example, some programs accommodate students with disclosed mental health disabilities by having them Skype once a week with school counselors. Another common practice is to use remote captioning to accommodate a student with a hearing loss in an overseas class.

7. Make sure the faculty and administrators leading trips or study abroad programs are fully equipped and trained to handle a student's disability-related accommodation needs. Provide training to overseas staff on disability issues, access, and the confidential nature of disability-related information. Intense predeparture training must be taken seriously.

8. After putting in place an accommodation plan, inform the departing student about overseas program contacts for disability-related accommodation needs or for addressing additional, unexpected access barriers.

9. Have an emergency backup plan in place should a student become disoriented, lost, or a danger to themselves and/or other participants while abroad. Consider what actions, and which faculty leaders are willing to take those actions, if the need to subdue a difficult situation arises.

10. Alleviate your trepidation to assist students with disabilities in studying abroad by becoming better informed. Research, research, and then, yes, do some more research to remain current with legal matters and trends for serving the needs of students with disabilities overseas. Become an avid reader of published works and media sources that advise and give resources for best practices in serving the needs of students with disabilities for study abroad.

CHAPTER SUMMARY

As revealed by the courts, medical risks and liability are a systemic concern with study abroad. *Paneno v. Centres*, for example, shows that coordinators must closely evaluate housing provided by their foreign partnering agencies prior to assigning partners with the care of students. The case also bared the limitations of a signed waiver as a method for protecting an institution from liability.

Student study abroad participants and coordinators should take notice of the Westmont College and the India Iguana lawsuits before going overseas. The cases verify the hazard of disease transmission overseas, and the absolute need for coordinators to require preventative immunizations from participants in advance of departure. Details about disease risks and other hazards that are unique to the region should be explicitly noted in risk-averting documents and predeparture orientation materials.

Accidental death is a legitimate concern with study abroad, and is often more common and readily accepted in regions overseas. The University of Pittsburgh Semester at Sea Program lawsuit punctuates this issue. Coordinators maintain that parental involvement in program orientation may offset this inherent danger and increasingly shield colleges from suits.

Court trends, as unearthed by the suit against University of Florida and the case of *King v. Board of Control of Eastern Michigan University*, seem to affirm that policies on duty of care for students at the home campus should also be present with study abroad programs.

Lack of full medical history disclosure by participants may upend study abroad programs, as exhibited by *Furrh v. Arizona Board of Regents*, leading to potential significant injury for the sufferer and other participants. Gaining full medical disclosure from study abroad participants is key, and a Health Disclosure Form (see Appendix L for an example) should be administered to participants prior to departure.

Disability support has become an increasingly important part of medical liability issues with study abroad. The type of student participant solicited by study abroad media has been narrow in focus. The image of a nontraditional-aged, rotund, and/or disabled student is void in nearly all advertising. In addition, it is not wise to overlook 11 percent of U.S. undergraduates who reported disabilities.[112]

U.S. courts and the Department of Education's Office for Civil Rights have sent mixed messages concerning their willingness to enforce extraterritorial application of Section 504 and the Americans with Disabilities Act. This is apparent when considering *Bird v. Lewis & Clark College*, and complaints filed against Arizona University, Husson College, College of St. Scholastica, and St. Louis University.

Overall, coordinators voice a genuine desire to serve students with disabilities who want to study abroad. Yet due to concerns with prohibitive program costs resulting from additional accommodations set for students with disabilities, many coordinators feel at a loss with finding viable solutions to aid these students.

To assist with this issue, and other matters that deter these students from gaining proper assistance with study abroad, a list of Resources for Coordinators to Use in Assisting Students with Disabilities and a Top 10 List of Best Practices for Coordinators to Serve the Needs of Students with Disabilities are provided.

NOTES

1. NACUANOTES. (2012, April 26). Federal disability laws: Do they translate to studyabroad programs? Retrieved from http://www.calstate.edu/gc/documents/NACUANOTES10.pdf.

2. 676 P.2d 1141 (Ariz. Ct. App. 1983).

3. 303 F.3d 1015 (9th Cir. 2002).

4. *Ariz. St. Univ.*, 22 N.D.L.R. 239 (2001).

5. Boorstein, M., & Wright, S. W. (1998). Fears about safety—and lawsuits—plague study abroad programs. *Community College Week 10*, 12.

6. *Paneno v. Centres for Acad. Programmes Abroad, Ltd.*, 13 Cal. Rptr. 3d 759, 762-63 (Cal. Ct. App. 2004).

7. *Id.* at 763.

8. *Id.* at 761, 763.

9. Rubin, A. M. (1996, May 10). Making it safer to study abroad. *Chronicle of Higher Education*, p. A49.

10. *Id.*

11. *Id.*

12. *Id.*

13. *Id.*

14. Rhodes, G. M., & Aalberts, R. J. (1994, January/February). Liability and study abroad: "Prudent" policies and procedures are the best insurance. *Transitions Abroad*, 65–67.

15. *Id.*

16. *Id.*

17. Institute of International Education. (2015). Press release: Study abroad by U.S. students slowed in 2008/09 with more students going to less traditional destinations. Retrieved from http://www.iie.org/Who-We-Are/News-and-Events/Press-Center/Press-Releases/2010/2010-11-15-Open-Doors-US-Study-Abroad.

18. Passport Health. (2015). Travel immunizations/travel health. Retrieved fromhttps://www.passporthealthusa.com.

19. No. IP97-0592 (S.D. Ind. Sept. 10, 1998).

20. *Bloss v. Univ. of Minn. Bd. of Regents*, 590 N.W.2d 661, 666 (Minn. Ct. App. 1999).

21. *Id.* (noting that the particular warnings about public transportation and travel at night were the exact circumstances that led to the student's injuries).

22.   Sherry, M. K., Mossallam, M., Mulligan, M., Hyder, A. A., & Bishai, D. (2013, December 3). Rates of intentionally caused and road crash deaths of US citizens abroad. Group.bmj.com. Retrieved from http://www.jhsph.edu/research/centers-and-institutes/johns-hopkins-center-for-injury-research-and-policy/publications_resources/Deaths of US travelelers Inj Prev-2013-Sherry-injuryprev-2013-040923.pdf.

23.   *Id.*

24.   Rubin, A. M. (1996, May 10).

25.   Complaint at 8–10, *Schulman v. Inst. for Shipboard Educ.*, No. 15-11689 (S.D. Fla. Apr. 20, 2015), *aff'd per curiam*, No. 11-11689, 2015 WL 4896597, at *9 (11th Cir. Aug. 18, 2015).

26.   *Id.* at 7.

27.   Father of U.Va. student who died studying abroad files lawsuit. (2013, November 2). *Richmond Times-Dispatch*. Retrieved from http://www.richmond.com/news/virginia/article_d966a9cb-da4f-5bb6-ba03-198c6bfc7cc7.html.

28.   Kast, R. (1997). In loco parentis and the "reasonable person." *International Educator 7*, 1.Rubin, A. M. (1996, May 10). Making it safer to study abroad. *Chronicle of Higher Education*, p. A49.

29.   Buckley, T. J. (1997, September 12), India crash wake up call for schools and parents. *USA Today*, p. A1.

30.   Rubin, A. M. (1996, May 10).

31.   Kast, R. (1997). Rubin, A. M. (1996, May 10).

32.   Buckley, T. J. (1997, September 12), p. A1.

33.   Semester at Sea—A deadly program (2011). Cherese Mari Laulhere Foundation. Retrieved from http://cherese.org/semester-at-sea.html.

34.   Kast, R. (1997). Rubin, A. M. (1996, May 10).

35.   *Id.*

36.   Rubin, A. M. (1996, May 10), p. A49.

37.   Rubin, A. M. (1996, May 10).

38.   Boorstein, M., & Wright, S. W. (1998), p. 13.

39.   221 F.Supp.2d 783 (E.D. Mich. 2002).

40.   *Id.* at 784–85 (describing the allegations of sexual harassment that detailed verbal, physical, and sexual abuse against female students during a study abroad program in South Africa).

41.   *Id.* at 785.

42.   *Id.*

43.   *Id.* at 791.

44.   *Id.*

45.   *Id.* at 790–91.

46.   *Id.* at 788, 790–91.

47.   676 P.2d 1141 (Ariz. Ct. App. 1983).

48.   *Id.* at 1142–43 (explaining that the student believed he was being held by the Mafia and attempted to escape from the group, and at least once used a knife to attempt escape).

49.   *Id.* at 1142.

50.   *Id.*

51.   *Id.* at 1146.

52.   *Id.* at 1142.

53.   *Id.*

54.   *Id.*

55.   *Id.*

56.   *Id.* at 1142–43.

57.   *Id.* at 1144.

58.   *Id.* at 1143.

59.   *Id.* at 1142.

60.   *Id.*

61.   *Id.* at 1143–44.

62.   *Id.*

63.   *Id.* at 1143.

64.   *Id.*

65.   *Id.*

66.   *Id.*

67.   *Id.*

68.   *Id.*

69.   *Id.*

70.   *Id.*

71.   *Id.*

72.   *Id.*

73.   *Id.*

74.   *Id.*

75.   *Id.*

76. *Id.*

77. *Id.* at 1144.

78. *Id.*

79. *Id.*

80. *Id.*

81. *Id.*

82. *Id.*

83. *Id.*

84. *Id.*

85. *Id.*

86. *Id.*

87. *Id.*

88. *Id.* at 1145 (quoting D. A. Cox, Annotation, *Right, Without Judicial Proceeding, to Arrest and Detain One Who Is, or Is Suspected of Being, Mentally Deranged*, 92 A.L.R.2d 570 Art. 2 (West 2015)).

89. U.S. Department of Education, National Center for Education Statistics. (2006). *Profile of undergraduates in U.S. postsecondary education institutions: 2003–04* (NCES 2006-184). Washington, DC: U.S. Department of Education. Retrieved from http://nces.ed.gov/fastfacts/display.asp?id=60.

90. National Center for Education Statistics. (2014, October). Profile of undergraduate students:2011–2012. U.S. Department of Education Institute of Education Sciences. Retrieved
   from https://nces.ed.gov/pubsearch/pubsinfo.asp?pubid=2015167.

91. U.S. Department of Health and Human Services: Office for Civil Rights. (2006). Fact sheet: Your rights under Section 504 of the Rehabilitation Act. Washington, DC: U.S. Department of Health and Human Services. Retrieved from http://www.hhs.gov/ocr/civilrights/resources/factsheets/504.pdf.

92. *Id.*

93. U.S. Department of Labor (2015). Disability resources: Americans with Disabilities Act. Washington, DC: U.S. Department of Labor. Retrieved from http://www.dol.gov/dol/topic/disability/ada.htm.

94. NACUANOTES. (2012, April 26). Federal disability laws: Do they translate to study abroad programs? Retrieved from http://www.calstate.edu/gc/documents/NACUANOTES10.pdf.

95. 303 F.3d 1015, 1020-21 (9th Cir. 2002).

96. *Id.* at 1017.

97. *Id.* at 1017–18 (noting that Bird needed to be carried to the bathroom from her bedroom, as well as up a flight of stairs to get to the cafeteria).

98. *Id.* at 1019. Bird also brought claims based on fraud, negligence, breach of contract, breach of fiduciary duty, intentional infliction of emotional distress, negligent misrepresentation, and defamation. *Id.*

99. *Id.*

100. NACUANOTES. (2012, April 26), p. 16.

101. NACUANOTES. (2012, April 26), p. 17.

102. NACUANOTES. (2012, April 26), p. 18.

103. NACUANOTES. (2012, April 26), p. 19.

104. NACUANOTES. (2012, April 26), p. 20.

105. NACUANOTES. (2012, April 26), p. 23.

106. NACUANOTES. (2012, April 26), p. 24.

107. *Ariz. St. Univ.*, 22 N.D.L.R. 239, 239 (2001).

108. *Id.*

109. NACUANOTES. (2012, April 26), p. 26.

110. NACUANOTES. (2012, April 26), pp. 26–30.

111. Soneson, H. M. (2009). Education abroad advising to students with disabilities.NAFSA: Association of International Educators. Retrieved from
   http://www.nafsa.org/uploadedFiles/NAFSA_Home/Resource_Library_Assets/Publications_Library/AdvisEAstudDis.pdf.

112. National Center for Education Statistics (2014, October).

Chapter Four

Sexual Assault Risks and Liabilities with Study Abroad

The reoccurring issue of *sexual assault*, another component of the LARGEST 3, continues to afflict study abroad. Associated lawsuits, brought forth in this chapter, show that courts expect colleges and universities to remain conscientious of study abroad activities that may endanger students and bring forth lawsuits relative to sexual assault.

Some closely surveyed cases include a St. Mary's College (2001) lawsuit (five female students were ambushed and raped while studying abroad in Guatemala), *Earlham College v. Eisenberg* (a student alleged she was sexually harassed and raped by her host father while participating in the college's study abroad program in Japan),[1] and *Bloss v. The University of Minnesota Board of Regents* (a student studying abroad in Mexico, en route to meet friends for a social evening, was raped at knifepoint by a taxi driver).[2]

This chapter explores the problem of sexual assault risks with study abroad (as shown by legal documents), outcomes from the lawsuits, and solutions to potentially protect students, coordinators, and their institutions. Expert opinion from coordinators and analysis of current risk-averting documents are brought forth for additional resolutions.

SEXUAL ASSAULT

Court documents unveil that *sexual assault* litigation is a dominant class of suits aimed at study abroad programs. Recent trends in the court system show that universities must remain vigilant of activities that might bring forth lawsuits relative to sexual assault abroad.

Risk-averting documents, including waivers of liability, tend to use the nonspecific term *injury* to encompass sexual assault. Two immediate questions come to mind. Is the definition of the word *injury* in a waiver far-reaching enough to protect an institution from liability when it comes to sexual assault? Does the use of the word *injury* adequately inform students of the potential risk of sexual assault with study abroad? These questions and others will be visited in the chapter.

St. Mary's College Lawsuit

A case involving St. Mary's College in Maryland brought forth immediate concern for whether sufficient safeguards were put in place to prevent the attack and rape of five female students participating in a program in Guatemala. The St. Mary's College lawsuit brings great implications for what study abroad coordinators might do to thwart sexual assault abroad, and what the courts expect from colleges and universities in the future.

In January 1998, while a group of students, faculty members, and the study abroad director were returning by bus to Guatemala City from a trip to a rural area, seven men in two pickup trucks forced the St. Mary's College group off the road.[3] The armed bandits robbed the participants, and five of the students were raped.[4] Following this, in 1999, three men were found guilty of the rapes in Guatemala, and each is serving a twenty-eight-year prison sentence.[5] Boorstein foresaw that "the rape of the five American college students . . . will fuel a growing movement to hold colleges liable for the safety of their students studying overseas."[6] This prediction came to fruition.

Demands for swift justice came with a lawsuit filed by three of the students on January 12, 2001.[7] In the suit, the students argued that insufficient precautions were taken for their safety, and that additional measures such as a convoy of several vehicles, an armed guard, and the selection of a safer route would have prevented the injuries.[8] College officials disputed that sufficient precautions had been taken, and since previous study abroad programs to Guatemala had been without incident, the injuries were unforeseeable.[9] In order to avoid drawing out the dispute, the college settled with the plaintiffs.[10]

In a statement sent to the entire college community through an email, then President Maggie O'Brien expressed, "The events that the group lived through in Guatemala would be doubly tragic if they served to increase, rather than minimize, that danger. We took every prudent safety precaution, both before and after the attack, and are confident that the College was not negligent in its duties to anyone on the trip; our hearts continue to go out to the victims of these terrible crimes."[11]

As tragic as this event was, it is difficult to determine irrefutable evidence showing improper safeguards by St. Mary's College officials led to this calamity. With the lawsuit having been settled out of court without trial, there is a lack of information. Still, there is enough information from the lawsuit to gain essential insights.

Let's revisit the claim that additional precautions such as a convoy of several vehicles, an armed guard, and the selection of a safer route would have prevented the injuries.[12] I can say from personal experience with designing and leading study abroad programs that having an armed guard to accompany a group is very uncommon. Simply, if you are in a region where an armed guard is needed to lead a group, then that is a region where the group should not have been taken.

It begs the question, "Did college officials fully research the countryside and its potential perils?" College officials maintain that since previous study abroad trips to Guatemala had been free of incident, the students' *injuries* were unforeseeable.[13] This also brings then the inquiry, "How many previous programs were successfully done in this region without issue?" Followed by the natural question, "Then how many successful programs to a region make for a clear measure that the region is safe?" This is a challenge for anyone to determine, especially if one was not directly involved in the design of the program.

Arguments for a convoy of several vehicles, or the selection of a safer route, are certainly manageable. Rather than having only a single coach to run off the road, perhaps a convoy of vehicles might have thwarted the criminals. The reason I note *perhaps* is because armed bandits were in two separate pickup trucks. With bandits possessing weapons and having *two* pickup trucks, would the convoy need to be made up of three or more vehicles?

Unless you have a very large group of participants, a coordinator would not think to supply multiple buses as a safety measure for study abroad. There were sixteen total participants for this program.[14] Program costs increase with procuring additional buses that would have empty seats. Participants would likely have wondered why the group was split into subgroups with multiple buses, as opposed to a single bus that could accommodate everyone. If a coordinator needed to apply this precautionary measure to avert attack, once again, the region should not have been traversed in the first place.

Other essential questions are, "If the head vehicle of the convoy was forcibly stopped by bandits, would the other vehicles stop as well, defeating the purpose of the protective convoy? Would drivers and participants in other vehicles be comfortable with leaving the group that had been stopped?"

To be clear, what those participants endured in Guatemala, particularly the five women who were sexually assaulted, was absolutely heartbreaking. These questions are only brought forth to illustrate how difficult it is to fully determine, had St. Mary's College officials put forth precautions for which they were sued, if the catastrophe could have been averted.

Perhaps more essential is whether proper vetting of the foreign agency occurred, a strong rapport between the college and agency was in place, and if a long history of safe exploration in the region had been worked out through St. Mary's College organizers. These measures are not only achievable but should also be mandatory. Coordinators stress the importance of such steps, among others, as best practices for avoiding risks and liabilities with study abroad, noted in chapters 7, 8, and 9. Yet let's explore the importance of reputable foreign providers here.

Depend on a Well-Informed, Trusted Foreign Travel Company to Give Updates on Regional Events and to Make Itinerary Arrangements

It is necessary to hire reputable travel companies to arrange safe travel in secure regions. All of the coordinators interviewed rely on the assistance of travel agents in various capacities, whether to arrange flights, secure tour sites, gain access to tour guides, find lodging, or procure meals. In addition, they are aware that choosing a company wisely and establishing a healthy working relationship with its members is essential for avoiding risks and liabilities.

Hopefully, St. Mary's College officials selected such a provider, and that provider put them in a safe environment. Also, the provider should have people that keep college program leaders fully aware of any past, current, or possible future disturbances in the area. With this information, potential hazards may be averted in the region. If a close relationship is established with the partnering member, this outcome should be expected.

Here is an example of support from my own experience. A study abroad group was scheduled to explore a volcano and park in Costa Rica. The site is heavily sought after by foreign visitors, and was a part of our program itinerary. Although it was not publicized, I was given news from my partnering agent, who remained in close communication with local residences near the park, that a couple of foreign hikers had been robbed and killed on one of the park's paths.

It was not information the U.S. State Department would have posted; it had just taken place. This insider's news was a relief for me. This program group was literally "on the doorstep" of the park, ready to enter, when I received the news and had to eliminate the activity. In the moment I realized how beneficial it was to partner with a foreign agent who could provide the "inside scoop" about a study abroad region and its surrounding area. Altering set study abroad plans to ensure participants' safety is a common practice for program leaders.

In relation to this topic, as unsettling as it may sound, *trial and error* is an essential component of study abroad. Trial and error never overrides common sense; in fact, common sense is what navigates its very approach. Make sure to read experts' thoughts on the merits of *trial and error* listed as best practice #23 in chapter 9.

Again, reputable travel companies should make program arrangements. Making venue arrangements on your own may increase potential hazards for participants. For example, Coordinator Pearl recalls a misguided, and potentially costly, attempt to make a program arrangement for her group while in Egypt:

> [I] had arranged for a ride on donkeys with participants along a river. [The group was] going on donkeys to a site away from the river as the [local guide] took them in a different path. [I] got concerned [and asked for the local guide] to follow the set path. [Angered, he] made [everyone] get off [the donkeys], and [left the group] in an unfamiliar town.

She continues and ponders,

> We didn't know where we were, and walked and [eventually] found our way [back to familiar territory]. And why would the [foreign guide] do that? It doesn't sound good. It is odd. So I think [we were] lucky. But the reality is those are the kind of issues that probably wouldn't happen on [this] continent.

Likely, the coordinator believed the group was "lucky" because they were vulnerable to robbery or attack when led from the more customary path. If you recall the St. Mary's University case, as the group drove from a rural area, perhaps well "off of the beaten path," they were forced off the road by bandits who robbed and sexually assaulted students.[15] A major grievance in the case was that the selection of a safer route could have prevented the injuries.[16]

Both the incident in Costa Rica (my own) and Egypt (with Coordinator Pearl) underscore the benefit that comes with having a reliable foreign partner to make program arrangements that is well familiarized with the environment. It should also be addressed that Coordinator Pearl holds a false sense of reality to think that these kinds of issues "probably wouldn't happen on [this] continent." Nefarious acts can occur on any continent, including our own. The experiences of other coordinators support this premise.

Coordinators Must Obtain Keen Cultural Awareness to Orient Students

Robbery and rape are not acceptable practices in any country, and I am not attempting to question the orientation methods of St. Mary's College officials in preparing students for study abroad in Guatemala. However, it seems an appropriate time to note that having an acute cultural awareness for a study abroad location is important so that you may properly orient students about potential dangers. Interviewed coordinators agree. Coordinator Levi claims that "one needs to be sure that students going abroad know firsthand about the problems . . . of the various countries they are going through."

To go further, not only does Coordinator Pearl inundate participants with information on unique risks but also goes a step beyond: "I give them scenarios." With ample orientation on dangerous scenarios, students may gain enough practical knowledge to avert the threats. For example, during orientation sessions some coordinators create potentially hazardous events in order to familiarize participants with self-defense techniques to ward off physical attacks, including threats of sexual assault. This chapter's section, Self-Defense Training as a Protective Measure, briefly touches on this.

Overall, creating overseas scenarios at orientation sessions adds work for instructors, but if this exercise assists just one student in escaping a dangerous situation, it is well worth the time spent. My experience has been that students highly embrace this approach to orientation.

Consult the U.S. State Department and Other Sources for Travel Warnings and Alerts

It is unclear if a travel warning or alert for Guatemala had been posted by the U.S. State Department in January 1998, the time when St. Mary's College had its study abroad tragedy. We will assume that college officials fully reviewed the U.S. State Department website in advance of travel. Remember, copious outside research of the country and its customs must also accompany U.S. State Department considerations. Presently, at first glance on the State Department website there is no current travel warning or alert for Guatemala. However, a deeper investigation into the website reveals more.

When navigating to the Safety and Security section for Guatemala on the U.S. State Department webpage, an essential safety warning can be found. It discloses that "the threat of violent crime in Guatemala is rated by the U.S. Department of State as 'critical.'"[17] The page cites that "the number of violent crimes reported by U.S. citizens and other foreigners has remained high."[18] This is important information to know. Similarly, coordinators need to scrutinize the U.S. State Department website to this degree with every program country.

All of the interviewed coordinators consult the U.S. State Department webpage in an effort to avoid dangers and potential lawsuits with programs abroad. Coordinator Trevor correctly assesses that "the coordinator and institutional officials must ultimately rule whether a region is safe or not, regardless of information posted by the State Department." Always rule on the side of caution.

The U.S State Department does not catch all potential risks. Recall my earlier account about a program in Costa Rica. Fortunately, I was forewarned about a fatal crime that occurred at a venue that was planned. A travel warning or advisory did not come from the U.S. State Department. Comparably, yet due to concerns with terrorist threats, Coordinator Trevor recalls having to cancel a program to Italy, just before departure:

> [Bombings occurred, but] Italy was not declared off limits. But our [school] president decided, "I cannot in good conscience allow this trip to happen. What if something happens?" Also, other college officials felt it was unsafe to travel there. Even though no travel warning had come out on Italy, a neighboring area seemed unsafe. So the college was responsible for reimbursing the students at the tune of $45,000.

Chapter 8's best practice #15, U.S. State Department Warnings, provides greater rationale for using the U.S. State Department webpage as a resource, accompanied by experiences from experts.

Although it is impossible for the U.S. State Department to report every hazard, its webpage remains an effective, essential tool for program participants, coordinators, and college officials to help evaluate potential threats in overseas regions.

Earlham v. Eisenberg

Earlham v. Eisenberg is a very pivotal case because it marks the first time that a student sought damages for a sexual assault abroad.[19] This is startling considering the number of sexual assault incidents that must have occurred prior that remained unreported. More lawsuits of this kind have followed since *Earlham v. Eisenberg.*

With a lawsuit brought by then-student Erika Eisenberg against Earlham College, a small Quaker institution in Indiana, courts addressed the question of whether a study abroad program and its institution are protected by a waiver when a student is sexually assaulted. [20]

Eisenberg alleged she was sexually harassed and raped while participating in the college's study abroad program in Japan in 1995. [21] She claimed that her host father, the head of the family to which the college assigned her in Tokyo, was the perpetrator of the assault. [22] She also charged that her repeated complaints of sexual harassment were not taken seriously. [23] In 1997, she filed a suit, seeking $3 million from Earlham and other organizations that ran the program. [24]

According to the suit, officials from the partnering college in Japan did not respond to her complaints until after she was raped on April 8, 1996; only then did they find her other accommodations. [25] Eisenberg also maintains that college officials never referred her to a medical doctor, police, or the U.S. embassy after the rape; rather, they compelled her to keep quiet. [26]

A contrasting account came from college representatives in Japan who steadfastly denied the allegations, arguing that Eisenberg was given the offer to move after she first complained of harassment, but she refused. [27] Again, the Earlham case tested the legality of risk-averting documents, particularly the waiver, as a means of protection for college officials. Earlham, like many other colleges with study abroad programs, has students sign a waiver absolving the college of responsibility in case of injury. [28]

The college asserted the waiver that Eisenberg signed in applying for the Japan program exempted Earlham from liability. [29] Eisenberg's attorney claimed "that the waiver cannot exempt a college from a civil-rights law such as Title IX of the Education Amendments of 1972,"[30] of which Ms. Eisenberg charged the school was in violation.

The court considered whether university programs of foreign study are held to the same standards of Title IX as programs run at the university's location and whether civil rights laws in America also apply to students while living and/or studying abroad. [31] Following this pivotal case, courts have been tackling this issue. They have increasingly held programs of study abroad and their institutions accountable for the same Title IX standards administered at the home campus.

With Erika Eisenberg's case, the parties settled the case for an undisclosed amount and on confidential terms. [32] Earlham's academic dean, Len Clark, complained, "These waivers are universal and colleges all over the United States need to know whether or not the waivers protect them from liability."[33]

The Universality of Language in Waivers

The universality of language in waivers is a concern. Nonspecific, stock language provided again and again in these documents by study abroad offices often falls short with suitably informing students about individual program hazards, and frequently fail to shield college officials from liabilities. One such example of unspecific language includes the declaration of being exempt from *any and all* liability.

Sample Waiver E (Appendix E) exemplifies this all-inclusive style:

I do release, waive, forever discharge and covenant not to sue the College, the Board of Trustees of the College, the officers, officials, employees or agents of the College (the "Releasees") from and against any and all liability from any harm, injury, damage, claims, demands, action, causes of action, costs . . .

The same stock language appears in Waiver B (Appendix B) to exempt the college and its affiliates from liability suits:

[The] Applicant releases fully and finally from any and all liability and claims, and covenants not to sue or cause to be sued in any judicial or administrative forum, the State of . . . the University, and their officers, agents, and employees with respect to any and all matters relating to or arising from Applicant's participation in the Program.

Experts concur that this method for waiver construction could improve. Coordinator Felix notes:

> The [waivers] that I've been noticing now have everything in there and include any airlines or bus services. Anything [or anyone that coordinators] hire or use, whether it public or private transportation, is mentioned in [the waiver stating] they are not responsible. So it's expanded to include almost everything but the grandmother that they are not going to be accountable for.

Coordinator Pearl reveals awareness that "a judge may throw out a waiver in a trial if it were to say too much," deeming it ineffective. Coordinator Levi also desires to shorten the length of his waiver, which he thinks is filled with extraneous details:

> [What] we use is a four- to five-page document that was developed by me with legal counsel from the college and it was reviewed every year, and brought up to date. And there were times I felt things needed to be reworded to be more appropriate to the time we were in the moment. And since the world is changing so much, we need to do some changing with the waiver form to address problems we have and have no control over.

He continues:

> I have complained to legal counsel about having [participants] read all that, and absorb all that, because I have seen forms only a page long. But they refused to change it based on the fact that even though it is repetitive, they feel it is important for a student to be signing a document they are sure the student has been reminded about what is [expected conduct].

Coordinators need to continue to contend this point with legal counsel. If the waiver is lengthy, formulaic, and repetitive, it may fail to protect students who are less likely to read it in its entirety, or fully absorb its message. In turn, this may create additional perils and future lawsuits, as previously shown with *Earlham v. Eisenberg* and *Paneno v. Centres*.

Construction of a separate waiver, per program, with succinct, regionally related details, brings increased safeguards to program participants. Every program is different, and in turn, has its own unique risks. Why shouldn't the risk-averting form reflect this? The merits of this approach are further demonstrated with the case of *Fay v. Thiel College* in the next chapter.

High Stakes Remain Following *Earlham v. Eisenberg*

It was argued that if Erika Eisenberg was successful with her lawsuit, than strict U.S. law that governs sexual harassment on campuses should be applied to all American students who study overseas each year, and the traditional waivers that they sign before going could be considered worthless.[34]

In the end, the parties settled the case for an undisclosed amount and on confidential terms.[35] Nonetheless, the lawsuit itself, without clear knowledge of its decision, was pivotal. It brought forth new questions of accountability for students who are sexually assaulted while abroad, and the effectiveness of risk-averting documents to protect institutions from liability.

If waivers are recrafted to curtail large degrees of vague, no-liability-whatsoever language, and include description of program-specific risks, they will likely increase in substance and value. Students may be more clearly informed of risks, and college officials will have more credibility. As you craft these forms, consult legal counsel.

Courts Are in Support of Risk-Averting Documents Spelling Out Regional Risks

Judges grow irritated with the wholly unanswerable tone commonly used in today's waivers. For example, recall in *Paneno v. Centres* an annoyed judge's rebuke of a program provider— "Centres for Academic Programmes Abroad, Inc., is attempting to avoid answering to any claim for negligence in California. We will not allow such trickery to be used to deny [the student] Paneno his day in court."[36] In turn, some college officials are taking the issue quite seriously.

Following *Earlham v. Eisenberg*, to his credit, the provost of Earlham College reexamined the program waiver and considered its language to be formulaic and nonspecific.[37] Succinct, program-specific risk-averting documents have proven to be successful with protecting colleges from liability, as shown with *Bloss v. The University of Minnesota Board of Regents*. Since this case was abundantly explored in chapter 2, only brief description and points of analysis are brought forth here.

Bloss v. The University of Minnesota Board of Regents

Again, while participating in the University of Minnesota's cultural immersion program in Cuernavaca, Mexico, student Adrienne Bloss traveled to meet friends for a social evening and was raped at knifepoint by a taxi driver.[38] She took the bus to and from school and to attend social and cultural events; on the night of the assault, Bloss left her host-family home, on her own, and hailed a taxi about one-half block down the street.[39]

The taxi driver told her the back door was broken and that she could get in the front seat; Bloss sat in the front with the driver, and while traveling to her friends' home, the driver pulled over to the side of the road and the rape occurred.[40] Bloss sued the university, holding it negligent for failing to secure housing closer to the Cemanahuac campus, imprudent in not providing transportation to and from the campus, and inattentive with imparting warnings about various serious risks, including the use of taxicabs in Cuernavaca.[41]

Yet through Cemanahuac, there were mandatory student orientation sessions, an Acceptance, Release, and Waiver document, and orientation materials that provided students with safety warnings and information concerning dangers of the city.[42]

The court opinion reveals that "the University demonstrated at its orientation session [that] it provides information about academic, health, travel, financial, safety, and social issues."[43] In addition, "The warnings included specific admonitions that it was dangerous for women to go out alone at night, [women] should call for a taxi at night rather than hail a taxi on the street, and that women should never sit in the front seat of taxis. These warnings specifically addressed the circumstances under which the student sustained her injuries."[44]

As a result, the university received a favorable ruling. The Court of Appeals of Minnesota reversed the initial judgment from the Hennepin County District Court (Minnesota) that denied the university statutory immunity in Bloss's suit for sexual assault.[45]

This court ruling was due in part to proper orientation being in place, *as well as* having risk-averting documents that specified regional threats in Cuernavaca, Mexico.[46] All coordinators and their institutions must give mandatory orientation sessions and should provide pro-gram-specific information in their risk-averting documents as a means to avert risks and liabilities. In making this point, it should also be emphasized that what happened to Adrienne Bloss was tragic and her desire for closure is valid. The university was given favor, but when a sexual assault is perpetrated there are no winners.

Fay v. Thiel College (case details are provided in chapters 2 and 5) also underscores the point that regional-specific, risk-averting documents must be in place to safeguard students and their institutions. Let's continue to move forward with more sexual assault cases that provide insight on how study abroad programs should be approached.

Nova Southeastern University v. Gross (2000)

Nova Southeastern University v. Gross[47] illustrates that court decisions that do not directly involve study abroad participants may still significantly influence overseas program ap-proaches. With *Nova Southeastern University v. Gross*, a Florida Supreme Court ruling af-firmed that universities are not exempt from liability just because a crime against a student took place off campus with a university-sponsored program.[48]

Nova Southeastern University graduate student Bethany Jill Gross was sexually assaulted in a Miami parking lot close to where she was doing an internship.[49] The court posed the question of "whether a university may be found liable in tort where it assigns a student to an internship site which it knows to be unreasonably dangerous but gives no warning, or adequate warning, to the student, and the student is subsequently injured while participating in the internship."[50]

The Florida Supreme Court held that a student injured during an off-campus internship program could sue his/her college because it had sufficient control over his/her actions.[51] Among other things, the school had the final decision over where students did their intern-ships.[52]

Legal experts confirm that the decision could lead universities to more closely scrutinize off-campus internships, including study abroad programs.[53] Peter Lake, a professor at Stetson University College of Law, believes the ruling "sent a shock through the system."[54] This precedent case is certainly worthy of consideration by officials of study abroad; coordinators, who are the main creators of study abroad programs, should serve notice that not only campus programs but also off-campus programs require full care and protection of students from sexual assault.

Needed Safety with Internships and Work Abroad

Nova Southeastern University Inc. v. Gross makes a proper segue to a related point—safe participation in internships and workforce development is a major aspect of study abroad and its offerings. There has been considerable growth with internship studies in study abroad, with close to seven hundred U.S. campuses reporting that twenty thousand of their students re-ceived credit for internships, volunteering, or work abroad in 2009 and 2010.[55] This represent-ed a 7 percent increase over the prior year's total, and almost triple the number reported a decade ago.[56]

Indeed, the same safeguards put in place for general study abroad must also exist with internships, workforce development, service learning, and all other components that make up the wide-ranging field of *study abroad*. For fuller information on internships and work abroad, and their accompanying risk-averting documents, simply return to the Internships and Work

Abroad as a Part of the Study Abroad Umbrella section in chapter 1; also, a sample Internship Agreement is provided in Appendix J.

Self-Defense Training as a Protective Measure

As a way to counter sexual assault threats that students may face abroad, coordinators may consider providing participants training with some self-defense techniques prior to departure. Among all of the sexual assault incidents and cases explored in this chapter, the honest truth is that there may not have been anything the victims could have physically done to alter their unfortunate fate. For example, with *Nova Southeastern University Inc. v. Gross*, the student who was raped in a parking lot close to her internship may not have had a real chance to stop her attacker.

However, this sad case does call to mind that self-defense training is another protective strategy that may be passed on to students to potentially thwart attacks. Coordinator Baron comes from a university where "we have a required international travel self-defense class for all students that attend our programs." This is a strong policy. The self-defense style, Krav Maga, serves this purpose well. Krav Maga was originally developed for the Israeli army and is ideal for expeditious training of study abroad participants. The reality-based system uses instinctive movements designed to teach extremely effective self-defense in the shortest possible time. [57]

Certainly I am not claiming that speedy training in Krav Maga will deter all potential sexual assaults and physical threats abroad. But such training is another helpful precautionary measure that may increase a person's chance of escape.

Slattery v. Antioch Education Abroad et al. (2009)

Again, in revisiting the major concern of sexual assault in study abroad, findings from *Slattery v. Antioch Education Abroad et al.* [58] serve to be very edifying. Stephanie Slattery, while a student at Eastern Michigan University, alleged that she was raped while participating in the University's Antioch Education Abroad (AEA) program in Mali, Africa. [59] A formal case was filed in September 2009 with the Ohio Southern District Court. [60] Slattery's sexual assault, disclosed in *Slattery v. Antioch Education Abroad et al.*, raises concerns about proper duty of care and accountability for participants overseas.

A significant part of Slattery's complaint was that proper orientation of inherent cultural and regional risks was missing. [61] Many higher-education officials believe that the results of this case could set a precedent, making study abroad programs increasingly liable for failing to warn students of cultural differences with their host countries. [62]

More specifically, while living in Mali as part of a program organized by Antioch University, Slattery alleges a bus driver working for AEA raped her after she accepted an invitation to have a cup of tea in his room. [63]

She received medical treatment in Paris, and upon return to Mali, she filed a formal complaint. [64] The suit stresses that AEA "actively advised, instructed and encouraged the program's students to interact with the local population, to learn the language and cultural differences, but negligently failed to advise . . . Slattery and others of the cultural belief in Mali that having tea alone in a man's apartment [is] considered implied consent to engage in sexual intercourse." [65]

As noted previously, the decision from *Nova Southeastern University v. Gross* is noteworthy because it put study abroad officials on notice that off-campus programs require full care and protection of students from sexual assault. If you recollect, a Florida Supreme Court held that a student injured during an off-campus internship program could sue her college because it had sufficient control over her actions.[66] The university, among other things, made the final decision as to where the students did their internships.[67]

Naturally, this begs the question, Does Slattery have a solid case against Antioch University and Antioch Education Abroad "because they had sufficient control over her actions" on where she did her studies? After all, according to Slattery, AEA makes the arrangements to "house, feed, and hire a bus driver for the students, among other functions."[68] The court could have been tasked with determining whether AEA is liable due to sufficient control over Slattery's actions.

In addition, study abroad program organizers should take notice that Slattery also sued AEA for negligent hiring and supervision, alleging it knew or should have known of the bus driver's "history of fathering multiple, illegitimate children with multiple women, and other disqualifying aspects."[69]

Plaintiffs complained that ADA's "negligent hiring and supervision practices, through its agent, directly and proximately caused Stephanie Slattery to be exposed to the assault and rape by the [hired] bus driver."[70] This point should serve to alert coordinators that they must be extremely diligent in vetting foreign partners, and remain fully aware of hiring practices by these groups.

A court document filed on October 28, 2011, shows the case was settled with the basic description, "STIPULATION of Dismissal WITH PREJUDICE by Defendant Antioch Education Abroad, Plaintiff Stephanie N. Slattery. (Freeze, Stephen) (Entered: 10/28/2011)."[71] The final outcome of *Slattery v. Antioch Education Abroad et al.* remains unclear.

However, details from the lawsuit itself brought forth a number of considerations for coordinators—the need for an equal duty of care for students with off-campus programs, close vetting of partnering foreign agents and affiliates, and ample warnings for program participants concerning regional risks accompanied by comprehensive orientation and well-constructed risk-averting documents.

Inappropriate Consensual Relations between Program Participants and Program Providers

The previously detailed cases have been about sexual harassment and sexual assault. Clearly, these are not consensual encounters. However, the issue of *consensual* contacts may also negatively impact a study abroad program and its participants. The fact is that inappropriate relations between student participants and program providers that are consensual are also common occurrences that study abroad coordinators may contend with.

What is disconcerting is that a relationship that starts off as consensual can evolve into something undesirable. Possibly, this was the situation with the student Slattery and the bus driver.[72] Regardless, the assault was detestable. Yet complaints made by Slattery can be constructively viewed to consider approaches that may be taken to avoid sexual harassment and assaults. Mainly, a study abroad participant and program leader/provider have to maintain a professional relationship. This sounds vague, so I will apply personal program experiences to bring clarity on the subject.

Two actual encounters from past short-term study abroad programs come to mind. One concerned a hired bus driver who assisted with a program in Western Africa, and another surrounded a tour guide with a program in Central America.

A single, nontraditional-aged student in her mid-twenties had become infatuated with the bus driver during a short-term study abroad program in Western Africa. For simplicity's sake, I will create the name Beatrice for the student. Beatrice chose to eat meals with the driver, as opposed to the group. A few meals shared with the driver and guide is fine, yet her desire to share every meal brought concerns. When encouraged to congregate with other program participants, Beatrice seemed dispirited.

Later, when I learned that Beatrice had visited the bus driver in his hotel room during a free evening, it was essential to explain to her the need for healthy boundaries between a participant and a program assistant. A sensitive yet firm warning was given to alter her behavior. Even though the student went to the driver's room on her own accord, she may still have been ignorant, as was Stephanie Slattery in the Antioch University case, of the driver's full expectations with the visit. Our discussion was an important one to have.

In a separate but similar incident, another student, who I give the pseudonym Kerry, also in her mid-twenties, received a lot of extra attention from the Central American tour guide. The guide went out of his way to frequently engage her in conversation, shared meals, and seating on the bus. The guide's affinity for Kerry was clear. When encouraged by program leaders to be more attentive to the *overall* group's needs, the guide publically altered his behavior. Unfortunately, one late evening I received a knock on my hotel door room from Kerry's anxious roommate.

On a side note, I make sure that participants know which room I am staying in case they need assistance. This is a point of contention with some program leaders. Many do not want to be found during their *free* time. However, I think it is necessary for participants to be able to find program leaders at any time in case a crisis arises. Like it or not, you are *always* the program leader, day or night, responsible for the well-being of your participants.

So returning to my account, Kerry's roommate anxiously relayed that none of the students, including herself, had seen Kerry since early evening. I looked at my watch. It was about 1:00 a.m. The roommate found this particularly odd since she and Kerry had spent all of their free evenings together up to that point.

My first inkling was to bang on the room door of the guide. I did. No answer. To my dismay, I realized by checking keys submitted to the front desk attendant that Kerry and the guide were the only group members outside of the hotel. I had no idea where he may have taken Kerry. My only recourse was to ask the front desk attendant to have the guide notify me when he returned.

To my relief and exasperation, the guide called me at around 3:30 a.m. and confirmed that Kerry had returned with him. The guide volunteered that he took Kerry out to a restaurant and they shared a romantic kiss, but no more. The full accuracy of his account remains in question. What was certain was that restaurants did not remain open that late in the sleepy town surrounding our hotel. I didn't hesitate to verbalize my displeasure with him.

Due to his actions, the guide had shirked his obligation to remain professional, betrayed the trust of the other students and program leaders, and compromised the program. It was enough to request a replacement guide from the tour company. The student was not blameless in the matter either. Her judgment was poor, which she acknowledged after being confronted.

Sadly, when I shared the guide's inappropriate behavior with the tour company manager, her first reaction was amused laughter. The remainder of the program went along without another hitch, but it was the last time that I used or recommended this tour company.

CHAPTER SUMMARY

Sexual assault is a common risk with study abroad, leading to numerous lawsuits; so much so that it is a component of the LARGEST 3. Examination of related complaints and lawsuits, provided in this chapter, reveal that courts expect higher-education institutions to be accountable for activities that may endanger students and bring forth sexual assault lawsuits. Courts are increasingly expecting a proper duty of care for students participating in off-campus programs, and are carefully scrutinizing whether sufficient safeguards are being put in place to prevent students from injury. This is well noted in the St. Mary's College lawsuit.

The point affirms coordinators' strict responsibility to procure reputable foreign travel agents to provide safe arrangements (i.e., St. Mary's College lawsuit; *Earlham College v. Eisenberg*; and *Bloss v. The University of Minnesota Board of Regents*), sustain keen cultural awareness of regions to explore (i.e., St. Mary's College lawsuit and *Slattery v. Antioch Education Abroad et al.*), and frequently consult travel information posted by the U.S. State Department.

The pivotal case of *Earlham College v. Eisenberg*, which marked the first time that a student sought damages for a sexual assault abroad, questioned if American-sponsored study abroad programs should be held to the same standards of Title IX and other U.S. civil rights laws as programs run on the institutions' campuses. The case also questioned the validity of a waiver to protect a study abroad program and its institution from culpability when its student is sexually assaulted.

Coordinators convey concerns with the universality of language in waivers. The belief is that nonspecific, stock language used in many current waivers fail to suitably inform students about individual program risks and do not serve to protect college officials from liability.

Paneno v. Centres, *Bloss v. The University of Minnesota Board of Regents*, and *Fay v. Thiel College* affirm that using a risk-averting document to avoid answering any and all claims for negligence is unwise; judges are growing more irritated with the wholly unanswerable tone commonly used in today's waivers.

Yet thorough predeparture orientation and well-crafted risk-averting documents with specificity of language beneficially warn students of dangers and safeguard institutions from liability, as established with *Bloss v. The University of Minnesota Board of Regents*.

Court cases that do not directly involve overseas participants can still have a clear impact on how study abroad should be conducted, as demonstrated by *Nova Southeastern University v. Gross*. The Florida Supreme Court declared universities are not exempt from liability just because a crime against a student took place off campus with a university-sponsored program. This should serve notice to study abroad program coordinators.

Internships, workforce development, and service learning all fall under the umbrella of *study abroad*. These high-impact learning approaches must also ensure safety for participants. *Nova Southeastern University v. Gross* highlighted this fact. Therefore, an Internship Agreement is provided in Appendix J as a possible guide to assist coordinators.

Slattery v. Antioch Education Abroad et al. also raises concerns with proper duty of care and accountability for participants on overseas programs. A significant complaint made by the sexual assault victim, Slattery, was that proper orientation of inherent cultural and regional risks was missing. In addition, this case closely intersects with the judgment made in *Nova Southeastern University v. Gross*; a student who is injured while taking part in an off-campus endeavor could sue his or her institution because it had sufficient control over the student's actions, and made the final decision over where the student participated in a program. [73]

An additional concern for study abroad program leaders to consider is not only nonconsensual relations but also consensual relationships between student participants and program providers. This occurs with more frequency than one may care for with study abroad, and two personal program instances are described as examples.

NOTES

1. No. IP97-0592 (S.D. Ind. Sept. 10, 1998).
2. 590 N.W.2d 661 (Minn. Ct. App. 1999).
3. Lawsuit filed against SMC (2001, February 6). *St. Mary's College of Maryland: The Point News.* Retrieved from http://smcm.cdmhost.com/cdm/ref/collection/SMCM/id/27667.
4. Kaplin, W. A., & Lee, B. A. (2011). *The law of higher education.* San Francisco: Jossey-Bass.
5. Lawsuit filed against SMC (2001, February 6).
6. Boorstein, M., & Wright, S. W. (1998). Fears about safety and lawsuits plague study abroad programs. *Community College Week 10*, 12, p. 12.
7. Lawsuit filed against SMC (2001, February 6).
8. Kaplin, W. A., & Lee, B. A. (2011).
9. *Id.*
10. McMurtrie, B. (2002, August 2). Maryland college settles lawsuit. *Chronicle of Higher Education*, p. A37.
11. Lawsuit filed against SMC (2001, February 6), p. 1.
12. Kaplin, W. A., & Lee, B. A. (2011).
13. *Id.*
14. Chen, D. (1998, January 19). 5 from Md. College sexually assaulted on Guatemala trip. *New York Times.* Retrieved from http://www.nytimes.com/1998/01/19/us/5-from-md-college-sexually-assaulted-on-guatemala-trip.html.
15. Lawsuit filed against SMC (2001, February 6).
16. Kaplin, W. A., & Lee, B. A. (2011).
17. U.S. Department of State (2015). U.S. passports & international travel. U.S. Department of State—Bureau of Consular Affairs. Retrieved from
   http://travel.state.gov/content/passports/english/country/guatemala.html.
18. *Id.*
19. Guernsey, L. (1997, April 11). A lawsuit raises difficult questions about liability and study-abroad programs. *Chronicle of Higher Education 43*, 31, p. A37, A39.
20. *Id.*
21. *Id.*
22. *Id.*
23. Pazniokas, M. (1997, March 27). Woman sues college, says she was raped while studying abroad. *Hartford Courant.* Retrieved from http://articles.courant.com/1997-03-27/news/9703270318_1_earlham-college-sexual-harassment-declaratory.
24. Guernsey, L. (1997, April 11).
25. *Id.*
26. *Id.*
27. *Id.*
28. Guernsey, L. (1997, April 11).
29. *Id.*
30. Guernsey, L. (1997, April 11), p. A38.
31. Guernsey, L. (1997, April 11).
32. *Id.*
33. Guernsey, L. (1997, April 11), p. A38.
34. Rape case threat to colleges. (1997, May 9). *The Times Higher Education.* Retrieved fromhttps://www.timeshighereducation.com/news/rape-case-threat-to-colleges/100898.article.
35. Guernsey, L. (1997, April 11).
36. *Paneno v. Centres for Acad. Programmes Abroad, Ltd.*, 13 Cal. Rptr. 3d 759, 766 (2004).
37. Guernsey, L. (1997, April 11).
38. *Bloss v. Univ. of Minn. Bd. of Regents*, 590 N.W.2d 661, 662 (Minn. Ct. App. 1999).
39. *Id.* at 662–63.
40. *Id.* at 663.
41. *Id.*
42. *Id.*
43. *Id.* at 666.
44. *Id.*
45. *Id.* at 667.
46. *Id.* at 666.
47. 758 So. 2d 86 (Fla. Dist. Ct. App. 2000).
48. *Id.* at 90.
49. *Id.* at 87-88.
50. *Id.* at 87.
51. *Id.* at 89.

52. *Id.*

53. Selingo, J. (2000, May 5). Florida court says colleges may be liable for off-campus injuries.*Chronicle of Higher Education*, p. A39.

54. Selingo, J. (2000, May 5), p. A39.

55. Donohue, D., & Altaf, S. (2012, May). Learn by doing: Expanding international Internships/work abroad opportunities for U.S. STEM students—A briefing paper from IIE's Center for Academic Mobility Research. Retrieved from http://www.iie.org/Research-and-Publications/Publications-and-Reports/IIE-Bookstore/Learn-by-Doing.

56. *Id.*

57. Krav Maga Worldwide. (2015). Self-defense. Retrieved fromhttp://www.kravmaga.com/programs/self-defense/.

58. Complaint at 1, *Slattery v. Antioch Educ. Abroad*, No. 2:09-cv-00828 (S.D. Ohio 2009) [hereinafter Slattery Complaint].

59. *Id.* at 2.

60. *Id.* at 1.

61. *Id.* at 4.

62. Heller, Matthew. (2009, September 30). Woman blames study abroad program for rape in Mali. *On.Point—A new take on legal news.* Retrieved from http://www.onpointnews.com/NEWS/Woman-Blames-Study-Abroad-Program-for-Rape-in-Mali.html.

63. Slattery Complaint, at 2.

64. *Id.* at 2–3.

65. *Id.* at 4.

66. *Nova Se. Univ., Inc. v. Gross*, 758 So. 2d 86, 90 (Fla. Dist. Ct. App. 2000).

67. *Id.* at 89.

68. Slattery Complaint, at 2.

69. *Id.* at 3.

70. *Id.*

71. *Slattery v. Antioch Educ. Abroad*, No. 3:10-cv-00010, 2010 WL 3264050 (S.D. Ohio Oct. 28, 2011).

72. *See* Slattery Complaint, at 2.

73. *Nova Se. Univ., Inc. v. Gross.*

Chapter Five

The Tragedy of Supervisory Neglect in Study Abroad

Put yourself in this scenario: You have been appreciating your time abroad with a group of fellow study abroad participants traversing a breathtaking country steeped with mountains, waterfalls, and seemingly endless flowing farms speckled with happy livestock, all while becoming educated about its rich, ancient civilization dating back as far as 950 BC.

Unfortunately, a nagging stomach bug keeps you from fully enjoying the experience, and you consider that while in a major city, you should get it resolved before heading to less populated regions, and consequently, smaller health facilities, that lie ahead for the next few days. So you seek the aid of your program leaders to help with a quick doctor's visit.

They are able to assist with getting you admitted into a medical clinic in the city, and fortunately so, since you speak almost none of the native language. Some basic tests are done, and you wait to hear what medicine the doctor will prescribe before whisking off with your group to encounter new adventures ahead.

To your utter surprise and disappointment, the doctor informs you and the program leaders that you need to remain at the health clinic for additional tests and rest. You are told that you should be in good shape when the group returns in three days. You're wary of not going with the group, and even more so, when you discover that all three of your group leaders plan to depart.

However, you do not want to be a burden to them, or the group. "Just sit tight and kick back for a few days," you muse. Plus, the program leaders know what they are doing. They have informed you that a kind, young woman, Ms. Helkison—a Lutheran missionary—has volunteered to stay with you the entire time until the group returns. She is fluent in the regional dialect. Wow, your very own caretaker and translator—and come to think of it, Ms. Helkison has remained dutifully by your side since your arrival to the clinic. If the leaders trust your care to her, you figure "why not?" Everyone has been very understanding and attentive here. It isn't some rinky-dink facility; you are getting good care in a major city.

Again, not wanting to spoil the time of the leaders, or be an unnecessary burden, with a cheerful attempt you wish the leaders well as they head out. Ms. Helkison reassures them of your care as they leave, along with the doctor. Though disappointed to miss the expected coming adventures of the program, you mentally unwind for the few noneventful days of rest and recovery ahead. Ms. Helkison devotedly sits bedside, prepared to stay the entire duration. She is a real saint.

Perhaps a half hour later the doctor comes back in to check on you. He addresses Ms. Helkison so that she can translate for you, and you are prepared to address the physician through her. A disconcerting look begins to form on Ms. Helkison's face as the doctor speaks.

"I've been informed that you need to be prepared for surgery, right away. Your appendix needs to be removed," she somberly says.

"What? I am just having a bit of stomach discomfort," you exclaim. "I would really rather they wait on this. Is the surgery absolutely necessary?"

Your heart is pounding out of your chest as you watch Ms. Helkison translate. The doctor solemnly shaking his head is the clear answer before Ms. Helkison responds.

"He says you are in immediate danger and time cannot waste."

Suddenly the clinic around you appears small and drab. You would rather be at a major hospital in the capital city.

"Ask that I please be transferred to a hospital in Lima."

Again, the same grave expression and nodding of the head back and forth by the doctor, eyes to the floor. Just a grunt of a response to the inquiry.

Already feeling both irritated and alarmed, the fact that the doctor is no longer even looking at you as he addresses Ms. Helkison is doubly disconcerting. You begin to question how easily your concerns are disregarded; you question if you are even respected.

In desperation you tell Ms. Helkison, "I want to fly home!"

The doctor has started to busy himself in the room in preparation for the surgery. He doesn't even seem open to fielding any more questions—just bent on moving to surgery.

"Tell him!"

Ms. Helkison meekly translates the request. Another barely audible grunt from the doctor to communicate his dissent.

In a choked voice, tears blurring the room around you, you sob, "Can I please call my parents first?"

A request that falls on deaf ears.

In a gentle voice, Ms. Helkison points to a wall with a small window and says, "There's a viewing room. I will be there the entire time. Do not worry."

Fay v. Thiel College

The above noted scenario, based on facts, is an attempt to capture the degree of angst that Amy Fay might have felt. Tragically, what followed was the most harrowing circumstance; Amy Fay had to endure her worst imaginable fears, and she was helpless to do anything about it. To attempt to dramatize such a distasteful occurrence is inappropriate, and should only be communicated in plain terms.

The report from a Common Pleas Court of Mercer County, Pennsylvania, in the case of *Fay v. Thiel College*, disclosed detailed description of Fay's (referred to as *the plaintiff*) trepidation and resulting injuries[1] endured during the absence of program supervisors:

> After the plaintiff was informed, through translation, that the doctor would be removing her appendix, the plaintiff went through a list of alternatives—the plaintiff asked if surgery was absolutely necessary; the plaintiff asked to be transferred to a hospital in Lima; the plaintiff asked to fly home; the plaintiff asked to call her parents in the United States prior to surgery.[2]

It continues:

> After all of her requests were denied, the plaintiff was then reluctantly prepared for surgery. The appendectomy was apparently authorized by Ms. Helkison—who, once again, was a Lutheran

missionary who was not in any way related to Thiel College or acting as an agent and/or representative of Thiel College. Ms. Helikson requested to observe the plaintiff's surgical procedure from the viewing room, but was not permitted to do so.[3]

The report resumes:

> After the appendectomy was completed, the plaintiff was sexually assaulted by the same surgeon who had performed the surgery and the same anesthesiologist who had administered the anesthesia—both of whom were men. . . . The plaintiff knows that she was sexually assaulted because she was fully conscious during and after her surgery. The anesthesiologist gave the plaintiff some type of local anesthetic, rather than a general anesthetic.[4]

Corrective Measures for Supervisory Neglect: *Fay v. Thiel College* as a Case Study

The case of *Fay v. Thiel College* returns in this chapter because there are various lessons that can be extracted from this case of *supervisory neglect*, not fully covered in chapter 2. First, let's reestablish that the supervisory neglect was so gross in this case that no risk-averting document would, or should, save the college from liability.

However, still instructive are court findings that show weaknesses with such documents. Perhaps, had the neglect not been so great, *and* the waivers of liability had been better constructed, the college would not have been seen as so utterly at fault. Fault with the waivers included 1) wording revealing a take-it-or-leave-it basis for participants,[5] 2) nonspecific language including that pertaining to unique regional risks, and 3) unclear delineation of the program leaders' roles and responsibilities to care for participants.[6]

Strengthening Current Waivers to Avert Supervisory Neglect: *Fay v. Thiel College* and Other Cases as a Backdrop

Recall in *Fay v. Thiel College* the program supervisors and the university were deemed liable for Fay's injuries, even with a signed waiver in place.[7] The language in the waiver of liability form stated, "As a condition of my participation in the study or project, I understand and agree that I am hereby waiving any and all claims arising out of or in connection with my travel to and from and/or my participation in this project or study that I, my family, my heirs or my assigns may otherwise have against Thiel College and/or its personnel."[8]

Both the plaintiff and defendant agree the waiver of liability form was presented to the plaintiff on a take-it-or-leave-it basis; the plaintiff either signed the form or she did not go on the Thiel-sponsored trip to Peru.[9] Because rejecting the transaction entirely was the plaintiff's only option other than accepting the contract, the court found the subject waiver of liability form invalid.[10]

The court ruling shows that language in a waiver should connote a shared experience with mutually agreed-upon responsibilities between participant and college to aid safety and structure for the study abroad experience. A take-it-or-leave it proposition discounts this partnership.

For example, the wording in Waiver E (see Appendix E) could be improved in this regard. As a condition for participants to engage in study abroad, or the "Activity," the waiver maintains that "in consideration of being permitted to participate in the Activity, I do release, waive, forever discharge and covenant not to sue the College." The assertion of "being permitted to participate in the Activity," followed by the absolute "forever," does not provide or give the impression of a negotiation of terms with participants. It is something courts do not look favorably upon, and could potentially leave a participant feeling entrapped.

The Malveaux Sample Recommended Waiver (see Appendix I) avoids take-it-or-leave-it statements, and uses clear language to strongly encourage signing of the waiver. It opens with the statement, "I understand that I am not required by Perilpure College (the College) to participate in this particular program."

To continue to avoid take-it-or-leave-it sentiments, the Malveaux Sample Recommended Waiver concludes with the declaration, "I acknowledge that I have read this entire document, and, that in exchange for the College's agreement to my participation in this program, I agree to its terms." No absolutes, no entrapment. Such wording relays a mutual understanding has been struck through "exchange" or "agreement" between participant and college. Again, to ensure that you have produced the best waiver for your institution's unique needs, consult legal counsel on waiver construction.

Get Specific!

In addition, if you recall, the court also rejected the medical consent form as a means for protecting Thiel College officials from liability, due in part to its language being too nonspecific.[11] The court stressed that a waiver "must spell out the intention of the parties with the greatest of particularity,"[12] and the consent form did not accomplish this.[13]

Issues with all-encompassing language in a waiver have haunted other study abroad program leaders and their institutions. This concern manifested itself with previous chapter cases—Westmont College (chapter 3) and *Earlham College v. Eisenberg* (chapter 4). With the latter case, a $3 million lawsuit followed; the provost reexamined the program waiver and considered its language to be formulaic and nonspecific.[14]

The major lesson is that in order to best inform the participant of risks native to the region while protecting the institution from liability, there should be separate waivers constructed for each study abroad program. Continue to evaluate and reevaluate, with legal counsel, the effectiveness of the waiver to aid student safety and impede liabilities.

Coordinator Desiree instructively expresses, "After each year's program we assess what went well and what could be improved. We identify if there were problems or potential for problems and work through to find solutions that minimize risks and enhance best practices."

Therefore, it is necessary to introduce specifics concerning foreign practices that contrast with U.S. policies in risk-averting documents to accompany predeparture sessions. With these specialized sessions, participants are provided information and forms that increase their awareness of the customs, laws, risks, cultures, and pertinent details about the foreign region.

Waiver E attempts to provide such insight: "I understand that each foreign country has its own laws and standards of acceptable conduct, including dress, manners, morals, politics, drug use, and behavior" (see Appendix E).

This is a good effort, but either the waiver has to specify the *types* of conduct, dress, manners, and so forth that the participant may encounter, and/or the program leaders will need to specify these standards in predeparture orientation sessions. Giving participants cultural competence is an effective strategy for off setting potential risks and liability issues.

If you recall from chapter 4, this approach proved beneficial for the university with *Bloss v. The University of Minnesota Board of Regents*.[15] In the lawsuit, student Bloss claimed she had not been properly warned of the risks involved in the region where she studied abroad, resulting in her sexual assault.[16]

However, the courts uncovered that the predeparture materials and orientations did in fact provide her forewarning about a culturally acceptable act in the United States—sitting in the front seat of a taxi—which is a dangerous deed in the region where she studied abroad; it served to be the circumstance that lead to her assault.[17]

Again, participant orientation that includes risk-averting documents that outline contrasting practices from those in the United States may offset program perils and potential lawsuits. Even beyond cultural and legal differences, far-reaching dangers such as common natural disasters, epidemics, and/or terrorist activities should be identified within risk-averting forms and during predeparture sessions.

Supervisory Neglect Makes Waivers Powerless

But let's not be naïve. Specific details about issues native to a region, inserted into a waiver, is not a magic formula for protecting study abroad participants and their institutions 100 percent of the time. As pointed out in chapter 3 and chapter 4, court cases exposed expansive, nonspecific, and ineffective language use in waivers of liability. However, even if the waiver did have specificity, it could not have protected the university in *Bloss v. The University of Minnesota Board of Regents*. For lack of a better term, "the college's goose was already cooked." The supervisory neglect was extreme; poorly constructed waivers only serve to be added ammunition for the courts to use against negligent institutions.

For instance, as previously noted with *Paneno v. Centres*, student Paneno fell from a sixth-floor balcony of the living quarters assigned to him and sustained severe injuries, including paralysis.[18] The court noted that the waiver avoided giving concrete details about which branch of CAPA would or would not be accountable for student injuries. In essence, CAPA attempted "to avoid answering to any claim for negligence in California."[19] The judge called this approach "trickery."[20] It is best to be clear and upfront in the waiver as to what group or entity is assigned to student injuries. You are not likely to fool the court by being wily with waiver construction.

Let's go further with *Paneno v. Centres* as it relates to details on overseas accommodations in waivers. Even if the waiver had specifically detailed ill-constructed and timeworn accommodations could pose a potential risk of injury for study abroad participants, should that institution or its partnering provider be shielded from liability? In fact, such a declaration may bring about additional questions of accountability, such as "Why would you place students in housing you knew to be potentially defunct?"

There is no winning formula with waiver construction to properly prepare a student for this type of risk, or to fully protect the institution from liability. In this case, there is no substitute for effective research of your foreign providers and their facilities to assure that safe and comfortable housing is assigned. This keeps you attentive to students' needs.

The importance of securing safe housing as an essential duty of care is also highlighted with the University of Florida lawsuit (reviewed in chapter 3). If you recall, while doing research in Bolivia, the student was severely burned when a kerosene lamp exploded.[21] The university showed a proper duty of care and did medevac the student to a proper medical facility.[22]

Underqualified and Ill-Trained Faculty Leaders Bring Supervisory Neglect

The case of *Fay v. Thiel College* does not stand alone as a reminder that coordinators need to better vet and train faculty leaders for programs abroad as a safeguard against supervisory neglect. *King v. Board of Control of Eastern Michigan University* (detailed in this chapter), *Bloss v. The University of Minnesota Board of Regents* (chapter 4), and a case against Radford University (detailed in this chapter) also bring forth concerns with ill-equipped faculty program leaders, who arguably were not properly vetted by coordinators for the program, were ill-trained for the task of leading study abroad, and/or were ignorant of their responsibilities.

Coordinators are impassioned about the topic. Coordinator Trevor bristles:

> Who is doing the trips? The college has to put a lot of faith in the person doing the trips. I don't
> know if there's some kind of background check. You don't want a bad character or with a criminal
> record doing these things. The school has to acknowledge that this person is our agent, this person
> is serving for the school in this capacity, and we trust this person. This person is not going to sit in
> their room and get drunk every night. This person is going to be reliable for the students if there is
> a problem. The person will attend to them right away.

Ill-prepared program leaders serve to be a source of great risk and liability to study abroad. The point segues into other cases concerning negligent supervision. As a means for reducing perils and legal issues in study abroad programs, courts advocate for coordinators to provide program supervisors with thorough training to offset poor program management. Expert perspective from coordinators, provided best practices, and instruction for properly developing risk-averting documents will periodically accompany the case descriptions that follow.

King v. Board of Control of Eastern Michigan University

The Federal District Court for the Eastern District of Michigan in *King v. Board of Control of Eastern Michigan University* upheld that a faculty supervisor's indifference to correct a hostile environment with a program to South Africa brought trauma to female participants due to sexual harassment and Title IX violations.[23] A major point of concern was whether Title IX, which prohibits sexual discrimination in educational programs receiving federal financial assistance, has *extraterritorial* application.[24]

Plaintiffs in this case were six African American women, students at Eastern Michigan University (EMU) at all relevant times, who participated in EMU's five-week study abroad program in South Africa.[25] EMU professors Dr. Klein and Dr. Okafor administered the program; the latter accompanied the students to South Africa while Dr. Klein remained in the United States.[26]

During the first week of the program, a male student by the name of McCauley entered a female student's room while she was sleeping without permission and without knocking.[27] The female student alleges that she awoke to find McCauley in her bed.[28] Also in the first week of the program, Frame, McCauley, and Miller, all males, allegedly referred to female students as "sweetie," "darling," and "sweetheart."[29]

When the female students asked to be called by their names, Miller and McCauley began to refer to them by gender-specific slurs, such as "sluts," "whores," "gold diggers," "pigeonheads," and "chickenheads."[30] When the female students objected, the men responded that they would call the women what they pleased.[31]

The plaintiffs alleged that such terms were a daily part of the men's vocabulary and interaction with the women.[32] The plaintiffs allege that Dr. Okafor was present during times when Miller and Frame referred to plaintiffs as "bitches," "hoes," "wideloads," "sluts," and so forth, and did nothing.[33]

In another incident, McCauley and Miller allegedly solicited South African women for sex from the tour bus, in the presence of Dr. Okafor.[34] McCauley and Frame offered women students for sale to South African men at a nightclub, and again when the group's tour bus stopped at a liquor store.[35] The plaintiffs alleged that Dr. Okafor was present on occasions when Frame leaned out the window of the tour bus and propositioned South African women for sex, and did nothing.[36]

A number of the female students approached Dr. Okafor in a dining hall and told him they had concerns about the program and asked for a group meeting to discuss them.[37] The plaintiffs asserted that they planned to discuss their concerns about Miller, McCauley, and Frame's conduct.[38] Dr. Okafor agreed to the meeting but did not attend; rather, he sent Miller in his stead, and Miller informed the students that he was standing in for Dr. Okafor and that any complaints about the program should go through him to Dr. Okafor.[39]

Dr. Okafor confirmed that he sent Miller as his representative to the meeting and asked Miller to report back to him, and that Miller did so.[40] Miller told Dr. Okafor that nothing of substance was discussed at the meeting, but this was not the case.[41] Allegedly, there had been a heated discussion concerning McCauley's entering the female student's room without permission.[42] Further, there had been discussion initiated by another female student concerning the men's inappropriate conduct.[43]

The plaintiffs asserted that Miller, McCauley, and Frame informed them that they would continue with their conduct if they wanted to and Miller told the women to "stop bitching."[44] A female student reported Miller's comment to Dr. Okafor, but nothing was done in response.[45] Further, program participant Travis Sloan asserted that he approached Dr. Okafor to complain that McCauley had threatened to slit his throat; he asserted that Dr. Okafor did nothing.[46]

Finally, the three troublesome students instigated a violent physical altercation with a number of male South African students.[47] The cause of this altercation was allegedly the men's continued verbal abuse of female students.[48] During this altercation, McCauley brandished a knife.[49] After this altercation, the six plaintiffs and another female student left the program more than a week before its scheduled conclusion.[50] Dr. Okafor finished the trip with six male students and one female student.[51]

The plaintiffs claimed a hostile environment surfaced that affected their ability to take full advantage of the educational program, and the faculty supervisor, Dr. Okafor, did nothing to correct the problem.[52]

Extraterritorial Application for Title IX with Study Abroad

The court confirmed that the female students were "persons in the United States" when a denial of equal access to EMU's resources, created by EMU's failure to address and stop the actions of McCauley, Frame, and Miller, happened.[53]

In addition, Title IX was "designed to eliminate (with certain exceptions) discrimination on the basis of sex in any education program or activity receiving Federal financial assistance."[54] "That is, allowing sex discrimination to occur unremedied in study abroad programs could close those educational opportunities to female students by requiring them to submit to sexual harassment in order to participate. This is exactly the situation that Title IX was meant to remedy: female students should not have to submit to sexual harassment as the price of educational opportunity."[55]

The court also affirmed that the female students had a valid sexual harassment claim in which harassment was so persuasive, severe, and offensive it undermined and detracted from the victims' educational experience; they were denied equal access to an institution's resources and opportunities.[56] The court maintained that the study abroad "programs were always under the control of Eastern Michigan University in every respect, rather than under the control of any foreign educational facility."[57]

In conclusion, as seen through *King v. Board of Control of Eastern Michigan University*, coordinators and their institutions are bound to extraterritorial application for Title IX with study abroad. Again, the court supported that EMU's program was always under the control of the university in every respect. Therefore, this backs that every moment of inaction by Dr.

Okafor, who represented the university, to stop the sexual harassment served as a form of negligence by the university.

Strong Faculty Leaders Are the Best Defense

The program leader, Dr. Okafor, time after time, had the opportunity to address this hostile environment yet did not. This case reveals that legal documents, such as waivers, fail to be effective when a program supervisor is inattentive. *King v. Board of Control of Eastern Michigan University* shows that a capable supervisor needs to accompany a well-written waiver of liability to assist in the protection of a university.

Coordinators understand the importance with having competent faculty leaders in place with study abroad programs, and tend to have confidence with their own faculty leaders' ability to manage study abroad programs. However, coordinators need to make sure they do not become lax in their vetting and training of those faculty leaders over time.

Let's revisit Coordinator Trevor's reflection: "The college has to put a lot of faith in the [faculty] person doing the trips. I don't know if there's some kind of background check. You don't want a bad character or with a criminal record doing these things. The school has to acknowledge that this person is our agent, this person is serving for the school in this capacity, and we trust this person. This person is not going to sit in their room and get drunk every night."

If only it were this simple. As shown with *King v. Board of Control of Eastern Michigan University*, the court did not bring to light a faculty leader who was a shady character, an alcoholic, or the like. Just the opposite—Dr. Okafor seemed to be an overly stoic individual whose inaction to squelch the volatile environment created a debacle of a program.

A faculty leader with a clean background check, who is a competent on-campus instructor with a pleasant personality, does not necessarily "make the grade" as a study abroad leader. Strong leadership skills, including a willingness to use one's authority to delve out swift sanctions to check potentially risky behavior or situations, sets the proper tone for a educationally enriching study abroad environment.

Good Cop/Bad Cop as an Approach to Leading Programs

The obvious benefit with having two faculty leaders in place per program is that each can take on responsibilities to assist the group during program activities. Another reason for two leaders is that each can provide constructive criticism for how well the other is leading the group. When leading a study abroad program, at the end of each day, I organize time with the other program leaders to discuss what went well and what could have been improved upon. We also discuss how we influence these outcomes.

Some coordinators prefer to establish, in advance of the program, the role that they would like to take as a program leader. With regard to this, some program leaders even see a good cop/bad cop approach as a potential method for leading study abroad programs. However, you cannot always have one faculty leader be a regulator and the other a conciliator for the group. A toned-down "good cop/bad cop" approach may serve to be an effective strategy for leading study abroad. There are mixed reviews on this approach.

For example, I co-led a program in Western Europe where the legal age for alcohol consumption was eighteen years of age, and we happened to be in a particular region of the country where beer was consumed like water. Students who were of legal age to drink in the country but underaged according to U.S. law were constantly being offered beer at mealtime.

My role and responsibility in serving as a "bad cop" was to remind students to kindly decline the offer, even if it made them look "uncool."

Incidentally, if parents are made aware of the environment ahead of time, parents of participants between the ages of eighteen and twenty-one could sign a separate waiver that gives consent for their son or daughter to "sample" beer in a responsible manner. It was specified that we do not endorse underaged (by U.S. standards) drinking, that it could not be the student's first drink, and it could only be a small sampling of beer with a meal in the presence of a program leader. If you ever consider doing something like this, you had better get approval from legal counsel first.

Do we as coordinators condone drinking by minors? No. Do we encourage parents to share a first drink with their child before sending them off to a beer garden abroad? No. We treated responsible students like they were adults—they met a reasonable legal drinking age in the region, were able to self-regulate, and had full support from their parents. The result was merely two "approved" students between the ages of eighteen and twenty-one sampled beer, and the rest of the participants were age twenty-one and over. Certainly it was not a major focus of the program, yet everyone enjoyed the run-of-the-mill cultural experience.

There must be weighed balance with a coordinator's expected program approach. Again, one program leader cannot only serve to regulate and the other to accommodate program participants. Early into our program, I had to correct my "good cop" faculty leader who purchased beer for students at a liquor store during a free evening. She took her role too far and lost her equanimity. I reminded her of her larger role and the expectations that come with being a program leader.

In the moment, she had felt justified in her actions because all of the students were "of age" (twenty-one years or older) and "it was a free evening to unwind." But the simple counter question, "Why can't they get their own beer if they are of age?" made her reconsider her actions. Going on beer runs for students, whether it is during their free time or not, does not send the right message.

Plus, in doing so, she may have unwittingly compromised her leadership role in the eyes of participants. Here, we needed an authority figure to help lead the program, not an adult buddy to the students. Years of experience has shown that student participants often come to resent leaders of programs who allow for too much liberty and not enough scholarly substance to a study abroad program.

All of this is to say that as program leaders, should you take on a "good cop-bad cop" approach, don't go so far in that you lose proper perspective and equanimity. You're a program leader; always conduct yourself like one. Many students will eventually thank you for a well-regulated study abroad program. They paid for a program to fully experience everything listed on the itinerary; it is your contractual promise to them. If they miss undertakings, it is by their own accord, not due to program activities being skipped.

A lack of regulation allows programs to unravel. Participants may begin showing up late for appointed times to depart from designated sites, leading to a domino effect of late or missed scheduled events, one after the other. Exasperated participants, by a program's end, have a right to demand partial or full reimbursement of program funds. Why not? They didn't get what they paid for.

Have the Flexibility to Change Course

Few participants or co-leaders desire a study abroad program with a leader who runs it with an iron first. There needs to be time set aside for absorption, change of pace, and/or connection to elements that bring a gratifying study abroad experience. Some venues elicit extended time for stay, others for reduced time. Sometimes even *reserved* venues are altered.

For instance, here is an example from a short-term study abroad program that I co-led to Peru. Our group arrived for a scheduled archaeological dig; to our amazement, the site was closed due to unexpected renovations. Our partnering agency had to quickly find a new, yet comparable, venue. We ended up going to a site where priceless artifacts were actively being unearthed. The energy of the archeologists, the intrigue with finding new artifacts, and the large degree of hands-on assistance by students allowed this site to outshine the original one. Therefore, itinerary adjustments can work in your favor.

Here is another example surrounding a short-term program that I co-led to Senegal and The Gambia. Our group needed to take a ferry from Senegal to The Gambia. We were not able to board the ferry until many hours after the scheduled time, so it became an impromptu opportunity to engage with locals on the docks. The cultural enrichment and long-term impacts acquired from those hours spent with community members far eclipsed anything on the *planned* itinerary.

More specifically, many of the young Senegalese men working on the docks were there because they were not able to pay for the required uniforms and books to remain in high school; as a result, they were at the docks looking for odd jobs. This came as a surprise for group members who took free public school education for granted. We also learned that these young men had attended a high school that we had visited earlier in the program.

That day, various program participants determined to assist these young men. A return to the high school, dialogue with the school principal, necessary paperwork, and a small pledge served to get those students through to graduation. Social media communication still remains between those program participants and the Senegalese graduates. You never know what positive impact may result from a *missed* opportunity (to board a ferry in this case).

This is the beauty of study abroad—continual unanticipated learning moments. Program leaders need to be open-minded, creative thinkers who are flexible enough to consider alternate plans when unexpected events occur abroad.

Clarity of Policies Transferring to Study Abroad Documents

To move in a slightly different direction, yet remain on topic with approaches that aid strong study abroad leadership, risk-averting documents should clarify college policies and regulations that transfer to the educational experience abroad. These policies may be stated directly and/or be provided through a web link.

For example, Sample Waiver B (see Appendix B) appropriately includes web links: "Applicant agrees to comply with all rules, regulations, and standards of conduct, including but not limited to violations of the Code of Academic Integrity (www.---.edu/code.html) and the Code of Student Conduct (www.--- conduct.html) fixed by the University, their agents, and employees who, in the event of violation, reserve the right to limit or terminate Applicant's participation in the Program."

Let's continue to scrutinize additional court cases that show the repercussions that might result when campus policies are flouted with overseas programs, leading to claims of supervisory neglect.

Radford University Case

Another suit that exposed the negligent act of a supervisor came with a Radford University sponsored program.[58] A faculty member at Radford University in Virginia took several students to the Bahamas to do research at an oceanographic facility with which Radford University had an affiliated agreement.[59] While there, the faculty leader drove some of the students in a truck down a narrow road, and a small car moving at a high speed collided into the truck.[60] As a result, the driver of the small car died; the students on the bus were uninjured.[61]

The parents of the deceased sued the faculty member and the university.[62] The faculty member was not entitled to representation under the state's insurance plan and had to retain and incur the cost to retain his own counsel.[63] It turned out to be a very costly affair; litigation went on for nine years.[64] The lawsuit was eventually settled out of court.[65]

Whether the faculty member personally made the decision or the university sanctioned the driving of the truck in the foreign country, the action was reckless. It endangered student passengers, caused the death of a civilian, and brought on an expensive, lengthy lawsuit. Study abroad program leaders should always have a hired driver from a reputable company to do the driving in all foreign locations. It is up to the coordinator to make sure arrangements for safe transportation are arranged in advance, and then the program leader must abide by set policies.

The University of Pittsburgh's Semester as Sea Program (detailed in chapter 3) in India also confirms that accidents on the road are a common risk factor with study abroad programs. However, the difference between the University of Pittsburgh's Semester as Sea Program and the Radford University case was *who* was negligent. Recall with the University of Pittsburgh's Semester as Sea Program that the hired driver was from a chartered bus company allegedly on duty between thirty and fifty hours, driving under the influence of alcohol and speeding, who lost control of the tour bus that crashed.[66]

It would appear that the program operators, more than the university and its faculty leaders, are liable for the tragedy. Of course, questions of proper vetting and selection of the sponsoring agency, Institute for Shipboard Education (ISE), which secures the transportation for the study abroad programs, should be a focus. Apparently so. Dissatisfied with the partnership, in 2005, University of Pittsburgh officials formally ended their relationship with the Semester at Sea Program.[67]

Due to the fact that a program leader was not driving the bus during the fatal accident in the University of Pittsburgh's Semester as Sea Program, it was logical not to fully introduce the case in this chapter on supervisory neglect.

University of Virginia Semester at Sea Program in the Caribbean

The University of Virginia took over as the academic sponsor of Semester at Sea in 2006.[68] It might not bode well for the University of Virginia and certainly not for Semester at Sea that another suit has been recently filed against the provider. David Schulman filed that lawsuit. He is the father of Casey Schulman, killed last year in the Caribbean, where she was studying abroad.[69] The lawsuit claims negligence by the Semester at Sea program, sponsored by University of Virginia and several others.[70] The suit seeks funeral expenses and compensatory damages.[71]

Additional details are that Casey Schulman, then a fourth-year student of the University, was swimming December 1, 2012, off Mero Beach, near Roseau, Dominica, when a small dive boat struck her.[72] Dominican authorities charged Andrew Armour, the boat's captain, with manslaughter more than six months later.[73]

"The trip was organized by students independently of Semester at Sea activities," a University of Virginia spokesman said at the time.[74] This Semester at Sea program is a twelve-to-fifteen-credit study abroad program that takes students around the world on the *Explorer*, a 590-foot ship.[75] In a statement, Semester at Sea president Les McCabe also said the snorkeling trip had been organized by a group of students and was not a Semester at Sea event.[76]

Court proceedings and the final outcome of this case will hopefully assist in determining whether supervisory neglect played a role in this tragedy. If so, the question that arises is, What changes need to be made to help ensure the safety of student participants with future programs?

Clear Delineation of Roles and Responsibilities with Program Leaders in Waivers

Risk-averting forms are often heavily consumed with verbiage that spells out the participants' responsibilities but light on expected responsibilities for program leaders. Coordinator Poppy rightly asserts that waivers need to make "demarcations of where our student's responsibility ends and the university's responsibility ends."

For instance, in Sample Waiver G (see Appendix G), the Student/Parent Liability Form avows, "The University strongly discourages students owning or operating vehicles while participating in study abroad programs." Yet the careless decision of a *faculty* member to drive a truck carrying students during a Radford University program led to the fatal collision that killed the other driver. [77]

A simple insertion of "program leaders and coordinators," to relate "The University strongly discourages students, *program leaders, and coordinators* from owning or operating vehicles while participating in study abroad programs," in Sample Waiver G, or any waiver for that matter, gives a more balanced understanding for the dual responsibility students *and* program leaders share in this regard. Such balance needs to be considered throughout waivers and their formulation. As always, feedback from legal counsel is recommended when constructing the language in waivers.

Thackurdeen v. Duke University (2014)

Concerns with supervisory neglect surfaced with the recent lawsuit *Thackurdeen v. Duke University*. A family remains devastated by the loss of one of its members, Ravi Thackurdeen. Ravi Thackurdeen was a scholar, researcher, tutor, and volunteer at Swarthmore College who lost his life on a Duke University Organization of Tropical Studies (OTS) program in Costa Rica in 2012. [78] Consequently, his family filed a formal suit, and these are the details of the tragedy and potential supervisory neglect that surrounds it.

Toward the end of the semester in Costa Rica, Duke and OTS took their students on a surprise celebratory trip to the beach at Playa Tortuga on the south central Pacific Coast. [79] The beach trip was not on the program's schedule, and students had no prior notice of it. [80]

Duke had been taking its students to this beach as part of its OTS program for three consecutive years. The students were told that it was safe to swim in the waters, and they were given only the following instruction: to swim parallel to the shore if they were caught in a rip current. [81] Ravi got caught in a rip current and drowned in Playa Tortuga that afternoon, one day prior to his scheduled return home from Costa Rica. [82]

The complaint also notes that almost every website or brochure that discussed visiting Playa Tortuga mentioned the dangerously strong rip currents and that swimming at the beach was not advisable. [83] What made Playa Tortuga even more dangerous is that there are no lifeguards on duty at the beach. [84]

Sad study abroad events disclosed in lawsuits such as this serve as more than enough motivation to write this book. I hope positive awareness results from disclosing these overseas tragedies and potential solutions to thwart the hazards will lead to a few less injuries or deaths to future study abroad students. We will need to wait for more information to come out regarding the *Thackurdeen v. Duke University* lawsuit. Hopefully, a court will be able to clearly determine if gross supervisory neglect played a major role in this tragedy, once both sides are heard.

Some immediate questions that would need to be addressed are: Did officials at Duke University do their due diligence in fully researching the reputability of the partnering organization, OTS? Did they have great familiarity with the sites where they took students? Did either Duke University officials or OTS members provide Ravi Thackurdeen advanced warning to avoid swimming at the beach area where he ended up drowning?

In addition, one should inquire: At the very least, was a general warning given during orientation classes and in risk-averting documents that swimming at beaches in Costa Rica, due to strong rip currents, is ill advised without specific approval from program leaders? Were set policies and procedures for Duke University followed during Ravi Thackurdeen's time abroad with the OTS program in Costa Rica?

Coordinators Must Do Copious Research Prior to Organizing Programs

Thackurdeen v. Duke University reports that drownings due to rip currents cause more tourist deaths in Costa Rica than all other causes combined.[85] Some statistics state that of the 150 to 250 drowning deaths that occur each year in Costa Rica, approximately 80 percent are caused by rip currents.[86]

This is an example of a key piece of information that the program leaders would need to be aware of through advanced research, especially if they are to take students to a beach. Of course, students would need to be apprised of this information. Again, hopefully court proceedings will determine the findings on this.

To their credit, most coordinators do the necessary research to stay current on essential safeguards and policies to protect their study abroad participants, such as Coordinator Desiree, who shares, "[I] do a lot of research on study abroad! I read a lot of books, benchmark best practices at other institutions across the country, and attend many workshops and conferences devoted to study abroad."

This is not an anomaly, but a common practice among coordinators. A good portion of a coordinator's time is spent researching program venues, accommodations, and other components in order to foresee potential risks for participants. Here are some of the resources that coordinators use to gain awareness on current events, safeguards, and best practices for study abroad:

- NAFSA (Association of International Educators) with its International Educator (IE) bimonthly magazine, other publications, conferences, and workshops
- The Forum on Education Abroad provides "Standards of Good Practice" and annual forums
- CCID (Community Colleges for International Development) in which community college coordinators network, participate in learning communities, and collaborate to advance global opportunities at the college level
- Statewide consortiums, organizations, and groups allow for constant consultation with other colleagues on current issues and best practices in the field.

However, there is room for improvement. Some coordinators remain too entrenched with constructing policies and safeguards on their own. By consulting colleagues from other institutions, and through conferring with departments, legal counsel, and other groups in their own institution, they will not need to approach study abroad as a lone entity.

Improved Transparency Needed among Study Abroad Coordinators

Roshni Thackurdeen, mother of Ravi, correctly asserts that "we need to make parents aware of issues with study abroad; we need to create laws and standards to protect our children abroad; we need to have transparency and reform across the board."[87] Even before this can be achieved nationally, it needs to occur on a regional level.

During interviews with fellow coordinators, whether from the West Coast, Northeast, Midwest, or South, I discovered that most were willing to share their knowledge, approaches, and risk-averting materials. However, this certainly was not across the board. Overall, coordinators need to be more transparent not only in sharing their knowledge but also in sharing their lack of knowledge.

Let me provide support for my critique. First, institutional waivers of liability are public documents, and second, I ensured (with both verbal and written guarantees) the identity of the institution would remain anonymous to any reader. Yet fellow coordinators still hesitated with sharing program shortcomings and current waivers used.

We don't run study abroad from out of a closet. This sort of uncommunicativeness, and perhaps distrust, does not serve the greater good of students and study abroad on a whole. This reticence is pervasive. A remark from Coordinator Braxton speaks to the issue: "I can honestly say our university has not had any major litigation from students involved with study abroad, or experiential learning programs off campus. I know when I have asked my university about this they are pretty low key about discussing any cases going to trial."

It is commendable that major litigation has not surfaced at his university. I am sure it is a great relief to the university considering that fighting a claim "can cost hundreds of thousands of dollars. And some college officials admit that they do not want to be in the position of fighting in court against students who were harmed while overseas."[88]

With an ever-increasing litigious culture aimed at study abroad programs in higher education, the second statement by Coordinator Braxton should cause one to pause. For university officials to deflect "[discussion on] any cases going to trial" being probed by *their own* coordinator shows a lack of transparency. An opportunity for a coordinator to gain insight from institutional officials on potential issues of liability, and subsequent impacts, should be open for discussion as yet another means to avert potential future program errors.

In addition, some fellow coordinators showed coolness when asked to share what providers and agencies they have used to assist with study abroad programs. For example, when I inquired about exemplary travel agencies that she uses for study abroad programs, Coordinator Poppy evaded the question, her rationale being, "I don't want the competition from other study abroad coordinators who desire assistance in arrangements for quality programs that I get at a very reasonable price."

Whose interest is being served here? It is better to fully disclose a reputable company used, and possibly lose a few opportunities, than to have colleagues furnish students with less-than-stellar providers. Less adept providers should not gain our business, and coordinators should point one another in the right direction. In turn, exclusively using trustworthy providers may offset some of the *negligence* that has surfaced with study abroad programs.

CHAPTER SUMMARY

Supervisory neglect brings great risks to study abroad students, and serious liability issues to colleges and universities. Its frequency makes it one of the LARGEST 3, along with medical risks and sexual assault.

Fay v. Thiel College illustrated a worst-case scenario that resulted from supervisory neglect. The court's recognition of misguided language used in risk-averting documents serves to be instructive; with it comes increased insight on how to bolster such forms. A waiver that works off a take-it-or-leave-it basis, remains vague about inherent risks in a region, and uses ambiguous language concerning program leaders' duties of care for participants are concerns.

Current sample waivers, as well as the Malveaux Sample Recommended Waiver, are provided in order to assist coordinators' construction of risk-averting documents. This should be accompanied by consultation with legal counsel. *Fay v. Thiel College, Paneno v. Centres*, and *Earlham v. Eisenberg* reveal various degrees of neglect, as well as the extent to which risk-averting documents can help or harm colleges and universities.

Yet when supervisory neglect is substantial, risk-averting documents, no matter how well crafted, are rendered powerless. *King v. Board of Control of Eastern Michigan University* and *Fay v. Thiel College* unveil gross supervisory neglect by program leaders. In addition, a case against Radford University validates the problems that may arise with poor decision making during programs.

Faculty leaders should have the ability to determine when it is best to serve as a *regulator* or *conciliator* of a study abroad group. Some leaders communicate with co-leaders about the role that they tend to embrace prior to the start of a program. Examples from past study abroad program scenarios attempt to bring clarity concerning proper balance with program leadership.

At times, reserved venues and expected program activities may have to be altered. Keep an open mind that people in other regions of the world are not always as punctual or pragmatic as Americans. Itinerary adjustments can work in your favor. Additional past program scenarios are provided to illustrate this point.

To support essential study abroad leadership, risk-averting documents should clarify college policies and regulations that carry forth to overseas programs. These policies may be noted directly or provided through a webpage link. The case involving Radford University underscores the need for clear policies to be in place for not only participants but also faculty leaders.

Accidents on the road are a common risk with study abroad programs, also revealed with the Radford University case, as well as with the University of Pittsburgh's Semester as Sea Program lawsuit; yet contrasting parties served to be negligent for each.

Following the University of Pittsburgh's Semester as Sea Program lawsuit came a second suit aimed at the University of Virginia Semester at Sea Program in the Caribbean (2012), bringing to question the reliability of this study abroad provider.

With the *Thackurdeen v. Duke University* lawsuit, a student taken to a beach not advised for swimming drowned to death, eliciting questions of supervisory neglect. At the same time, coordinators tend to spend a good amount of time, as a part of their job, conducting research and attending conferences in order to stay up to date on proper safeguards for study abroad participants.

Coordinators helped to generate a brief list of resources that may aid awareness of current events, safeguards, and best practices with study abroad. However, greater transparency and increased willingness to share resources is needed among coordinators in order to most efficiently serve the needs of student participants.

NOTES

1. *Fay v. Thiel Coll.*, 55 Pa. D. & C.4th 353 (Com. Pl. 2001).
2. *Id.* at 356.

3. *Id.*
4. *Id.*
5. *Id.* at 359.
6. *Id.* at 362, 369.
7. *Id.* at 369.
8. *Id.* at 357–58.
9. *Id.* at 359–60.
10. *Id.*at 361.
11. *Id.* at 369.
12. *Id.*
13. *Id.*
14. Guernsey, L. (1997, April 11). A lawsuit raises difficult questions about liability and study-abroad programs. *Chronicle of Higher Education 43*, 31, p. A37, A39.
15. 590 N.W.2d 661, 662–64 (Minn. Ct. App. 1999).
16. *Id.* at 663.
17. *Id.* at 666.
18. *Paneno v. Centres for Acad. Programmes Abroad, Ltd.*, 13 Cal. Rptr. 3d 759, 763 (Cal. Ct. App. 2004).
19. *Id.* at 766.
20. *Id.*
21. Kast, R. (1997). In loco parentis and the "reasonable person." *International Educator 7*, 1.Rubin, A. M. (1996, May 10). Making it safer to study abroad. *Chronicle of Higher Education*, p. A49.
22. *Id.*
23. *King v. Bd. of Control of E. Mich. Univ.*, 221 F. Supp. 2d 783, 791 (E.D. Mich. 2002).
24. *Id.*
25. *Id.* at 784.
26. *Id.*
27. *Id.*
28. *Id.*
29. *Id.*
30. *Id.*
31. *Id.*
32. *Id.* at 785.
33. *Id.* at 786.
34. *Id.*
35. *Id.*
36. *Id.*
37. *Id.* at 785.
38. *Id.*
39. *Id.*
40. *Id.*
41. *Id.* at 786.
42. *Id.*
43. *Id.*
44. *Id.*
45. *Id.*
46. *Id.*
47. *Id.*
48. *Id.*
49. *Id.*
50. *Id.*
51. *Id.* at 785.
52. *Id.* at 784.
53. *Id.* at 791.
54. *Id.* at 790.
55. *Id.*
56. *Id.* at 791.
57. *Id.*
58. Kast, R. (1997).
59. *Id.*
60. *Id.*
61. *Id.*
62. *Id.*
63. *Id.*
64. *Id.*

65. *Id.*

66. Semester at Sea—A deadly program (2011). Cherese Mari Laulhere Foundation. Retrieved from http://cherese.org/semester-at-sea.html.

67. Hart, P., & Thomas, M. A. (2005, June 9). Pitt to end pact with Semester at Sea program. *University Times: University of Pittsburgh.* Retrieved from http://www.utimes.pitt.edu/?p=942.

68. Father of U.Va. student who died studying abroad files lawsuit. (2013, November 2). *Richmond Times-Dispatch.* Retrieved from http://www.richmond.com/news/virginia/article_d966a9cb-da4f-5bb6-ba03-198c6bfc7cc7.html.

69. Complaint at 5, *Schulman v. Inst. for Shipboard Educ.*, No. 15-11689 (S.D. Fla. Apr. 20, 2015), *aff'd per curiam*, No. 11-11689, 2015 WL 4896597, at *9 (11th Cir. Aug. 18, 2015).

70. *See id.* at 9–10, 13.

71. *Id.* at 22.

72. *Id.* at 7.

73. Father of U.Va. student who died studying abroad files lawsuit. (2013, November 2).

74. *Id.*

75. *Id.*

76. Marklein, M. B. (2012, December 4). Death highlights risks of study abroad programs. *USAToday.* Retrieved from http://www.usatoday.com/story/news/nation/2012/12/03/study-abroad-safety/1742503/.

77. Kast, R. (1997).

78. Complaint at 3, 6, *Thackurdeen v. Duke Univ.*, No. 14-cv-6311 (Aug. 8, 2014 S.D.N.Y.)

79. *Id.* at 5.

80. *Id.*

81. *Id.*

82. *Id.* at 6.

83. *Id.* at 12–13.

84. *Id.* at 13.

85. *Id.*

86. *Id.*

87. Vigliotti, J., & Givens, A. (2014, September 22). I-team: Parents demand transparency from college study abroad programs after sons' deaths. Retrieved from
http://www.nbcnewyork.com/news/local/Study-Abroad-Program-Wrongful-Death-Regulation-Investigation-Thackurdeen-275787101.html.

88. Van Der Werf, M. (2007, June 6). A wide world of risk. *Chronicle of Higher Education 53*, 30, p. A1.

Chapter Six

Increasing Concerns with Cyberthreats, Identity Theft, and Terrorist Acts

This chapter delves into growing issues that threaten all aspects of study abroad, including overseas internships, workforce development, service learning, or general study abroad. Cyberthreats, identity theft, and terrorist acts are not new problems; however, in recent years they have become increasingly worrisome for American travelers. One section of this chapter considers the cyberthreats and identity theft that have resulted from improved technology, and ways that study abroad participants can protect themselves from being victims.

A second section delves into our changing world landscape, which requires American travelers to be alert to regions that may become unsafe for travel, particularly due to terrorist threats. Regions once considered safe havens may not be suitable for study abroad today. The political and economic climate of various countries has been shifting.

A current global refugee movement across the world—from Afghanistan, Eritrea, Libya, Pakistan, Syria, and Somalia to name a few—is occurring due to people's pursuit for improved living conditions. American travelers need to be aware of changes taking place around the world, and in particular, with regions where terrorist activities have increased.

Terrorism is well defined in the chapter in order to show that its outreach extends far beyond extremist groups in the Middle East. Study abroad participants need to be wary of potential kidnapping. Human trafficking, whether it is labor trafficking or sex trafficking, is a serious threat. In addition, Americans are often perceived as being wealthy and serve as targets for gaining ransom.

Overall, this chapter sets out to explore increasing cyberthreats, identity theft, and terrorist acts that impact American travelers, and gives potential solutions to elude these dangers.

THE GENERAL ISSUE OF CYBERTHREATS

It is worthwhile to begin with considering the general issues that come with cyberthreats by considering our government's response. President Barack Obama issued an executive order on April 1, 2015, declaring foreign cyberthreats to U.S. economic and national security a "national emergency."[1]

Four categories of cyberbehavior could trigger sanctions under the executive order: 1) harming or significantly compromising critical infrastructure services, 2) significantly disrupting a computer network via, for example, a distributed denial-of-service attack, 3) causing a significant misappropriation of funds or economic resources by, for example, stealing credit card information or trade secrets, and 4) using such trade secrets for commercial gain.[2]

Among the four categories, the third most critically impacts study abroad participants. I have had a few students go overseas and upon return discover that their debit card, credit card, or online accounts had been hacked.

In addition, due to concerns with increasing cyberthreats, President Obama charged the Director of National Intelligence (DNI) with establishing a Cyber Threat Intelligence Integration Center (CTIIC). The CTIIC will be a national intelligence center focused on "connecting the dots" regarding malicious foreign cyberthreats to the nation and cyberincidents affecting U.S. national interests, and on providing all-source analysis of threats to U.S. policymakers.[3]

It is believed that cyberthreats are among the gravest national security dangers to the United States.[4] Our citizens, our private sector, and our government are increasingly confronted by a range of actors attempting to do us harm through identity theft, cyberenabled economic espionage, politically motivated cyberattacks, and other malicious activity.[5]

Prior to departure, students of study abroad will need to be informed about the kind of cyberthreats that exist; cyberattacks are certainly not a threat limited to home. Cybersecurity is a top-tier issue that is getting the type of attention and resources given to terrorist defense. In creating the CTIIC, the administration is applying some of the hard-won lessons from our counterterrorism efforts to augment that "whole-of-government" approach by providing policymakers with a cross-agency view of foreign cyberthreats, their severity, and potential attribution.[6]

HOW CYBERTHREATS DIRECTLY HARM AMERICANS PARTICIPATING IN STUDY ABROAD

Cyberthreats immensely impact Americans overseas, and identity theft is a growing worldwide problem. Travelers are very vulnerable because they are obligated to carry vast personal documentation at all times, use unsecured Internet connections, and share their credit cards with merchants who know that the travelers may never return.[7] Identify theft has been particularly problematic at hotels, as well as with simple activities including using free Wi-Fi, business kiosks, ATMs, and cell phones.

Hotels with Free Wi-Fi

Hotels are frequently used by groups who take part in short-term study abroad. The unfortunate news is that if participants stay at a hotel that offers free Wi-Fi, they can become victims of cybertheft. A report from California-based security firm Cylance reveals a serious vulnerability in a commonly used Internet router that can be found at hotels around the world.[8]

In various cases of identity theft through hotels, Cylance found that the affected router, the ANTLabs InnGate, was integrated with the hotel's Property Management System.[9] Therefore, a hacker could find the way to data such as hotel guests' credit cards.[10] Cylance experts maintain that this has the potential to impact millions of customers ranging from everyday vacationers and data center IT staff to tradeshow attendees.[11]

So an immediate solution that comes to mind is to avoid certain hotel chains or regions of the world that pose this threat. Unfortunately, there is no way to predict what hotels are safe and which are not. According to Brian Wallace, senior researcher for Cylance, "Take it from us that this issue affects hotel brands all up and down the spectrum of cost, from places we've never heard of, to places that cost more per night than most apartments cost to rent for a month."[12]

For example, the average price for a room at the high-end New York City Mandarin Oriental hotel is $850 a night.[13] In 2015, nearly all of the Mandarin Oriental's twenty-four locations worldwide might have been subject to a cyberattack, and all of the chains in the United States—including New York, Washington, DC, Boston, and Las Vegas—were affected.[14] As a result of the security breach, hackers were able to obtain guests' credit card information.[15]

Stolen credit card numbers often end up on black markets around the world, and the ones stolen from the Mandarin Oriental could fetch big bucks due to the chain's upscale clientele;[16] and in fact, it was confirmed fraudulent charges began appearing on a number of past guests' credit card accounts.[17]

Steps are being taken by businesses to put the appropriate protections in place; however, online thieves are committed to finding ways around the defenses.[18] That means that there remains no guarantee of protection from identity theft when staying at a foreign hotel. Clearly this issue also impacts study abroad participants.

To offset potential collateral damage, coordinators should have participants pay program organizers for accommodations in advance of check in. Then, a single credit card can be used to check in everyone. This should be possible when working through a reputable travel agency.

However, a separate issue also comes to mind. Hotel staff will often use the passport numbers of guests to check them into the computer system. If hackers are able to access this data, they can also create a lot of havoc. Therefore, if a hotel has this check-in policy, I recommend that you do not provide passport numbers and negotiate an alternative approach that does not put your group at risk for identify theft.

Identity Theft through Wi-Fi, Registration Kiosks, ATMs, and Cellular Networks

Keeping private information from being entered into a hotel data system is one way for coordinators to protect participants; unfortunately, identity theft can still occur. Wi-Fi, business kiosks, and cellular networks can be compromised and used against travelers. Whether at a hotel, restaurant, or business that offers free Wi-Fi, students who log in can be victimized.

Michael Robinson, an expert in computer forensics and cybersecurity, asserts that hackers can create a fake wireless access point that an unknowing victim will log onto assuming that it is the official business' Wi-Fi.[19] At that point, hackers can take information entered or exchanged on laptops and wireless devices while individuals are connected to the imposter Wi-Fi, including login passwords and credit card numbers.[20]

Logging into a bank account, work email, or other sensitive account should be avoided if at all possible while traveling.[21] If you have no alternative, choose what you type over these open connections very carefully.[22]

If it is essential for you to use your own laptop and free Wi-Fi during travel, protect your connections. Some websites let you log in over open networks; always try to use HTTPS://www.website.com instead of HTTP://www.website.com (the *S* stands for *secure* and indicates that the data is encrypted for more protection).[23] You can also get a plug-in for your browser such as HTTPS Everywhere (Firefox, Chrome, and Opera only), which will do this automatically.[24] Another possible solution is SurfEasy VPN, which helps encrypt your data when you're using a public connection from your own computer.[25]

Kiosks have also been used to gain access to individuals' private information during travel. Hotels, car rentals, airports, and many other businesses use kiosks to allow customers to check in or register. Robinson points out that if those kiosks have USB ports that are running and open, a predator can gain access into the system. [26] Apparently, if the hacker hits the shift key a number of times in a row, they can get an error message to pop up; this gives them special rights into the computer. [27] Then, the predator can start processing and stealing data. [28]

I wish that I could provide a clever solution to defend against this problem, but I do not have one. Take the time to wait in line and have a business representative assist you as opposed to using a kiosk.

Another recent trend among identity thieves has been to install card readers in an ATM by which they can access your card number and PIN. [29] This happens most often at nonbank, "generic" ATMs (in hotels, convenience stores, etc.), which have less oversight and are therefore more vulnerable than bank-run and hosted ATMs. [30]

To avoid identity theft, limit your ATM use to banks while overseas. Prior to going abroad, make sure to contact your own bank to inform them of your departure. If there are sudden changes in your account activity, including unexpected transactions abroad, it can generate a fraud alert and cause your account to be frozen.

The simple use of one's cell phone or smartphone can also put someone at risk with identity theft. Robinson details that while you are talking on a cell phone, a nearby predator can create a fake cell phone tower and steal all of your traffic, listening to your calls and stealing all of your text messages and email. [31]

Loss or theft of cell phones is a rather common problem with study abroad. Cell phones often contain information that put you at risk. They typically have apps that give access to personal information, and people leave them lying around quite a bit. [32] Here are steps to protect yourself in case you lose possession of your cell phone while abroad:

- Set a password on the phone so someone who finds or steals it cannot use it.
- Before traveling, consider deleting any especially sensitive apps, such as banking apps, social networks and others; they are easy to reinstall when you get home.
- Specifically log out of all apps before going out and about.
- Remain wary of suspicious emails and websites; studies indicate folks are much more likely to click on malware links on their cell phone than on their computer. [33]

With existing technology, coordinators need to include warnings prior to departure about cyberthreats in orientation sessions and materials in order to protect student abroad participants. Honestly, not every threat can be detected. However, with foreknowledge of many potential cyberthreats, students might be able to protect themselves from identity theft while abroad.

Physical protection from identity theft should be coupled with the technological protections that have been outlined. Good old-fashioned pickpocketing still remains prevalent with study abroad. For measures to protect against physical theft of valuables, do not forget to review in chapter 8 best practice #14, Passport, Cash, and Protection of Other Valuable Items.

THE IMPACT OF TERRORISM AND POLITICAL STRIFE IN THE WORLD

The global landscape is altering all of the time, and Americans need to stay abreast of ongoing changes in foreign regions prior to going overseas. Political unrest and terrorist activities have been contributing to this altering landscape.

The United Nations Refugee Agency estimates that currently 59.5 million people have been forcibly displaced worldwide. [34] In 2014, an estimated 13.9 million people were newly displaced due to conflict or persecution.[35] Some of the causes for this uprooting is continued fighting in the Syrian Arab Republic, an Islamic State offensive across multiple parts of Iraq, renewed fighting in the Democratic Republic of Congo, discord in South Sudan, and conflict and security concerns in Afghanistan.[36]

Current study abroad participants need to remain highly informed about world events in order to determine ideal locations for secure study. Coordinators must be able to advise them on their choices.

THE DIFFICULT TOPIC OF TERRORISM ABROAD

Admittedly, this section is limited with providing experiences from coordinators who conduct, or have conducted, study abroad in regions with the presence of past or existing terrorist activities. One of the questions that I posed to coordinators during interviews was "Can you explain any experiences, positive and negative, with programs to locations that may contain potential threats of terrorist groups and/or activities?" It was a hot-button topic. A vast majority chose to skip the question. Guaranteeing that they and their institution's identity would remain anonymous did not help to produce answers.

I touch upon the lack of transparency of coordinators in the chapter 5 section, Improved Transparency Needed among Study Abroad Coordinators. I undoubtedly "hit a brick wall" when I brought forth the subject of terrorism abroad. Information shared on the topic came incidentally from general questions about potential risks and liabilities with study abroad. But with mention of the *t* (terrorism) word, coordinators often became reticent, or felt the need to consult a supervisor, who would not give consent to answer the question.

Regardless of this limitation, I felt it was essential to address the major issue of *terrorist threats* and its impact on study abroad. This section may be light on coordinator feedback, but it remains informative on the subject matter. Really, I do not know how a book on risks, liabilities, and repair of study abroad could be written and not address the increasing concern with terrorist acts against Americans overseas. With amplified media coverage on the savage acts and growth of such groups as the Islamic State in Iraq and Syria (ISIS) and al Qaeda, one must consider how this is impacting American students overseas.

TERRORIST THREATS ARE NOT A NEW PHENOMENON, BUT ARE AN EVER-INCREASING CONCERN

The threat of terrorism abroad is not a new occurrence for American study abroad students. As Evans (1991) points out, "The vulnerability of group travel was realized in December, 1988, when a terrorist bomb killed thirty-five Syracuse students over Lockerbie, Scotland."[37] Students were returning from study abroad onboard Pan Am Flight 103 that crashed due to an organized terror attack, or bombing.[38]

What is disconcerting is that in recent years, terrorism is on the rise globally. Clearly, this could lead to increasing danger for American students studying abroad who may be targeted. More specifically, in 2002, 725 people were killed worldwide in terror attacks; by 2010, the number was 13,186.[39] In 2014 the death toll was 32,727.[40] The number of attacks has also grown dramatically, from 9,707 in 2013 to 13,463 in 2014.[41]

U.S. citizens are prime targets for terrorists' kidnappings, and the U.S. State Department urges Americans to be on high alert when they're traveling abroad.[42] In addition, the U.S. State Department fears that ISIS and other extremist groups have "increased attempts to finance their operations through kidnapping for ransom."[43]

There is little chance of survival for Americans who are taken captive by ISIS. The most recently murdered American by ISIS was Kayla Jean Mueller.[44] The twenty-six-year-old was kidnapped while trying to help people whose lives have been upended by the long Syrian civil war.[45] She was taken in August 2013.[46] ISIS reportedly demanded more than $6 million for her freedom, a figure in keeping with the impossibly high ransoms it has placed on other U.S. citizens it has held.[47] The Obama administration has a firm policy of not paying ransom for hostages and has even advised the families of Americans held in Syria that they could be criminally prosecuted if they pay for their loved ones' releases.[48]

As an obvious safeguard, study abroad participants should remain far from regions that contain ISIS and other extremist groups. However, terrorist threats have spread outward to other countries that have not traditionally had this risk.

TERRORIST THREATS IN TRADITIONAL SAFE HAVENS FOR STUDY ABROAD

Even more disturbing is that terrorist attacks are streaming into what were once considered safe havens for student study abroad. Considered a trustworthy destination for study abroad, Western Europe still remains the most popular region of choice for students. Yet this area of the world has been riddled with fresh terrorist attacks linked to extremist groups. Some recent terrorist incidents have included a series of coordinated attacks in Paris, France that left 130 dead in a single day,[49] ; shootings at the *Charlie Hebdo* weekly newspaper office in France,[50] and at a Jewish museum in Brussels.[51]

COORDINATORS AND PARTICIPANTS MUST BE ATTENTIVE TO TERRORIST THREATS WHEREVER THEY GO

Since acts of terrorism can take place in any region of the world without clear warning, coordinators and study abroad participants must be heedful of this threat *wherever* they go. The streaming of terrorist acts into Europe has had an impact on study abroad programs, including those run by interviewed experts.

For example, a student in London taking public transportation to class was the unlucky victim of a terrorist attack. Legally limited in his ability to discuss the incident, Coordinator Trevor briefly describes "[An] incident abroad occurred when a student was in London at the time of [terrorist] bombings. He was actually on the top part of a Double Decker [bus] in which the bomb went off. The first three rows were totally destroyed. He was in the fourth row. His ears continued to ring a long time after this." Sitting just one row from the demolished section of the bus, the student was extremely fortunate in not sustaining more serious injuries or death as a result of the explosion.

Coordinator Eve also discusses an act of terrorism on public transit that took place during a program to Spain. In this scenario, it was on a subway—the same that her students took to go to class each morning. She reminisces, "I had students who [were] in Spain when bombings [in] the train stations [occurred] . . . There was only one student that couldn't be located. She was supposed to be gone, and had signed out, but had not [left for the train station as expected] . . . The student was eventually located." It was by lucky chance that the student was delayed in getting to the train station to commute to school.

The growing concern for terrorist acts abroad has forced coordinators to reexamine program choices, even in areas with little to no threats. For example, Coordinator Trevor and college officials deemed Italy unsafe for travel, even though no incidents or U.S. State Department warnings applied to the region. Due to the fact that neighboring France had terrorist activities, they cancelled the program:

> [We consider] what the State Department declares . . . Italy was not declared off limits. But our [school] president decided, "I cannot in good conscience allow this trip to happen. What if something happens?" Also, other college officials felt it was unsafe to travel there. Even though no travel warning had come out on Italy, a neighboring area seemed unsafe. So the college was responsible for reimbursing the students.

Regardless of what the U.S. State Department declares, coordinators and college officials are the ones who need to research and scrutinize the safety of regions. Terminating a program, though difficult at times, is a necessary action that program officials must be willing to take. Never feel you must stay the course when a sudden detrimental change occurs in the overseas environment. The top priority is to safeguard program participants. Decisions and policies that safeguard students should be clear and decisive.

AMBIGUOUS SUPPORT FOR STUDENTS TO STUDY ABROAD IN REGIONS WITH U.S. STATE DEPARTMENT WARNINGS DUE TO TERRORIST THREATS

As a general rule, to avoid potential injury or death, a student should not be permitted to study in a region with a U.S. State Department warning. This subject is more fully considered in best practice #15, U.S. State Department Warnings, in chapter 8. Yet the question of whether students should still be afforded the opportunity to study in a region that has been issued a warning due to terrorist threats remains under debate with experts.

All coordinators agree that students should be advised not to study in such areas. However, some coordinators still condone study abroad in the regions. This sends mixed messages to students. What level of support are the students being given?

Let us consider the subject more closely. Coordinator Baron will "not allow students to travel to countries and/or regions that are on the U.S. State Department's Travel Warning List." Should the region be taken off the U.S. State Department list, he "will send students to . . . an area that experiences periodic terrorist activities." This begs the question, "If the country has had past terrorist issues, but doesn't in the present, is it once again safe for study abroad?" Again, it is a murky area that coordinators, their risk assessment team, legal counsel, and college administrators need to work out in accordance with their set policies and educational philosophy.

Then, there are coordinators who will tolerate overseas participation in regions with existing U.S. State Department warnings resulting from terrorist threats. For example, Coordinator Poppy will allow a student to study in a place with a U.S. State Department warning if the person "signs an agreement in which [the student] acknowledges awareness of the State Department warning, and decided not to heed it, releasing the institution from all responsibility of liability should an unfortunate occurrence result." She acknowledges that "Kenya [is a location that I have approved for students to go] while there was a U.S. State Department warning for the region."

Comparably, Coordinator Lonna avows that "[our university] will not ever set up a program that is on the U.S. State Department travel warning list. So that is one automatic. If the government says Americans shouldn't be traveling there, [our university] probably shouldn't be sponsoring programs there." This seems straightforward enough.

However, as Coordinator Lonna continues to address the subject, the university policy becomes more ambiguous. "If the student wants to go to that country on their own, they can.

So the biggest example of that would be Israel. There are many Jewish heritage students who are here who are interested in studying abroad in Israel. We'll let them do that as long as they sign a waiver saying there is a U.S. State Department travel warning and they apply directly through [an] institution [abroad]; and we'll let them transfer their credits back. But we won't set up a university presence there with that warning in place."

Quite simply, if university members agree to transfer credits back to their home institution, then they have condoned study abroad in that foreign location. By having the student sign a waiver to study in a potentially risky region, in order to protect the university, it makes one question if the student has become a secondary concern. Sure, making the student aware of a U.S. State Department warning is simply obligatory. If the risk assessment team, including legal counsel, approve of students studying in areas deemed risky by the U.S. State Department with the signing of a waiver, it is their prerogative.

However, they may want to consider that by claiming "we [do] *not set up* a program that is on the U.S. State Department travel warning list," it does not relieve the institution from all accountability. Why? The institution acknowledges that the student is studying in that region with the intent of transferring credits back to the home institution. There is responsibility and a potentially heavy price to pay in taking those credits. Hopefully, the coordinator and university officials view this in the same manner.

Each study abroad office and their committee members needs to find their own balance. What is the psychology at the college? Do the policies and procedures at the home campus mirror the approach abroad? Students are certainly game to explore less traditional or risky locations to further their growth and to serve as ambassadors of the world. I believe that they are the greatest ambassadors we have to show America's best side. Many coordinators naturally want to keep as many regions as possible open to students. Their office may be more favorably looked upon for having more program offerings.

Yet all of these motivations are trumped by this question: "Does putting students in a certain country bring additional risks not inherent to study abroad?" In other words, "Does that location bring greater potential harm to the student than most other regions in the world?" These are the questions that must be honestly answered prior to approving a location to send a student abroad.

ALWAYS USE A TRUSTED TRAVEL AGENCY WITH AN OFFICE IN THAT COUNTRY TO MAKE ARRANGEMENTS

Using a familiar, reliable travel agency to make arrangements for you in a foreign country is always recommended. If you decide to take participants to a region of the world with potential terrorist threats, it becomes increasingly essential that the travel agency have a main office in the foreign region. Should a sudden threat arise, a local group needs to be in place to immediately assist.

For example, one program leader of a short-term study abroad program in Egypt made such an on-the-spot arrangement without the help of an established travel agency in the region. This opened the group to potential threats. More specifically, due to the group leader's misstep, the group walked around lost in parts unknown for a time. In a region where negative sentiments are felt toward Americans, a group of U.S. students who are aimlessly walking about become an open target. The program leader knew that the group was in this vulnerable position while lost. Coordinator Pearl recollects:

[On] a trip to Egypt [I] arranged for a ride on donkeys with participants along a river. [However, the group was] going to a site away from the river . . . The [foreign guide] took them in a different path. Concerned, [I requested that the foreign guide] follow the set path. [He became angered and] made us get off [the donkeys], and [left the group] in a town. We didn't know where we were, and we walked and [eventually] found our way [back to familiar territory]. And why would the [foreign guide] do that? It doesn't sound good. It is odd. So I think [the group] was lucky.

Perhaps there was no intended foul play by the foreign guide. Perhaps he merely desired to extend the donkey ride to justify charging the group more money. Perhaps the unfamiliar town where the group walked aimlessly about contained no citizens who harbored hostile sentiments toward Americans.

However, all of these considerations become legitimate concerns when touring a region with a past history of political unrest and terrorist activities. I am not aware of what the U.S. State Department's stance was for Egypt during the time of this program, but at present, an alert exists, principally along the Israeli border. I would advise not to bring a group to the area while this alert remains. For coordinators at institutions that would do so, the stakes are high. Make sure that a reliable travel company with a strong presence in the region secures program activities; it should also be a travel agency with which you have had a long, successful history.

VARIOUS FORMS OF TERRORISM

It is essential to point out that not only must coordinators remain vigilant of terrorist acts *wherever* they go, but they should also be fully aware of various *types* of terrorist threats. Terrorist acts are not limited to bombings or shootings perpetrated by fringe groups. The Federal Bureau of Investigation's definition of *international terrorism* is instructive in laying out forms of terrorism:

> Activities with the following three characteristics: 1) Involve violent acts or acts dangerous to human life that violate federal or state law; 2) Appear to be intended (i) to intimidate or coerce a civilian population; (ii) to influence the policy of a government by intimidation or coercion; or (iii) to affect the conduct of a government by mass destruction, assassination, or kidnapping; and 3) Occur primarily outside the territorial jurisdiction of the U.S., or transcend national boundaries in terms of the means by which they are accomplished, the persons they appear intended to intimidate or coerce.[52]

Within this definition, "acts dangerous to human life," including "kidnapping," is a form of terrorism. Kidnapping, for the purpose of ransom or human trafficking, is a major concern with study abroad. A reported twenty-one to thirty million men, women, and children are enslaved today due to human trafficking.[53] Victims of kidnapping can also be held captive for a short period of time, but the results can be equally devastating for the sufferer, if not deadly.

Kidnapping is on the rise in various parts of the world. For example, in 2013, Mexico alone officially recorded 1,698 kidnappings, the highest number ever for the country.[54] Yet government officials concede that only a small percentage of victims—one in ten by some estimates—reported the crime, as police are sometimes involved in kidnappings and are not trusted.[55]

Recently, a member of the U.S. Marine Corps was one of four individuals kidnapped at the same time by the criminal group Los Zetas in Cancun, Mexico.[56] The criminal group intended to contact family or associates of the victims to demand ransoms for the victims' safe return.[57] Two of the victims were able to elude their captures and report the incident to the federal police; the authorities responded and were able to save the U.S. Marine and the remaining victim. [58]

Similarly, a recent kidnapping and attack of an American took place in Manali, India. [59] A thirty-year-old woman was raped by three men. [60] The woman arrived and stayed at a guest-house with three other women in the resort town of Manali. [61] She left to meet a friend at Vashisht in the evening, which is about two miles north of Manali. [62] At 1:00 a.m. she was looking for an auto-rickshaw to return to the guesthouse when three men in a truck offered to drive her to Old Manali. [63] Instead, they took her to a secluded spot and raped her. [64]

Another recent case of an American abduction occurred in Rio de Janeiro, Brazil. [65] An American student was kidnapped, robbed, and raped in front of her shackled French boyfriend during a horrifying six-hour ordeal on a minibus in Brazil. [66] The couple had boarded the minibus near the tourist-heavy Copacabana beach around 1:00 a.m. [67]

Three men hijacked the vehicle and forced everyone else off. [68] The male victim was allegedly cuffed and beaten with a crowbar—then made to watch as the woman was repeatedly raped. [69] The attackers also seized the victims' credit cards and used them to withdraw cash from ATMs across the area. [70] The terrifying ordeal ended when the accused rapists dumped the terrified couple in Itaborai, more than thirty miles away from Rio. [71]

These are just a few recent cases of terrorist acts committed against Americans abroad in parts of the world that would generally be considered safe. I bring them forth to show the seriousness of the problem, and to illustrate the range of locations where terrorist acts can occur.

EMERGENCY RESPONSE PLAN IN PLACE AS A PRECAUTION

Coordinators need to have an emergency response plan in place to aid participants should political unrest or a terrorist attack surface. In fact, coordinators stress this with best practice #17, Emergency Response Plan, in chapter 9. An emergency response plan is meant to assist with the abrupt threat of not only natural disasters or pandemics but also terrorist threats.

Part of this emergency response plan should include preemptive steps taken to safeguard students prior to going overseas, including registering participants with the U.S. embassy.

Once a participant is registered with the U.S. embassy, emergency messages, travel alerts and warnings, fact sheets, and other information in relation to the country are provided to the participant. [72] This branch will also evacuate U.S. citizens in emergency situations. [73]

Yet another preemptive measure for safeguarding students is having foreknowledge of American military bases abroad. Not every coordinator is aware that when sudden civil unrest or acts of terrorism occur in a country, the U.S. Air Force will evacuate American citizens.

Study abroad coordinators and institutional officials should have an emergency campus committee or response group to assist when emergencies arise with study abroad programs. This is explained by Coordinator Poppy: "An on-campus committee [looks] at emergency response here at [the college]. [Study abroad officials] work with that committee to [form] an emergency response plan [in] the event of an emergency that [is] all outlined for the faculty [who intend to lead study abroad] in handbooks so they know that before they go [abroad]."

Should the program leader be unable to do so, the campus response group must be ready to carry out emergency plans on behalf of the group *while* abroad. A program leader's ability to communicate may be compromised at the foreign location; the response group needs to know the group's daily itinerary, consider dangerous events, and take steps to aid the group from home.

POST POLICIES AND APPROACHES TO ASSIST STUDENTS WITH TERRORIST THREATS

In an attempt to address the issue of terrorist threats abroad, study abroad and international education offices should be open to posting policies that specifically address terrorist concerns overseas. For example, the Office of International Education at the University of Colorado, Boulder, aptly does this. The Office provides an online posting of "Policy in Case of Political or Social Unrest, Terrorism, and the Threat of War."[74]

The Office outlines three major approaches to deal with emergencies or other events that could jeopardize the security of students on the study abroad programs. Some of the approaches reiterate what we have previously considered. One approach is to give students the website for the U.S. Department of State's Background Notes and to urge students to read the U.S. Department of State's Consular Information Sheets.[75]

The second approach outlined by the Office is to furnish students with the U.S. Department of State's Travel Registration website information for participants to register with the country's embassy where they are studying abroad should a consular officer need to be contacted in case of an emergency.[76]

A final approach the Office takes is should a U.S. State Department Warning be issued, the study abroad program staff will evaluate and communicate with program contacts on site so that appropriate action can be taken.[77]

These are basic guidelines that all members of international education and analogous departments of higher education should take as precautionary steps in case sudden threats, including terrorism, surface during a study abroad program.

CHAPTER SUMMARY

The issue of cyberthreats has been identified as a "national emergency" by the U.S. government. As a measure of protection, President Obama has put forth the Cyber Threat Intelligence Integration Center (CTIIC), a national intelligence center focused on detecting malicious foreign cyberthreats to the nation and cyberincidents affecting U.S. national interests.

Cyberthreats considerably affect Americans who are overseas, and identity theft is a global problem. Identify theft has been particularly problematic with hotel stays. Also, study abroad participants who use free Wi-Fi, business kiosks, ATMs, and cell phones also open themselves up to identity theft. However, protective solutions are provided for the use of each.

At present, we are in a unique period of history. The global landscape is quickly changing around us. Refugees around the world have been forcibly displaced or have chosen to depart their homelands to find better living conditions. As Americans entering foreign regions across the globe, we need to stay well informed about not only changes in populations but also, more importantly, understand potential political unrest and terrorist activities within the altering world landscape.

The topic of terrorism, and how to safeguard against it, proved to be a difficult point of discussion for many coordinators who desired to avoid the subject. The threat of terrorism abroad is not a new phenomenon, yet has become a major focus of concern with intensified media coverage, increasingly callous terrorist acts, and with the expansion of sects such as ISIS and al Qaeda. American overseas students must remain alert of possible dangers.

Acts of terrorism can take place in any part of the world, without prior warning. Coordinators and study abroad participants must have this mentality when going overseas. Areas in the past that were considered safe havens have recently had issues with terrorist threats, particularly parts of Western Europe.

As a general rule, experts agree that a student should be discouraged from studying in a region with a U.S. State Department warning. Yet some coordinators still afford students the opportunity to do so. Therefore, the question of whether a student should be given the chance to study in a region that has been issued a warning due to terrorist threats still remains up for debate with coordinators.

Utilizing a customary, dependable travel agency to make travel arrangements is a best practice for safety. As study abroad groups prepare for departure, they must be fully informed on the various *types* of terrorist threats that exist. The Federal Bureau of Investigation's expansive definition of *international terrorism* helps to bring clarity. Within this definition, "acts dangerous to human life," including "kidnapping," is a form of terrorism that poses a significant threat to study abroad participants.

Coordinators must have an emergency response plan to assist participants should political unrest or a terrorist attack arise. Part of this emergency response plan should be to take preemptive measures to safeguard students, prior to going overseas, including registering participants with the U.S. embassy and having advanced knowledge of military bases abroad. As a measure to further edify students, it is recommended that study abroad and international education office members openly publicize terrorist concerns and protections online, along with orientation sessions and in risk-averting documents.

NOTES

1. Lyngaas, Sean. (2015, April 1). Obama declares foreign cyber threats a "national emergency."*The Business of Federal Technology.* Retrieved from
    http://fcw.com/articles/2015/04/01/obama-cyber-threats.aspx.
2. *Id.*
3. White House Office of the Press Secretary. (2015, February 25). FACT SHEET: Cyber threat intelligence integration center. Retrieved from https://www.whitehouse.gov/the-press-office/2015/02/25/fact-sheet-cyber-threat-intelligence-integration-center.
4. *Id.*
5. *Id.*
6. *Id.*
7. 11 ways to prevent identity theft while traveling. (2015). *IndependentTraveler.com.* Retrieved from http://www.independenttraveler.com/travel-tips/travelers-ed/11-ways-to-prevent-identity-theft-while-traveling.
8. Clark, Carolyn. (2015, April 13). The serious cyber security threat that could hurt hotels. *Leading Meeting Professionals: Professional Convention Management Association.* Retrievedfrom http://www.pcma.org/news/news-landing/2015/04/13/the-serious-cyber-security-threat-that-could-hurt-hotels. Halleck, Thomas. (2015, April 3). Mandarin Oriental hacked: Luxury hotel chain admits credit card numbers were stolen in security breach. Retrieved from http://www.ibtimes.com/mandarin-oriental-hacked-luxury-hotel-chain-admits-credit-card-numbers-were-stolen-1836574.
9. *Id.*
10. *Id.*
11. *Id.*
12. *Id.*
13. Halleck, Thomas. (2015, March 4).
14. *Id.*
15. *Id.*
16. *Id.*
17. *Id.*
18. Clark, Carolyn (2015, April 13).
19. Durso, Christopher. (2014, December 1). Cyber-security basics. Professional ConventionManagement Association. Retrieved from http://www.pcmaconvene.org/departments/working-smarter/cyber-security-basics/.
20. *Id.*
21. *Id.*
22. 11 ways to prevent identity theft while traveling. (2015).

23. *Id.*
24. *Id.*
25. *Id.*
26. Durso, Christopher. (2014, December 1).
27. *Id.*
28. *Id.*
29. 11 ways to prevent identity theft while traveling. (2015).
30. *Id.*
31. Durso, Christopher. (2014, December 1).
32. 11 ways to prevent identity theft while traveling. (2015).
33. *Id.*
34. UNHCR: The UN Refugee Agency. (2015). Facts and figures about refugees. *The United Nations High Commissioner for Refugees*. Retrieved from http://www.unhcr.org.uk/about-us/key-facts-and-figures.html.
35. *Id.*
36. *Id.*
37. Evans, R. B. (1991). "A stranger in a strange land": Responsibility and liability for studentsenrolled in foreign-study programs. *Journal of College and University Law 18*, 2, p. 306.
38. Syracuse University Pan Am Flight 103/Lockerbie air disaster archives. (2010). Syracuse University. Retrieved from http://archives.syr.edu/panam/.
39. Miller, A. D. (2015, August 7). Reassessing the threat from terrorism—Abroad and at home.*Wall Street Journal—Washington Wire*. Dow Jones & Company. Retrieved from
     http://blogs.wsj.com/washwire/2015/08/07/reassessing-the-threat-from-terrorism-abroad-and-at-home/.
40. *Id.*
41. *Id.*
42. Wagner, M. (2014, October 11). Americans abroad at "high risk" of ISIS kidnappings, terroristattacks, U.S. warns. *Daily News*. Retrieved from http://www.nydailynews.com/news/national/americans-high-risk-isis-kidnappings-u-s-article-1.1971063.
43. *Id.*
44. Shoichet, C., Hanna, J., & Brown, P. (2015, February 11). American ISIS hostage Kayla Mueller dead, family says. *Cable News Network (CNN)*. Retrieved fromhttp://www.cnn.com/2015/02/10/world/isis-hostage-mueller/.
45. Harris, Shane. (2014, November 2014). A 26-year-old woman is ISIS's last American hostage. *The Daily Beast*. Retrieved from http://www.thedailybeast.com/articles/2014/11/16/a-26-year-old-woman-is-isis-s-last-american-hostage.html.
46. *Id.*
47. *Id.*
48. *Id.*
49. BBC News. (2015, December 9). Paris Attacks: What Happened on the Night. Retrieved from www.bbc.com/news/world-europe-34818994.
50. Onyanga-Omara, J. (2015, January 7). Timeline: Terror attacks in Europe over the years. *USA Today*. Retrieved from http://www.usatoday.com/story/news/world/2015/01/07/terror-attacks-europe/21384069/.
51. *Id.*
52. Federal Bureau of Investigation. (2015). Definitions of terrorism in the U.S. Code. Retrievedfrom https://www.fbi.gov/about-us/investigate/terrorism/terrorism-definition.
53. Allies Against Slavery. (2014–2015). Around the world and around the corner slavery stillexists. Retrieved from http://www.alliesagainstslavery.org/slavery.
54. Partlow, J. (2014, August 15). Kidnappings in Mexico surge to the highest number on record.*Washington Post*. Retrieved from https://www.washingtonpost.com/world/the_americas/kidnappings-in-mexico-surge-to-the-highest-number-on-record/2014/08/15/3f8ee2d2-1e6e-11e4-82f9-2cd6fa8da5c4_story.html.
55. *Id.*
56. Reed, T., & Stewart, S. (2013, December 26). Mexico: Tactical adaptions in virtual kidnapping. *Security Weekly*. Retrieved from https://www.stratfor.com/weekly/mexico-tactical-adaptations-virtual-kidnapping.
57. *Id.*
58. *Id.*
59. Bagri, N. T., & Varma, V. (2013, June 4). American tourist gang-raped in Manali, police say. *New York Times*. Retrieved from http://india.blogs.nytimes.com/2013/06/04/american-tourist-gang-raped-in-manali-police-say/?_r=0.
60. *Id.*
61. *Id.*
62. *Id.*
63. *Id.*
64. *Id.*

65.   Moran, L., & Ortiz, E. (2013, April 2). U.S. tourist in Brazil kidnapped, robbed and raped in front of boyfriend on bus during 6-hour nightmare: Police. *New York Daily News*. Retrieved from http://www.nydailynews.com/news/crime/u-s-student-kidnapped-raped-bus-brazil-article-1.1305356.

66.   *Id.*

67.   *Id.*

68.   *Id.*

69.   *Id.*

70.   *Id.*

71.   *Id.*

72.   U.S. Department of State. (2015). U.S. passports & international travel.

73.   *Id.*

74.   University of Colorado, Boulder. (2015). The Office of International Education's policy in case of political or social unrest, terrorism, and the threat of war. Retrieved from http://studyabroad.colorado.edu/index.cfm?FuseAction=Abroad.ViewLink&Link_ID=7D547AD8-B6BF-5897-E81FB545DEFB9202.

75.   *Id.*

76.   *Id.*

77.   *Id.*

Chapter Seven

The Experts' Advice: Best Practices #1–6

This chapter, as well as chapters 8 and 9, highlight essential insights gathered from personal interviews with higher education experts (coordinators, directors, and administrators) of study abroad, global studies, and international education, who tackled such questions: "How can risks and liabilities be minimized in study abroad? What inspired you to provide career service to students? What influence do legal issues have upon your work approach?"

Other inquiries pondered by the experts include: "How do you explain/understand the major risks involved with conducting a study abroad program for students and their institutions? How can risks and liabilities be affected through the use of a waiver and other forms?"

For simplicity's sake, I refer to the experts—whether coordinators, directors, or administrators in the field of study abroad, global studies, or international education—as *coordinators* throughout. Again, each coordinator has been given a pseudonym. With this section of the book, the experiences and analyses of coordinators receive primary attention, followed by court cases and scrutiny of current risk-averting documents.

The immense amount of advice from coordinators is organized into twenty-three of the most essential steps or best practices for reducing study abroad risks for students and for deterring potential lawsuits. These best practices often reiterate essential points made in earlier chapters. The first set of best practices, 1 through 6, is provided in this chapter:

- Predeparture Orientation
- Parent/Guardian Involvement
- Faculty Leaders
- Foreign Institution Partnerships
- Reputable Travel Companies/Agencies
- Professional Organizations/Conferences

If you want to be reacquainted with the background of the experts, including their institution type, gender, number of years administering study abroad, and selected regions where they provide study abroad, refer to table 2.1: Key Demographic Characteristics of Coordinators, as needed in chapter 2.

Straightforward, commonsense advice often accompanies the legal and practical instruction. For example, Coordinator Felix advises study abroad leaders to "cover your rear end a bit, and not make something up on the spot [with a program] . . . So I would always prefer a program to consider the ethical, rather than the legal . . . I don't care if drugs and prostitution in Amsterdam are legal. Hey, that doesn't mean it's okay for [participants] to do it. Where the [heck] is your ethical code not to do it?"

Coordinators believe that program leaders and participants should heed each of the twenty-three best practices in order to avoid hazards for students and liability issues for institutions. Much of a coordinator's job is researching best practices to ensure the safety of students, and to safeguard their institution from liabilities. I think that Coordinator Desiree speaks on behalf of all coordinators when she relates, "[I] do a lot of research on study abroad! I read a lot of books, benchmark best practices at other institutions across the country, and attend many workshops and conferences devoted to study abroad."

Program glitches make for experiences that allow coordinators to become more efficient with offsetting study abroad risks. For example, Coordinator Eve recounts, "One of the students [studying in Mexico] claimed that the son of the host family in which she was living invited her to the top of the roof to look at the sunset . . . made an advance on her, and she called home all upset, and her mother called me. So we called the foreign school . . . and the student [was immediately] taken from that family and put with a different family."

When safety and the educational environment are compromised, swift action must be taken to avoid potential risks. The raw analysis that comes from the voices of coordinators gives energy, authenticity, and soul to each best practice. With this chapter come the first six of twenty-three best practices recommended by experts for minimizing risks and liabilities with study abroad.

BEST PRACTICES FOR AVOIDING RISKS AND LIABILITIES IN STUDY ABROAD

1. Predeparture Orientation

Every coordinator asserts that predeparture orientation sessions are necessary to avoid perils and legal issues with study abroad. In fact, both Coordinator Lonna and Coordinator Felix maintain that predeparture orientation is the best available practice to avoid risks and liabilities, and Coordinator Eve feels that the greatest danger for a program starts with ineffective orientation sessions:

> I think [the most] major risk . . . is going to be for students who do not take seriously all of the information we try to give them about safety. A good portion of the predeparture orientation deals with safety, and it deals with everything from drugs, alcohol, how to conduct themselves, avoiding places where it's just all Americans, and being careful with traffic.

She continues:

> And not going with someone who is offering you this great deal—"I can take you to this great place where nobody else can go," and that kind of thing. So we do a lot to try to warn students, not to frighten them, but to let them know they need to be at least as cautious as they are in the United States.

In fact, prior to departure, Coordinator Arianna, Coordinator Baron, Coordinator Braxton, Coordinator Desiree, Coordinator Levi, Coordinator Lonna, and Coordinator Pearl make predeparture sessions mandatory for participation in study abroad. Coordinator Desiree especially emphasizes the importance of safety with her sessions: "At the initial orientation meeting we talk about why it is important to be safe, what could happen if [students] are not, and that while the college makes their safety a priority, that it requires [students'] due diligence as well to achieve it."

Similarly, Coordinator Lonna puts discussion of risky behavior at the forefront of orientation sessions:

> We try to be as upfront as possible with our students—there are some safety concerns, some health concerns—and in our orientation we really spend a lot of time talking about the laws of physics still apply abroad, just as they do here. You'll be fine if you keep a low profile. Try to blend in and you'll be okay. Luckily, we haven't had problems.

However, even when American travelers think that they are doing a good job with keeping a low profile, it is often not the case. For example, my student Ben shared an unfortunate encounter he experienced while studying abroad in Russia during our postprogram interview.

Existing political tensions between U.S. officials and Russian president Vladimir Putin may have played a role in Ben's ill-fated encounter. It was the fall season in Russia, so temperatures were cool and a jacket was necessary. Ben's jacket was a light blue color, and all of the Russian citizens wore black. Ben desired to keep a low profile; however, his jacket was like a neon sign flashing "foreigner, foreigner, foreigner."

He did not have the money to purchase a new jacket, so he was resigned to standing out. Well, one day, he went into a McDonald's in St. Petersburg. As Ben began to give his food order, the McDonald's attendant spat in his face and sneered, "You're not wanted here you American bastard." Ben was shaken by the very hurtful encounter.

This was also a lesson for me to be more conscious with advising students about attire, among other items, as a means to blend in with the overseas environment. But the fact is that no matter what measures you take, you might still not be able to fully conceal that you're a foreigner. Plus, unfortunately the world is full of people who behave poorly, like the McDonald's attendant. Ben was smart to calmly walk away to avoid further conflict.

To further confirm this point, here is an example. I appreciate attending the annual National Cherry Blossom Festival in Washington, DC, which draws a lot of tourists from around the world. I credit my overall travel experience with giving me the ability to guess, with reasonable accuracy, what region of the world people are from, before they ever speak. I detect this through their mannerisms. So even if Ben wore a black jacket, it is quite likely that the community would still have sniffed out his American status.

Not to belabor the point, but while teaching English as a Foreign Language (EFL) in Thailand, as a six-foot, copper-toned man walking around a small Thai community (the average height for a Thai person is five feet, five inches), it was abundantly clear, all of the time, that I was a foreigner. However, the point is that the best attempt should be made to meld in to a society when studying overseas. By attempting to dress, speak, and conduct yourself similar to the natives, you tend to be positively viewed for giving respect to their culture.

Coordinator Levi correctly asserts that "predeparture orientation sessions familiarize study abroad participants with intercultural dialogue or the best manner to communicate with individuals overseas." Both Coordinator Levi and Coordinator Eve believe orientation sessions are the proper forum to prepare participants for differing cultural experiences abroad. In particular, Coordinator Levi contends that "these orientation sessions avert risks and liability by outlining what should be the proper conduct of student-participants."

Coordinator Felix maintains that students feel taken advantage of when they are not given proper orientation prior to study abroad: "Our kids really resent if they go abroad and we don't tell them what is going to happen to them. If we say to them you are going to live in tents, they'll be all right because we told them. But if they get abroad and we didn't tell them, they'll kill us. Lay it all out . . . I don't want to sell a program. I want you to know everything and find out if you want it or not."

Also, laws and regulations abroad are reviewed at sessions with Coordinator Poppy. She avows that "distributing physical documentation on safety at predeparture sessions is the best practice to combat risks and liability suits." Coordinator Pearl agrees, and similar to other coordinators she tends to hold one or two sessions per program. She notes, "[I do] about a two-hour orientation for anyone who is going under our auspices."

The Ideal Approach to Predeparture Orientation Sessions

However, one, even two sessions are not enough to fully prepare participants. Three sessions are more appropriate. Four hours is my recommended time per session, with a break worked in. So a total of twelve hours over three sessions is ideal. This amount of time is most suitable to appropriately prepare participants for overseas study, but if you attempt to fit twelve hours into a marathon session, chances are participants will get exhausted and lose concentration, if not become seriously annoyed.

Some students, justifiably, may not remain for the entire duration of the session. If they do not physically depart, they would certainly "mentally check out" of your grueling meeting. This is not the way you want to introduce your program. Even two sessions, lasting six hours each, seems a bit exhausting. Therefore, three sessions work best.

The First Orientation Session

The first session must provide tasks that participants must quickly address. More specifically, participants should be oriented on such items as immunizations to acquire, health insurance to obtain, and passport and visa requirements. International students who do not have an American passport would need additional advising. Initial questions and answers about the program itinerary, discussion about the schedule of payments for the program, and other logistical matters may also be covered in the first session.

In addition, the first session is a time to go over your role as a program leader, as well as establish the role and responsibilities of participants. Short, risk-averting documents may be read aloud, with questions fielded after. Also, specific details about the overseas area—standard attire, laws, weather, electric voltage use, cultural differences, ATM accessibility, Wi-Fi availability, recommended cash to carry, tipping expectations, and much more—should be introduced in this session. Inherent risks associated with the overseas location can start to be presented. The second and third orientation sessions can continue to reiterate all of the aforementioned items.

It goes without saying that "icebreakers" and activities that familiarize participants with one another is a healthy approach to the first orientation session. Try to develop cohesiveness with the group from the start. Hopefully the group builds on the initial connection made during orientation while abroad. It is important that they have a strong rapport going into the program because potential challenges while overseas can bring out the testy side of people.

Something happens when having to share meals, travel time, venues, activities, service-learning work, academic discussions, and not to mention sleeping quarters, for days or even weeks at a time. The outside veneer that participants present at orientation peals away. Strong personalities rise to the surface, insecurities may emerge, and cliques could develop. And I am not just referring to participants. These elements have surfaced with some past *faculty leaders*, leading to some rather awkward conversations to redirect their focus.

I am a strong believer that everyone deserves respect; demand this with how participants treat one another. This generally keeps overbearing personalities in check and cliques from forming with everyone making the best effort to be generous with sharing knowledge, meals, and experiences with one another.

The Second Orientation Session

The second orientation session is less introductory and more educational in format. This session may include a guest speaker or lecturer. A member from the partnering travel agency, an ambassador, or someone native and quite familiar with the overseas location may serve as a speaker. This is also a time for faculty leaders to shine. They have just completed instruction of the semester course that merges with the study abroad program. Now they should lucidly connect the course curriculum with the coming study abroad program.

It was not fully mentioned prior, but there should be a cataloged, full-credit-bearing course that directly links to the short-term study abroad program. Institutions vary on how many credits may be earned with a short-term study abroad component to a course. The study abroad program, whether an option or mandatory part of the accompanying semester course, serves as a ten-day-to-one-month culminating experience to the class.

Academic elements of the semester course curriculum that students had read, viewed online, assessed by PowerPoint, and considered with discussion now come to life. What was once mere theory advances into practice, or hands-on scholarship. For example, a geology professor on a program to Iceland instructed on various volcanic land surfaces and glacier formations with the semester course. Yet he felt that a semester in the classroom was incomparable to the learning students acquired during their twelve-day accompanying program abroad.

He vowed there could never be a substitute for going to Iceland and getting your hands dirty atop volcanic, palagonite tuff. The scarce surface is found in few places on Earth; otherwise you'll have to go to Mars.[1] Or the experience of traversing diverse glacier surfaces, while pausing at times to drink from a puddle in order to rehydrate. This professor's account of the incomparable educational experiences that come with study abroad is emblematic of those shared by other past program leaders.

The Third/Final Orientation Session

Returning to the need for three orientation sessions, the third and final session allows for faculty leaders to lecture on any remaining academic information that ties in to the study abroad program and its itinerary. If homework assignments were given during the first or second session, they may be returned with feedback during the final session. The third session allows time to collect all of those essential forms from the first session—waivers, health forms, emergency contacts, a copy of the photo page of the passport, and so forth—that may not have been fully gathered during the second session. Remind participants that immunizations should have already been administered.

The third orientation session is used to confirm that every participant knows the meeting spot for departure at the airport, the modes of transportation available to reach the airport, remaining items to pack, and lingering questions to address. You should provide clarification on whether you are handling check in for the group at the airport or if they are to check in individually. Acceptable weight, size, and amount of baggage permitted by the airline must be specified in advance.

Be clear about how much cash for tips will be collecting from participants at the airport prior to departure; tour guides and bus drivers should be fairly compensated for their work. I have noticed that by the middle to end of a program, often people are tipping less due to depleted funds. I don't want the final bus driver and tour guide with a program to automatically receive less as a result. Therefore, I collect tips in the beginning to guarantee that an equal monetary amount goes to all of the hard-working program helpers.

Last, this final wrap-up session should leave the group feeling comfortable that no unresolved matters remain prior to departure. Coordinators need to keep the "lines open," allowing participants to contact them until everyone is at the airport and ready to depart. These are just some immediate ideas that accompany orientation sessions. However, it is clear that having just one session, or even two, brings potential risk, with participants not being wholly prepared for their time abroad.

Support from the Courts

Court results support that well-conducted predeparture orientation sessions minimize risks and liabilities in study abroad programs. *Bloss v. The University of Minnesota Board of Regents* and *Slattery v. Antioch Education Abroad* are example cases.

Bloss v. The University of Minnesota Board of Regents

Disgruntled student Adrianne Bloss, with *Bloss v. The University of Minnesota Board of Regents*, alleged that the university failed to sufficiently warn her of the dangers at the site abroad.[2] She sued university officials for negligence with not providing secure housing closer to the Cemanahuac campus, insufficient transportation to and from campus, a failure to adequately warn about risks, and in protecting her from foreseeable harm.[3]

However, the court gave favorable ruling to the university. The expressed opinion was that undisputed evidence in the program materials, the release form and program orientation, and Cemanahuac's orientation materials all warned students about their safety.[4]

Bloss testified she had received explicit written and oral warnings related to safety in Cuernavaca at mandatory orientation sessions prior to the start of the program.[5] The warnings included specific admonitions that it was dangerous for women to go out alone at night, that women should call for a taxi at night rather than hail a taxi on the street, and that women should never sit in the front seat of taxis.[6] These warnings specifically address the circumstances under which the student sustained her injuries.[7]

The use of a predeparture orientation, along with orientation materials, proved favorable in protecting the program and institution from liability. The use of thorough, instructive predeparture orientation sessions and materials may significantly reduce risks (but unfortunately this was not the case for Bloss) and liabilities with study abroad.

Slattery v. Antioch Education Abroad

The failure to properly orient student Stephanie Slattery on an important cultural norm prior to engaging in study abroad triggered the lawsuit *Slattery v. Antioch Education Abroad*. Slattery, while a student at Eastern Michigan University, alleged that she was raped while participating in the University's Antioch Education Abroad (AEA) program in Mali, Africa.[8] As part of the study abroad program, AEA advised and encouraged the students to speak and interact with the local population to learn the language and cultural differences.[9]

Slattery was invited by the bus driver to have a cup of tea in his room.[10] She joined him, and the driver forcefully assaulted and raped Slattery.[11] Afterward, Slattery was flown to Paris, France, for medical treatment, and upon return to her group in Mali, the students were informed and warned by AEA, for the first time, "to never be alone with a male in his room because in Malian culture it is considered to be implied consent to have sexual intercourse."[12]

In the lawsuit Slattery declared AEA negligent in its failure to inform and warn her of this cultural difference prior to the study abroad program; she asserts the harm done to her could have been avoided had she been forewarned.[13]

Program leaders must do a great amount of research in an attempt to uncover and inform participants of the potential threats that exist at a study abroad location. Unfortunately, not all hazards are known in advance. The hope is that enough major risks are disclosed during orientation sessions to give participants proper safeguards.

2. Parental/Guardian Involvement

According to coordinators, it is essential to involve parents and guardians of student participants in orientation sessions to offset program risks and liabilities. In order not to place limits on caretakers, the label *guardian* should be applied with orientation and materials. For example, in my most recent orientation session, a grandmother sat in because she was the most influential parental figure in the student participant's life. To be clear, when I make reference to *parents* in this section, this also includes guardians.

In an effort to have parents attend orientation classes, Coordinator Eve, Coordinator Levi, and Coordinator Felix invite them to the sessions. Coordinator Eve details a discussion with a group of students at a program orientation session that motivated her to open future sessions to parents:

> One of the students said, "My mother wanted to come to an orientation. I told her 'No mom, you'd embarrass me if you come.'" But then some of the others said, "Yea, my parents might like to come." And [a student asked the other students] "Now if they had a [special] session, how many of your parents might come?" And most of [the other students] said [their parents would [come]. One of them said, "My mother's six hours away; she wouldn't come."

Coordinator Eve continues to recount the discussion:

> So by the time we got to the end, one said, "Would you consider doing an evening orientation session for our parents?" And I said, "Yea, we could do that" . . . [Later,] I contacted the students and said, "Talk to your parents over Thanksgiving and if they'd like it and I could see what works; [having them participate with orientation] could ease some of their concerns."

With parental involvement, Coordinator Eve and Coordinator Levi maintain there is less chance for risks to be taken by students, and a decreased likelihood of lawsuits that are most often filed by parents. According to Coordinator Levi, "Sometimes it is very necessary for me to contact parents to reassure them of the safety of the area where their children are going and discuss with them the financial arrangements so that we can be aggressive at it. Also to find out if there are any particular medical problems their son or daughter has we can address before leaving."

Coordinator Trevor also likes to assure parents that safe measures accompany study abroad: "I'm not going to bring [students] to London and say 'see you in two weeks.' That is one of the things I want to make clear to parents. Every day is regulated. They do have two free days, but by the end the kids know London pretty well. And tell them what to do on their days off. It's pretty regulated."

Coordinators desire parents to have informative background information on the program provider and content. Coordinator Eve "mails the parents brochures about outside agencies, such as the Council on International Educational Exchange (CIEE), that assist in organizing programs." Coordinator Baron also wants parents to know that program agendas are carefully selected: "We have a document that outlines how our institution assesses and approves international travel itineraries. We send this to all students and parents."

Coordinator Poppy also uses mail and personal orientation sessions for "orienting parents of participants on the expected code of conduct, the policy handbook, and manuals pertaining to the program." These are intelligent strategies with conducting orientation sessions that all coordinators should consider using.

Parental involvement with programs has potential advantages. Parents may disclose additional information about health concerns for a son or daughter, echo program policies, and encourage their child to be a more proactive participant in orientation sessions.

Confirmation from the Courts

The inclusion of parents in activities that advocate program safety might assist with reducing perils to participants and lawsuits aimed at the institution. But there certainly is no guarantee of this. Court cases illustrate that parents often prompt the filing of lawsuits on behalf of student study abroad participants.

University of Pittsburgh Semester at Sea Program

A study abroad tragedy with the University of Pittsburgh Semester at Sea Program prompted various lawsuits from parents. While taking part in the university's program, four U.S students were killed and three injured in a crash of a chartered bus in India. [14] Anne Schewe, a mother of one of the students who died in the India bus crash, stated, "We [mothers] are madder than hell our daughters were killed." [15]

An initial lawsuit came in 1996, filed against program operators. [16] Following this were other lawsuits that most likely came from exasperated parents. In fact, as recently as March 2011, one of those separate lawsuits resulted in a Pennsylvania court finding Semester at Sea / ISE Institute for Shipboard Education negligent in a wrongful death claim of student Cherese Mari Laulhere. [17]

Make Waivers Inclusive of Parents

Overwhelmingly, current waivers used by coordinators smartly include statements that consult parents about risk-deterring measures with study abroad programs. The majority of the sample waivers address parents or legal guardians.

Waiver E (Appendix E) even gives voice to the parent:

I: (a) am the parent or legal guardian of the above participant/student; (b) have read the foregoing Release (including such parts as may subject me to personal financial responsibility); (c) am and will be legally responsible for the obligations and acts of the student/participant as described in this Release, and (d) agree for myself and for the student/participant to be bound by its terms.

Waivers with language that evokes parental involvement serve as a strong accompaniment to orientation classes and materials. As a result, parents may become strong advocates for safety and healthy participation by students with study abroad programs.

3. Faculty Leaders

Faculty often assist in leading study abroad programs, and coordinators (i.e., Coordinator Eve, Coordinator Lonna, and Coordinator Poppy) express anxieties about programs led by faculty members who are too lax in their duty of care for participants, who are not carefully vetted from the start, and who are not properly oriented with potential dangers and matters of liability prior to departure.

To prevent these issues, Coordinator Eve has one-on-one office meetings with potential program leaders in order to gain clarity regarding their qualifications. She has seen "past study abroad programs that had faculty leaders who let students go where they wanted, at any time . . . [And viewed] poor supervision of students by faculty which raised risks and potential liability suits." Coordinator Pearl agrees that "students who study abroad should not be able to go wander off on their own for a long period of time."

Coordinator Tabitha worries about issues of liability that come with inattentive faculty leaders:

> I've heard of situations where students went abroad and the [faculty member] responsible for coordinating the trip went off on their own and was not near the incident that occurred with the student. So that, I think, will totally release any liability of release that was signed because . . . I believe that person needs to be involved in all aspects and ensure they are not separated from students, or they're in close proximity of students so that they can jump in and take care of whatever situation might have occurred. But if that person is nowhere in sight and something happens . . . that whole liability is null and void.

In a well-organized program with a cohesive group, there should not be many opportunities for students, or faculty leaders, to stray from the program for an extended period of time. Coordinators and faculty leaders must establish proper guidelines prior to the start of a program.

Naturally, any participant who wants to remain at a program venue for an extended period or desires to take part in a separate educational activity outside of the planned itinerary should get approval from program leaders. Often, students will gather research for projects, and faculty participants will seek data for professional development. As a leader, try to remain flexible. If participants are engaged in the program's learning objectives, seriously consider their additional requests for augmenting scholarship.

On a slightly different matter, coordinators should not make assumptions while training faculty leaders. Coordinators cannot assume that faculty leaders will exercise the formers' own commonsense approaches. In other words, as you train faculty, do not omit any expectations, even when they may seem obvious. For instance, a faculty program leader of a Southeast Asian program thought that it was acceptable to make arrangements to leave his co-leader and group for a couple of days in order to present a scholarly paper at a conference in Central Asia.

Aside from being immensely inconsiderate to the group and fellow faculty leader, the act would have put the program and college at risk. If you don't believe this behavior brings risks and liabilities, return to chapter 5, The Tragedy of Supervisory Neglect in Study Abroad.

Coordinator Trevor raised a slightly different concern. He is wary of faculty leaders with shady backgrounds:

> The college has to put a lot of faith in the [faculty] person doing the trips. I don't know if there's some kind of background check. You don't want a bad character or with a criminal record doing these things. The school has to acknowledge that this person is our agent, this person is serving for the school in this capacity, and we trust this person. This person is not going to sit in their room and get drunk every night.

With regard to this, the vetting of potential faculty leaders should occur well before their proposal is submitted. I put out an annual collegewide call for proposals to faculty who would like to merge study abroad into their semester courses. Prior to submitting a proposal, they must hold an interview with me and have the endorsement of their supervisor. During this meeting, I am already asking questions about their character, along with academic and global qualifications, for leading a study abroad program. This includes colleagues that I personally know well. This is followed up by workshops that faculty must attend prior to submitting a proposal. The workshops are meant to bolster their submissions.

Coordinator Poppy also gives training, information packets, and workshops on safety to faculty program leaders:

> A good university will make sure the faculty member is given the proper information and training so that they understand what [their] responsibilities are before going abroad. So I'm a firm believer that, along with faculty-led programs, you need to have university faculty workshops about liability issues and about safety issues. So this is just part of the preparation [for study abroad programs].

It may not be in the form of a formal workshop, but Coordinator Lonna is also effective with "[scheduling] a two-to-three-hour lunch meeting with [faculty leaders] to discuss the best practices for leading a safe program." Any training that can improve a faculty leader's knowledge about safety and best practices abroad is encouraged.

Displeasure from Court Officials

Court trends show increasing intolerance for negligent behavior from study abroad program supervisors. The issue, which is one of the LARGEST 3, is prevalent and necessitates an entire chapter (chapter 5) to scrutinize.

The penalizing of negligent supervisors by courts is welcomed and appreciated. This will serve to improve risks and liabilities with study abroad programs, compelling inept program leaders and institutions to give a proper duty of care for participants.

Radford University

A case in point comes with the Radford University lawsuit that exposed the negligent act of a supervisor.[18] A faculty member made a poor choice to drive a truck full of participants that had a collision with a car, leaving the car's driver dead.[19] The action of the faculty member endangered student passengers, resulted in the death of another individual, and brought on an expensive, lengthy lawsuit.[20] Only hired drivers from licensed travel agencies should transport students while abroad. It is a difficult lesson learned.

King v. Board of Control of Eastern Michigan University

Lax supervisory conduct can violate Title IX regulations and bring a hostile environment to a study abroad program, as was the case with *King v. Board of Control of Eastern Michigan University*.[21] A federal district court for the eastern district of Michigan noted that the faculty supervisor's indifference to correcting a hostile environment of sexual harassment on a program to South Africa brought trauma to female participants.[22]

Full details of the case are disclosed in chapter 5. However, here are some specifics about the case. Six African American female students at Eastern Michigan University (EMU) participated in the university's five-week study abroad program in South Africa.[23] Within the first week of the program, a male student by the name of McCauley entered a female student's room and bed without invitation, and male students Frame, McCauley, and Miller referred to female students as "sweetie," "darling," and "sweetheart."[24]

When the female students asked to be called by their names, male students began to refer to them by gender-specific slurs.[25] The program leader, Dr. Okafor, was present during times when Miller and Frame referred to female students as "bitches," "hoes," "wideloads," "sluts," and so forth, and did nothing.[26] He was also present when McCauley and Miller allegedly solicited South African women for sex from the tour bus, yet did nothing.[27]

Female students approached Dr. Okafor in a dining hall to voice their concerns about the program and asked for a group meeting to discuss them; he agreed to the meeting but sent Miller to stand in for him.[28] After a heated discussion about the men's inappropriate conduct, Miller, McCauley, and Frame informed the women that they would continue with their conduct, and Miller told the women to "stop bitching."[29] A female student reported Miller's comment to Dr. Okafor, but nothing was done in response.[30]

Further, program participant Travis Sloan asserted that he approached Dr. Okafor to complain that McCauley had threatened to slit his throat; he asserted that Dr. Okafor did nothing.[31] Other volatile events took place, which elicited no response from the program leader.

The program concluded with seven students leaving the program more than a week before its scheduled conclusion, and Dr. Okafor finished the trip with six male students and one female student.[32] Not surprisingly, some of the female students brought litigation against the university. In court, the plaintiffs claimed a hostile environment surfaced that affected their ability to take full advantage of the educational program, and the faculty supervisor, Dr. Okafor, did nothing to correct the problem.[33]

The court ruled in favor of the plaintiffs, determining that the plaintiffs were persons in the United States who were allegedly denied the benefits of an education at EMU.[34] The court denied the defendant's motion to dismiss the plaintiff's Title IX claim of sexual assault.[35]

The court also pointed out that the plaintiffs had a valid sexual harassment claim in which harassment was "so persuasive, severe, and offensive" that it undermined and detracted from the victims' educational experience; they were denied equal access to an institution's resources and opportunities.[36]

Also, the court maintained that the study abroad program was always under the control of Eastern Michigan University in every respect, rather than under the control of any foreign educational facility.[37] In turn, every moment of inaction by Dr. Okafor, who represented the university, to stop the sexual harassment served as a form of negligence by the university.[38]

King v. Board of Control of Eastern Michigan University is a clear case of supervisory neglect. A coordinator who is unwilling to alter a hostile environment violates Title IX regulations. The court determined that equal protections under the law must be afforded to students overseas. Courts are increasingly embracing this principle, and it is imperative that faculty leaders are fully vetted and trained prior to leading a group abroad. In addition, there should never be a sole program leader, as was the case with *King v. Board of Control of Eastern Michigan University*.

Fay v. Thiel College

In another case example, *Fay v. Thiel College*, the court of common pleas of Mercer County, Pennsylvania, determined that colleges and universities should be held accountable for negligent actions by program leaders.[39] The court viewed Thiel College to be neglectful when faculty supervisors left student Amy Fay unattended for three days in a foreign clinic, resulting in her being sexually assaulted and exposed to needless surgery.[40] Full description of the case is contained in chapter 2.

The Radford University lawsuit, *King v. Board of Control of Eastern Michigan University*, and *Fay v. Thiel College* embody cases that unearth concerns with supervisory neglect by faculty members leading study abroad. The results proved to be unfavorable for each college and university.

4. Foreign Institution Partnerships (for Long-Term Study Abroad)

To avert risks and lawsuits, coordinators maintain that they must be well informed with the policies and practices of partnering foreign institutions. These groups assist with long-term study abroad program options for students.

Coordinator Levi acknowledges that past students have complained about his college's partnering foreign institution and the anemic educational experiences that it brought. As a result, Coordinator Levi takes "a hands-on approach to partnering with foreign institutions that make up consortiums." He also "attempt[s] to visit the foreign sites."

Some of the consortiums that coordinators disclosed as partners include the American Institute for Foreign Study (AIFS), the College Consortium of International Studies (CCIS), the Centers for Education Abroad (CEA), Center for International Studies (CIS Abroad), Education First (EF Tours), and International Studies Abroad (ISA).

Coordinator Levi stresses that you must have a close working relationship with foreign institute officials to assure students receive a quality education:

> [Our institution partners with] two nationally and internationally recognized organizations in which [we] send students abroad and have [established a] center abroad. Those [foreign institutions] have been thoroughly researched and are accredited by Middle States in our area. One is CEA and the other one is CCIS. They are both educational agencies that send students abroad, and have excellent facilities abroad to adjust academic standards, grading, and whatever.

He also enthusiastically relays:

> I'm always interested in the students' programs that are available. I want to know about the teaching staff, and I want to know what is required of the student. I can get that information from these organizations because they will provide me with what information I require.

The more invested you are with your foreign provider, the more information you will gain from them, and in turn, more protection for student participants and the institution may follow. Therefore, serve as a member on the board of one of your main providers. This has allowed me immense access and understanding for the policies of partnering institutions.

Coordinator Eve also carefully scrutinizes the policies and set arrangements by foreign institutions. This is motivated by a past incident in which a host family member in Mexico sexually harassed a study abroad participant:

> One of the students claimed that the son of the host family in which she was living invited her to the top of the roof to look at the sunset. . . . He made an advance on her, and so she called home all upset and her mother called me. So we called the [foreign] school. We told her she had to contact the [foreign] school—take care of it and report it and all. She did, and the [foreign] school investigated it. We were constantly back and forth [by phone] with [those] school officials, with the student, with the parents, and so forth.

Coordinator Eve despondently recounts:

And the student [was] immediately [taken] from that family and [the foreign school] put her with a different family. But she was freaked out and decided she was coming home. So [our college] made arrangements, and paid the supplemental difference in airfare to exchange her ticket . . . And it didn't go anywhere [in the form of a lawsuit] . . . It was a pretty bad situation with parents and grandparents involved . . . It seemed to take care of itself with her coming home. We offered to pay the ticket for her to come home. I could see no sense in saying she had to stay [there even after] she was in a different house.

Unfortunately, sexual harassment and sexual assault are major issues with study abroad. A nearly identical incident to what Coordinator Eve recounted occurred with one of my students studying abroad in Costa Rica. She had to conclude her study abroad program early as a safety precaution. For greater depth shared on issues of sexual harassment, and particularly sexual assault abroad, please return to chapter 4, Sexual Assault Risks and Liabilities with Study Abroad.

Again, here is what the experts relate. Coordinator Tabitha feels impassioned that "coordinators should continually discuss and share academic objectives with partnering foreign institutions." Coordinator Poppy declares, "I refuse to work with a foreign institution unless it allows programs to be closely scrutinized. [This means] a college representative is able to frequent the foreign institute and negotiate terms if academic standards are not met." In addition, she expects foreign institutions to "provide on-site counselors and advisors for study abroad participants."

To ensure student safety, Coordinator Pearl says, "A residence administrator from [our] home institution works in the housing unit of study abroad students in the host country."

When considering the positive vetting process of Coordinator Poppy and Coordinator Pearl, the reality is that not every institution has the resources for personnel to frequently visit the various campuses at foreign institutes, or have satellite campuses in place for the home institution to send employees.

This is ideal but often not realistic. That is why close vetting and research of the foreign agency must take place. Close vetting includes investigating the experiences of other coordinators who have worked with the agency. Also, communicate with past study abroad participants who have taken part in their academic system. In addition, converse with foreign faculty, administrators, and host families who work within the agency. And yes, *some* physical visits are necessary—both prior to and while partnering with the agency—to develop a strong rapport with the foreign partner while scrutinizing accommodations to ensure the safety of students.

Foreign institutions, or consortiums, are pivotal for securing long-term study abroad for students. Make sure that every student who does a semester overseas is assigned an academic advisor. As a coordinator, you should sustain steady communication with a participant's academic advisor in order to know the student's academic and social progress. In addition, your student should have mandatory meetings with the foreign advisor. Our study abroad students do blogging with me through our college's online system. Try to get the academic advisor to also blog with you.

Going in a slightly different direction, Coordinator Poppy correctly contends that "every college and university has to understand its own philosophical approach to academia, and make sure that the academic goals and environment of the foreign institution are aligned with those at the home institution." Indeed.

Share your home institution's academic policies and procedures with the foreign institute, and expect the same of them. These goals and objectives for student success should line up.

For proper transferability, course descriptions and credits for overseas classes must coincide with home institution offerings.

Coordinator Poppy also emphasizes that "study abroad coordinators must advise students about the educational approach, class structure, and class offerings offered by foreign institutes to ensure that students make the proper choice about which programs best suit their needs."

Well stated. Collaboration between the study abroad coordinator, home school academic advisor, transcript evaluator, and foreign institute advisor should come together to properly direct and place a student in the appropriate study abroad program. Prior to a student departing for overseas studies, they must have all four aforementioned people's approval for the selected program and classes of choice. A home institution transcript evaluator, prior to student departure, should determine course equivalencies. Then, after successful completion of foreign courses, credits will transfer to the student's official transcript at the home institution.

For a clear and instructive start to the study abroad experience, a student should be provided a well-composed study abroad application form. In order to give guidance, I have provided a sample Application for Semester or Year-Long Study Abroad form (see Appendix M). To assure collaboration occurs between coordinator, academic advisor, and transcript evaluator, approval signature spaces are provided for each on the form. Other considerations, such as financial aid use, are noted. It is important to have a close working relationship with members of your financial aid office to assist study abroad students.

Verification by the Courts

As verified by court proceedings, risks and liabilities are minimized in study abroad programs when coordinators link themselves with reputable foreign institutions and carefully scrutinize the facilities of those providers. The opposite impact can occur when due diligence is neglected. Issues with proper housing afforded to students surfaced with the University of Florida,[41] *Earlham College v. Eisenberg*, *Paneno v. Centres*, and *Slattery v. Antioch Education Abroad*.

University of Florida

A student participant in the University of Florida's Bolivia program was provided accommodations by a foreign institution, and while staying in her designated housing she was severely burned when a kerosene lamp exploded.[42] As a result of the injury, the university chartered a plane to bring the student back to the United States at a cost of $50,000.[43] The lawsuit is considered with greater detail in chapter 3.

Earlham College v. Eisenberg

In addition, *Earlham College v. Eisenberg* brought to light the need for coordinators to closely examine accommodations furnished by partnering foreign institutions for overseas students. Earlham College student Erika Eisenberg alleged she was raped by the Japanese host father where she was residing.[44] This was followed by $3 million lawsuit filed against Earlham College and other organizations that ran the program.[45] Full details on the lawsuit are in chapter 4.

With *Earlham College v. Eisenberg*, the foreign institution assigned host families and living quarters to student participants. This is a common practice with study abroad. Reserved housing in dormitories and off-campus stay may also be assigned through foreign agencies. Coordinators should have a close enough working relationship with foreign partners to gain access to background checks and to hold interviews with potential homestay family members. Allegedly, two other students complained of sexual harassment from the same host father, and the host father showed Eisenberg pictures of himself with prostitutes. [46]

Paneno v. Centres

Paneno v. Centres also brings attention to the fact that coordinators need to be vigilant in securing reliable foreign agencies to obtain safe housing arrangements for study abroad students. With *Paneno v. Centres*, a state appellate court in California exposed an ineffective arrangement made between Pasadena Community College (PCC) and its partner, Centres for Academic Programmes Abroad (CAPA); the major lawsuit resulted from inept housing provided by CAPA that led to the serious injury of student Rocky Paneno. [47]

The case is thoroughly reviewed in chapter 2; however, here are some pertinent points with the case to consider in this section. Paneno traveled to Italy and commenced the academic component of the program in Florence, Italy, where he lived in an apartment with roommates who were also participating in the program. [48] Again, PCC provided the accommodations for Paneno through CAPA. [49]

On October 21, 2000, Paneno and a friend were on the apartment's balcony; when Paneno leaned against the balcony railing, a portion of it gave way, and Paneno fell six stories. [50] He sustained serious injuries, including paralysis, as a result of his fall. [51] On August 10, 2001, Paneno initiated a lawsuit against CAPA and PCC for premises liability and negligence. [52] The judge ruled CAPA and PCC were both liable for Paneno's damages, with the court disposition revealing that Paneno was entitled to his costs on appeal. [53]

Coordinators should have access to accommodations of participants. If they are unable to inspect the facilities personally, they should communicate with housing officers who work in the facilities.

Slattery v. Antioch Education Abroad

Not only must there be oversight of the foreign institution that provides housing assignments to students, but there should be scrutiny of the people whom the foreign institution hires. *Slattery v. Antioch Education Abroad* made clear that coordinators and their institutions should expect background checks on the employees of foreign institutions.

While living in Mali as part of a study abroad program organized by Antioch University, student Stephanie Slattery alleges a bus driver working for Antioch Education Abroad (AEA) raped her after she accepted an invite to have a cup of tea in his room. [54]

In the lawsuit, Slattery faulted AEA for delegating "its hiring duties to their agent in Mali, which resulted in the negligent hiring and supervision of Dramane Coulibaly, whose history of fathering multiple, illegitimate children with multiple women, and other disqualifying aspects were known or should have been known by [AEA's] hiring agent." [55]

The suit highlights that close vetting, including background checks, needs to occur with a foreign institute's employees.

5. Reputable Travel Companies/Agencies (for Short-Term Study Abroad)

Carefully selecting a travel agency and establishing a healthy working relationship with its members is important for avoiding risks and liabilities. Travel agencies are pivotal in helping coordinators organize short-term study programs. Coordinators rely on the assistance of travel agents in various capacities, whether to arrange flights, secure tour sites, gain access to tour guides, procure lodging, or reserve meals, among other things.

A hands-on approach to building short-term study abroad programs is recommended. When proposing a study abroad program our institution's faculty members are put through a lengthy application and interview process prior to being approved by a selection committee.

A superior faculty proposal that is selected will then be presented to reputable international agencies to price out. The agencies must be willing to advance this tailor-made program, which has been designed to fit the individual needs of our students, program disciplines, and institution.

There are plenty of international travel agencies with premade cookie-cutter programs to choose from. Selecting one is an easy solution but may not best serve the exclusive needs of your institution. Coordinators and faculty leaders must consider national trends, research scholarly sites, merge semester course curriculum to the study abroad experience, match appropriate disciplines to combine with the itinerary, and take various other steps to create a valuable program. At the same time, travel agencies are necessary to help build programs.

For example, Coordinator Trevor has led a short-term program to England every year for over fifteen years and uses his experience to make most travel arrangements. Yet he still desires some assistance from travel agencies with certain arrangements: "I do the travel arrangements, [but] I go to a travel agent that gets the flights for me because I don't want to sit on the phone for x number of hours with British Airways. But I found this company that leases the flats [and] I found the company that leases buses. So I get a good rate there. [Also,] specifically [for] London I get tube passes."

Attempting to procure venues on your own is ill advised and can bring potential dangers to the study abroad group. For example, Coordinator Pearl recollects a misguided, on-the-spot attempt to make arrangements that put the group in harm's way. "[I] took a [group] to Egypt about five years ago [and arranged a ride on donkeys beside a river]. [The group was] going on donkeys to a site away from the river . . . [The foreign guide] took them in a different path."

The situation further declined. "[I] got concerned [and asked him] to follow the set path. [Angered, he] made them get off [the donkeys], and [left the group] in a town. They didn't know where they were, and they walked and [eventually] found their way [back to familiar territory]. And why would the [foreign guide] do that? It doesn't sound good. It is odd. So I think [we were] lucky. But the reality is those are the kind of issues that probably wouldn't happen on [this] continent."

It seems that Coordinator Pearl gained helpful insight to avoid making program arrangements without the aid of a dependable travel agency. However, Coordinator Pearl holds the flawed perspective that these kinds of issues "probably wouldn't happen on [this] continent." My experiences and those of other coordinators prove that dubious acts can also take place throughout North and South America. Coordinator Pearl should not let her guard down at *any* location.

Coordinators also agree that professional travel agencies assist with molding the safest, most academically inclined programs that result in fewer disappointed participants, less risks, and decreased lawsuits. Direct, open, recurrent communication between you and the partnering travel agency can help to establish a close working relationship. In turn, the travel agency's members will likely have greater awareness of the foreign region, so close communication with them can help to decrease potential perils you could face.

Here is a personal past program scenario that supports the argument for establishing a strong rapport with a partnering travel agency to reduce potential hazards with study abroad. During a short-term study abroad program to Costa Rica, my group prepared to visit a planned site to a popular park with a volcano.

Although it was never publicized, I was given news from my accompanying agent, who happened to keep close communications with local residences near the park, that a couple of foreign hikers had recently been mugged and killed on one of the park's paths. With this sudden, unexpected outbreak of violence, the program activity had to be eliminated.

Again, this was not public information. The reality is that in some countries this kind of event may be concealed by news sources. Though tragic, the event was not part of a string of crimes, so perhaps it was not considered extremely newsworthy. At that moment, I was thankful for the fellowship I had with the foreign agent. It also confirms that partnering with travel agents who know internal happenings is crucial.

6. Professional Organizations/Conferences

Many of the coordinators maintain that perils and potential lawsuits with study abroad are reduced when colleagues actively participate in the regional and national conferences of study abroad and international education organizations. Some of the organizations that they mentioned include the Association of International Educators (NAFSA), the Forum on Education Abroad, the Council on International Educational Exchange (CIEE), and the Community College for International Development (CCID), to name a few.

According to coordinators, conference attendance gives essential access to professionals, administrators, educators, and attorneys in the field. Through organized workshops and meetings, coordinators gain increased insight on honing their professional practices, resulting in increased safety measures for students and improved knowledge about legal matters that impact study abroad.

In fact, Coordinator Poppy directly credits workshops at professional conferences for giving her the edification to obtain an administrative position in international education: "While I was still a faculty member, I joined NAFSA. And with workshops at NAFSA I began to really build [my] resume within international education, as well as experience. [Then], I came to now be [in my current position]."

Coordinator Pearl credits outside organizations with giving her guidelines to construct risk-averting documents: "[In order to protect the college from] liability as much as I can, I've been researching documents, pulling out information, reading, and [viewing] background information . . . It's not one [aspect] I know much about. But I've been creating generic forms that have now been sent to our attorney. And I've got them from NAFSA and all sorts of resources that can literally help us cover that piece of it."

Coordinator Pearl is a trailblazer in the field. The model used by a national cohort served as the prototype for a statewide organization that she created with study abroad coordinators and international educators. Creating such a cohort saved her from tedious work and expanded her program options:

> I wanted to start [the organization] because I found that it is very time consuming and expensive to [construct] study abroad programs all over. And [for] many of the short-term ones, as well as my own at times, it is difficult to find the students. So instead of recreating the wheel everywhere, I looked into [already existing programs] . . . It is cost prohibitive sometimes. So if [the cohort] bands together and helps each other, our students have much more options and each college doesn't have to do so many [programs].

Professional conferences with colleagues who discuss safety are akin to camp counselors sitting around a campfire exchanging ghost stories. The difference is that my colleagues' tales are not fictitious. Coordinators say that they appreciate hearing the horror stories of other coordinators at professional conferences. It gives them important insights.

For example, after speaking with other coordinators at conferences, Coordinator Felix learned his program and institution have been fortunate: "We have a non-litigating [student] population. They just don't litigate. Thank God. So we don't have a lot of experience in that. When I go to the NAFSA conference and hear about what some of the suits are, I say 'you got sued on that?' And I think we've done worse than that and never got sued."

Thus, according to experts, attending professional workshops and conferences provides coordinators with added insight for refining practices to increase student safety, and allows for essential information exchange with colleagues, higher education officials, and in-state consortium groups. These conferences also provide professional workshops that assist with bolstering risk-averting documents.

CHAPTER SUMMARY

The first six of twenty-three best practices to avoid risks and liabilities in study abroad, acquired from the acumen of coordinators and administrators of study abroad, global studies, and international education, are provided in this chapter. Rich conclusions from experts unveil much.

Educational and supplemental materials provided to participants through comprehensive predeparture orientation sessions serve to deter risks and liabilities in study abroad. Whenever possible, parents and guardians of participants, who also happen to be the main financers of programs and engineers of lawsuits, need to be invited to these sessions and be provided orientation materials.

Adept, well-trained supervisors must be put in charge to lead programs, and coordinators should research and carefully scrutinize the background of faculty, agencies, and foreign institutions with whom they work. Open, frequent dialogue with partnering travel companies and their affiliated members can help avert disasters overseas. The travel agents should be well aware of regional risks and be willing to fully disclose those hazards. In addition, steady participation in professional organizations and conferences is essential for coordinators to remain current in their field. Plus, it should naturally be a part of their job.

The good news is that best practices provided by experts do not end here. Continue on to chapters 8 and 9 for additional best practices!

NOTES

1. Allan, C. C., Gooding, J. L., Jercinovic, M., & Keil, K. (1980, September 19). Altered basaltic glass: A terrestrial analog to the soil of Mars. Department of Geology and Institute of Meteoritics, University of New Mexico. Retrieved from
   http://www.mars.asu.edu/christensen/classdocs/Allen_Alteredbas_icarus_81.pdf.
2. 590 N.W.2d 661, 663 (Minn. Ct. App. 1999) ("The student sued the University for negligence in its failure to secure housing closer to the campus, failure to provide transportation to and from campus, failure to adequately warn about risks, and failure to protect students from foreseeable harm.")
3. *Id.*
4. *Id.* at 666.
5. *Id.* at 663, 666 (finding that the program offered instruction in Spanish, as well as a written waiver for students).
6. *Id.* at 666.
7. *Id.*
8. Slattery Complaint at 2, *Slattery v. Antioch Educ. Abroad*, No. 2:09-cv-00828 (S.D. Ohio 2009).
9. *Id.*
10. *Id.*
11. *Id.*
12. *Id.* at 2–3.

13. *Id.* at 4.

14. Kast, R. (1997). In loco parentis and the "reasonable person." *International Educator 7*, 1.Rubin, A. M. (1996, May 10). Making it safer to study abroad. *Chronicle of Higher Education*, p. A49.

15. Buckley, T. J. (1997, September 12). India crash wake up call for schools and parents. *USA Today*, p. A1.

16. Rubin, A. M. (1996, May 10).

17. Semester at Sea—A deadly program. (2011). Cherese Mari Laulhere Foundation. Retrieved from http://cherese.org/semester-at-sea.html.

18. Kast, R. (1997).

19. *Id.*

20. *Id.*

21. 221 F.Supp.2d 783, 791 (E.D. Mich. 2002).

22. *Id.*

23. *Id.* at 784.

24. *Id.*

25. *Id.* These terms included "cows," "bimbos," "pigeonheads." *Id.*

26. *Id.* at 786.

27. *Id.*

28. *Id.* at 785.

29. *Id.* at 786.

30. *Id.*

31. *Id.*

32. *Id.* at 785.

33. *Id.* at 786.

34. *Id.* at 791.

35. *Id.*

36. *Id.* (quoting *Davis v. Monroe Cty. Bd. of Educ.*, 526 U.S. 629, 631 (1999)).

37. *Id.*

38. *Id.*

39. 55 Pa. D. & C.4th 353, 363 (Pa. Com. Pl. 2001) (noting that this duty arises as a part of the special relationship assigned to program leaders when students sign a consent form to study abroad).

40. *Id.*

41. Kast, R. (1997). Rubin, A. M. (1996, May 10).

42. Rubin, A. M. (1996, May 10).

43. Kast, R. (1997). Rubin, A. M. (1996, May 10).

44. Guernsey, L. (1997, April 11). A lawsuit raises difficult questions about liability and study-abroad programs. *Chronicle of Higher Education 43*, 31, p. A37, A39.

45. *Id.*

46. *Id.*

47. 13 Cal. Rptr. 3d 759, 761-63 (Cal. Ct. App. 2004) (detailing the allegedly defective balcony of the apartment assigned to Paneno while studying in Italy).

48. *Id.* at 762.

49. *Id.*

50. *Id.* at 763.

51. *Id.*

52. *Id.*

53. *Id.* at 766.

54. Slattery Complaint at 2, *Slattery v. Antioch Educ. Abroad*, No. 2:09-cv-00828 (S.D. Ohio 2009).

55. *Id.* at 3.

Chapter Eight

The Experts' Advice: Best Practices #7–15

This chapter continues where chapter 7 left off, and where chapter 9 will ensue. Three chapters are necessary to present the wealth of information that comes with the twenty-three most essential best practices to reduce risks and liabilities with study abroad, stemming from experts' encounters and advice. Additional support comes from legal trends and current risk-averting documents. Best practices #7 through #15 include:

- Foreign Laws and Cultural Awareness
- Participant Selection Process
- Consultation with the Institution's Legal Office
- Reentry Orientation
- Program Procedures
- Participant Medical History
- Institutional Administrators/Committees
- Passport, Cash, and Protection of Other Valuables
- U.S. State Department Warnings

Just as it was the case in the previous chapter, the transparent discourse from coordinators is illuminating, honest, and passionate. Here is #7 through #15 of the twenty-three best practices.

MORE BEST PRACTICES FOR AVOIDING RISKS AND LIABILITIES IN STUDY ABROAD

7. Foreign Laws and Cultural Awareness

According to most interviewed coordinators, keen cultural awareness of the foreign location for intended study is essential. Then, participants can be fully oriented so that their overall learning experience is augmented, and risks and liability issues may be deflected.

Coordinator Braxton rightly asserts, "I think when you travel abroad you always have to be alert to the politics of the country." For Coordinator Felix, the foreign culture directly influences the academic approach of a program. "[In our institution] we approach first and foremost learning the culture through academics. We'll require if you are to study in Belgium, you will study Flemish while you're there. Namely, we want to make sure [students] learn the culture first and foremost. [While] in Thailand, [our college] has a requirement for Theology. We want you to study Buddhist Theology while you're there and Buddhist culture."

To go further, Coordinator Levi asserts that familiarity with a foreign culture and its laws protect institutions from legal risks. "[Students] must abide by all the laws that are in that country. If [they] are caught in a drug charge in some countries, they may [be] thrown in the slammer and you may not hear from them for a very long time. So one needs to be very sure that students going abroad know firsthand about the problems and laws of the various countries they are going through."

Coordinator Pearl furnishes participants with as much material and information as possible to make them aware of the unique risks posed in a foreign location:

> [We hope to make participants] understand the way of the world now. I don't think it's even something we have to watch in [our location at home]. We can have problems here, but I think if they understand [that] the little children running around in these [foreign] cities [are] going to pickpocket them, [they] began to get a different perspective.

She continues:

> So I give [students] scenarios, I give them forms, I do orientations . . . and I give [participants] websites to read like the State Department website. I'm going to give them a total list of websites [and] books—things they can do. I'm going to show them anything I can and answer questions to get them [as prepared] as I can.

Thus, familiarizing students with foreign laws and giving them multifaceted awareness of cultural differences overseas is essential. Coordinators also make a point of this in their waivers. A majority of their sample waivers reveal this. For example, Sample Waiver E (Appendix E) conveys:

I understand that each foreign country has its own laws and standards of acceptable conduct, including dress, manners, morals, politics, drug use, and behavior. I recognize the behavior that violates those laws or standards could harm the College's relations with those countries and the institution therein, as well as my own health and safety. I will become informed of, and will abide by, all such laws and standards for each country to or through which I will travel during the Activity.

However, this waiver, like other waivers used (see appendices), could be more specific about the *kind* of concerns that are native to that region, and the program's accompanying orientation sessions would *have to* be regionally specific in disclosing laws, standards, and potential risks.

What is significant is that within their waivers, nearly all coordinators provide statements that maintain that attentiveness to foreign laws and cultural practices is required, and unanimously agree that this awareness by students and program leaders is essential to offset hazards and legal issues with study abroad.

Legal Cases That Highlight the Significance of Knowing Foreign Cultural Practices and Regulations

Again, study abroad participants need to be fully oriented about acceptable cultural practices in their study abroad region. This issue was essential to the case of *Bloss v. The University of*

Minnesota Board of Regents. What may be considered safe practices by U.S. standards served to be tragic when applied by student Adrienne Bloss in Cemanahuac, Mexico.

Bloss left her host-family home, on her own, and hailed a taxi about one-half block down the street.[1] She was traveling to meet friends for a social event.[2] The taxi driver told her the back door was broken and that she could get in the front seat.[3] Bloss sat in the front with the driver, who then pulled over to the side of the road and raped her.[4] Bloss sued the university for inattentiveness in imparting warnings about various serious risks, including the use of taxicabs in Cuernavaca.[5]

However, orientation given to Bloss gave "warnings [that] included specific admonitions that it was dangerous for women to go out alone at night, that [they] should call for a taxi at night rather than hail a taxi on the street, and that women should never sit in the front seat of taxis. These warnings specifically addressed the circumstances under which [Bloss] sustained her injuries."[6]

The assault is tragic, and the reason that Bloss did not heed the warnings about taxicab use in Cuernavaca remains unanswered. However, the case draws attention to the fact that it is crucial for study abroad participants to understand foreign cultural practices to safeguard themselves from potentially hazardous situations.

Slattery v. Antioch Education Abroad et al.

Student Stephanie Slattery also sued her university for failing to disclose an essential cultural difference at her study abroad location; she claimed this resulted in her being raped.[7] More specifically, while a student at Eastern Michigan University, Slattery alleged that she was raped while participating in the University's Antioch Education Abroad (AEA) program in Mali, Africa.[8] A formal case was filed in September 2009 with the Ohio Southern District Court.[9] The case raised concerns as to whether Slattery was adequately informed about accepted cultural norms in the region and whether her sexual assault in Mali was preventable.

Slattery alleges the bus driver working for AEA raped her after she accepted an invite to have a cup of tea in his room.[10]

She received medical treatment in Paris, and upon return to Mali, she filed a formal complaint.[11] The suit stresses that AEA "actively advised, instructed and encouraged the program's students to interact with the local population, to learn the language and cultural differences, but negligently failed to advise . . . Slattery and others of the cultural belief in Mali that having tea alone in a man's apartment [is] considered implied consent to engage in sexual intercourse."[12]

In short, a part of Slattery's complaint was that proper orientation of inherent cultural and regional risks was missing.[13] A court document filed on October 28, 2011, shows the case was settled with the basic description, "STIPULATION of Dismissal WITH PREJUDICE by Defendant Antioch Education Abroad, Plaintiff Stephanie N. Slattery. (Freeze, Stephen) (Entered: 10/28/2011)."[14]

The final outcome of *Slattery v. Antioch Education Abroad* remains unclear. However, what is clear is that study abroad participants must be well oriented on cultural practices in the overseas location so that potential threats can be avoided. It is essential that coordinators conduct extensive research on program locations in order to best orient students about regional risks.

Thackurdeen v. Duke University

With *Thackurdeen v. Duke University*, the lawsuit charges Duke University officials with carelessly overlooking and failing to warn students about a significant hazard in the study abroad region.

Toward the end of the semester in Costa Rica, Duke and the Organization of Tropical Studies (OTS) took their students on a surprise celebratory trip to the beach at Playa Tortuga on the south central Pacific Coast.[15] Caught in a rip current, Ravi Thackurdeen drowned in Playa Tortuga that afternoon.[16]

It is asserted that "Ravi's death was 100% preventable by Duke and OTS."[17] A point of backing is that the dangers of Playa Tortuga were well known and Duke University and OTS should have been aware of them.[18] Almost every website or brochure that discussed visiting Playa Tortuga mentioned the dangerously strong rip currents and that swimming at the beach was not advisable.[19] The students were told that it was safe to swim in the waters, and they were given only the following instruction: to swim parallel to the shore if they were caught in a rip current.[20]

This lawsuit clearly brings forth the point that institutions and their affiliates must have solid regional awareness of the overseas location and must properly advise students on regional dangers.

8. Participant Selection Process

Coordinators insist that by approving exceptional students for study abroad, there is less chance with lackluster program participation or poor behavior that leads to overseas hazards. A selection committee should accept socially mature, academically inclined participants who have a positive rapport with employees at the home institution and will take on an ambassador-like mind-set while abroad.

Just as ineffectual participants can bring decline to a program, adept participants can dramatically improve one. Consider Coordinator Eve's recollection of a mature student who aided a program director. The study abroad student helped to pacify emotional peers reacting to a terrorist attack:

> I had students who [were] in Spain when [there was] the bombings [in] the train stations, . . . [After the crisis occurred], the program director . . . said, "Your student [Lisa] was so wonderful. She was helping to calm the other students [during the crisis]. I felt like I had another study abroad advisor there." And he said, "She's just wonderful anyway. She would come in just on an ordinary day and come in and say, 'How are you doing?'"

Coordinator Eve concludes her account:

> And [the program director] said, "That's so strange to me because usually I'm the one asking everyone else how they're doing. And she'd come in [and ask], 'How are you doing? I have a half hour; can I do something to give you a hand?'" [The program director] had a good relationship with Lisa, and was used to having her around the office. So when this emergency happened, she really stepped in.

This type of narrative confirms the invaluable impact a mature student can bring to a study abroad program. To acquire such students, coordinators contend that there must be high academic and interpersonal standards for participants. This is the reason that Coordinator Levi conducts "at least two one-on-one interviews with a student who wants to study abroad; academic history, travel experience, work experience and extracurricular activities [are] topics discussed." Coordinator Desiree also "has a rigorous application process to vet participants for good standing in the college, both academically and behaviorally."

Coordinator Eve describes the academic standards expected of students who do long-term study abroad:

> All of the courses [abroad] must be taken for a letter grade and must be taken for credit. And those grades count in their GPA, so they know they are not there just to goof off. In fact, sometimes [our students] come back appalled by the students who go just to have a good time, and don't care about the courses . . . Things like that. So, the quality of the student, and our selection process for the students who go abroad, is pretty stringent.

She continues, relating the thorough selection process for students:

> They meet with me at least four times individually, [and much more] coming with questions. But at least four times. Then they need letters of recommendations from their advisor, and two other faculty members. They must have a GPA of 2.75, and then once they submit their application, it goes to a study abroad committee. And the study abroad committee is made up of faculty, the registrar, the director of international programs, me, the student services, and financial aid.

This seems like a thorough selection committee, minus one institutional member—the student. Students should also have a presence in study abroad selection committees. This is implied with Coordinator Eve's allusion to "student services" as part of her committee, but it is not overtly clear. In addition, tap into seasoned study abroad students who have recently returned from overseas studies. Such students give the committee balance; they are tuned in to the student environment on campus as well as the academic culture abroad. Their experience makes them effective with discerning appropriate student candidates for study abroad.

A comprehensive selection process is doubly beneficial because not only does it provide clear understanding of the student's *academic history* but also involves numerous contacts— faculty, the registrar, the director of international programs, student services, financial aid— with people who can help to determine the *character* of the student.

This has also been Coordinator Eve's experience with the process: "So we have people from the whole span of the department who are looking at this application and may know the student in different ways. So when a student is accepted to go abroad, [they] really [have] to prove [themselves]. So the quality of the student we send makes a big difference so we don't tend to have a lot of problems."

Coordinators maintain that a personal history between the student and employees of the institution will help to check certain risks and liabilities that could result from poor-behaving, immature students.

Coordinator Trevor feels that this can be established through interviews: "Well, a student has to be made aware of their sense of responsibility when they're abroad and their expected conduct. Okay. That comes as a result of the kind of individual you are sending abroad. And usually when you conduct these interviews with students for weeks on end before going abroad you'll have a very good sense of the kind of student you are sending abroad. Um, I really get to know the student well."

Likewise, Coordinator Eve appreciates that "all of the study abroad participants' academic achievements, work etiquette, and levels of maturity are known . . . and [I] intentionally pursued work at an institution where there was a family-type environment in which closeness developed between students and administrators." She works at a small institution where "everyone knows one another."

This rationale also supports my belief that you need to have at least one mature student serve on your study abroad selection committee. Students know students. For example, during a recent student study abroad scholarship selection meeting, each committee member reviewed applications of potential candidates, then verbally justified their top five selections to the rest of the committee. Administrators and faculty members had consistently selected a student, who I will name Boris, as their top choice. However, the two student committee members, Cheryl and Sebastian, rebuffed this selection.

Cheryl and Sebastian agreed that their fellow student applicant, Boris, looked good on paper. Yet they warned against the selection due to unfavorable experiences with Boris on campus. More specifically, to illustrate his leadership skills, Boris praised his work in student governance. Cheryl happened to have served on the Student Government Association (SGA) at the same time as Boris. Apparently, while in SGA, Boris failed to complete various essential tasks expected with the post.

Sebastian, who had no prior connection to Cheryl, also had a past unfavorable interaction with the applicant. Sebastian served on the Honor Roll Committee with Boris. Boris had also cited, in his application, instrumental work done in this committee. Yet Sebastian shared a different story of shirked duties by Boris as a member of the Honor Roll committee. Both selection committee members, Cheryl and Sebastian, had direct interactions with Boris that faculty and administrators lacked; their assessment brought reason to reexamine the once-favored applicant.

This pause caused a faculty committee member to retrace Boris's efforts in a former class. Boris had attended the course only a short time before voluntarily withdrawing. Additional investigation from the faculty member revealed a pattern of incomplete work by Boris prior to dropping the class. This presented another red flag. The input of Cheryl and Sebastian directly influenced this additional scrutiny. Their direct extracurricular interaction with the applicant, which other committee members lacked, was pivotal in foregoing this selection for a more dependable student. As shown, greater balance with a selection committee might result with student representation.

Lets return to the advice of coordinators. Coordinator Eve and Coordinator Levi explicitly tell program participants that they are to serve as ambassadors of America while abroad. They hope that this will assist with cultivating positive behavior among participants, and in turn, help to avert potential risks and liabilities. Coordinator Levi concurs, "[Participants] have to understand [they] are a guest of the country [they] are going to."

Concurrently, Coordinator Eve apprises participants of their roles as overseas guests: "[In our programs] we always say when you're abroad you're not just representing yourself— you're representing your family, you're representing the school, and you're representing the country. God knows, we need an improvement in our representation and so forth abroad."

Overall, coordinators agree that a rigorous selection process that accepts mature, academically driven students that understand their role as guests in another country reduce risks and resultant liabilities in study abroad. At the same time, coordinators expect to work with participants who have already established a positive rapport with institution officials.

9. Consultation with Institution's Legal Office

Every coordinator recommends getting input from the college attorney or legal office when constructing risk-averting documents as a measure to protect the institution. Coordinator Braxton reveals, "To be honest, I count on other legal offices on campus with specialty staff to be the experts to offer assistance or advise where needed." Coordinator Lonna describes a tight-knit relationship with legal counsel: "[Study abroad officials] are very close friends and colleagues with our legal office. We're in touch with them all the time. We need the expertise and advice of our legal office here."

This type of camaraderie, as felt by Coordinator Lonna, comes with strong backing from the legal office: "[Our institution] has a legal office that is very supportive of study abroad programs, and [they] want to do everything they can to protect the university while also not limiting the international opportunities offered to our students. . . . So in our own programs, definitely students on those programs all sign waivers saying they understand there are some risks inherent in study abroad and even though we do all we can to protect them, some things do happen outside of our control."

However, there is also tension in the relationship between coordinators and legal counsel. Coordinators admit that a natural resistance occurs between the two entities because coordinators tend to want more direct, emotive language in the waiver. In contrast, officials in the legal office tend to desire lengthy, legal communication. As Coordinator Levi clarifies:

> Of course you never have control over student behavior. And the waiver form, even though it is lengthy, [may assist with risks and liabilities]. I have complained to legal counsel about having [participants] read all that and absorb all that because I have seen forms only a page long. But [legal counsel] refused to change it based on the fact that even though it is repetitive, they feel it is important for a student to be signing a document . . . [that] reminded [them] about [expected conduct].

Each party recognizes the essentiality of the other to create the best risk-averting document and willingly work through differences in order to gain instructive feedback. Coordinator Pearl reports that "[I] just created generic waiver forms that were sent to the attorney, and [am] looking forward to receiving input."

Coordinator Lonna is accurate in her claim that "study abroad office members [tend] not to have any legal training and need the expertise and advice of the legal office." Therefore, she is "pleased to have a legal office that is very supportive of study abroad programs, and believes [that] the aid of the legal office, through dialogue and constructing waivers, helps minimize risks and liabilities."

Knowing the importance of this partnership, Coordinator Poppy emphasizes that "study abroad coordinators must coordinate with a risk management team and the institution's legal office, along with faculty and the dean's office." Coordinator Baron concurs. "We [are pleased to] have a general counsel's office that reviews our program contracts and initiatives." Similarly, Coordinator Felix expresses relief that "the legal office [is] very supportive of the study abroad program at [my] institution."

It is not only waivers but also *all* risk-averting documents that should be passed on to school-appointed attorneys to scrutinize. Coordinator Poppy accurately points out that "it has become increasingly important to have the legal team peruse [not only] waivers [but] other legal documents prior to program use."

The expanse of legal cases and suits examined in chapters 2 through 5 expose the ever-increasing litigious society that we now live. Intensifying risks and liabilities are likely the result of record-breaking study abroad participation, and there is no end in sight for this trend.

10. Reentry Orientation

Many coordinators desire reentry orientation or exit interviews with study abroad participants who return from overseas. The meetings are meant to aid participants with reverse culture shock, according to Coordinator Eve and Coordinator Poppy. Coordinator Felix and Coordinator Levi insist that reentry orientation furnishes coordinators with additional opportunities to address potential issues not discussed before or during study abroad that could lead to lawsuits.

Particularly with students returning from long-term study abroad programs, Coordinator Felix uses exit interviews to ascertain grievances so that he may improve the quality of future programs: "[I want to know] what went wrong so [that] we can correct [it] because after I meet with [returning participants] I'm going to meet with the administrators and say, 'Well this is what went wrong; can we rectify this for the next group?'"

Exit interviews can be done in a formal or informal setting. I prefer a more formal, attentive meeting in my office with a student who recently returned from long-term study abroad. The reverse culture shock that comes with spending three to twelve months abroad is typically more intense than a short-term study abroad homecoming.

At the conclusion of a short-term study abroad program, I often have exit interviews with participants in a lax group setting, such as a "potluck reunion." The reunion allows for program participants to exchange experiences (good and bad) with one another, swap images and video, and share a large communal meal. Much of the meal consists of dishes made by participants that originate from the foreign country they just explored. When I do my exit interviews at this gathering, participants are often unaware of my intentions. Discussion is casual and friendly. Yet like Coordinator Felix, I am searching out details about what went well and what did not with the program.

Regardless of whether it is long-term or short-term study abroad, I have all students complete a program evaluation form. This helps to unearth any remaining unspoken sentiments by participants. How you choose to conduct these essential exit interviews is up to you, depending on your leadership style. Coordinator Felix says:

> Over a beer [they] can tell me the positive. But for the interview it's mostly what went wrong, how we can fix it, things like that. How did we fail at adequately preparing you for the experience? How did the on-sight director do? Whatever went wrong, let us hear it. We might [get a] report on every program, every year. So based on exit interviews, it's the students living there for six months to a year telling us what it was like.

Coordinator Poppy acknowledges that "post-orientation sessions [are] important, and the study abroad participants [have] difficulty becoming readjusted with their home environment when they return." She shares that faculty also see disorientation with students who return from overseas:

> It's very interesting because I [had a] faculty member [tell] me, "I have so many things happening with students that are coming back to my classes this semester who've been studying abroad, and they come in . . . and are enthusiastic about their studying abroad. But they are just not in sync with the university anymore. They're not in sync with their friends. What can I do when they come back to assist them?"

Coordinator Poppy prescribes a holistic method for assisting such students: "And my response is 'doing activities for reentry is great, but reentry actually begins with predeparture, so a part of it is about planning and preparation before a student goes and while a student is on site so that you are not dealing with as pronounced a transition when they come back.' [It is part of that] sort of holistic approach to the entire process."

I can recall my own reacclamation trials as a novice of overseas travel and study abroad. Following two years spent in Southeast Asia, I was completely floored by American interactions. I perceived hostility among people where there was none. With customary speech, people's voices came across as loud, their gestures aggressive, and their tone inhospitable.

After years of access to various open-air markets and lush countryside regions, a return to the concrete jungle was jolting. A deflating realization came to me—if I wanted to continue to obtain healthy food, my once therapeutic daily walk through multiple outdoor, fresh food markets would need to be replaced with a lengthy automotive commute to an overpriced Whole Foods Market.

Again, numerous coordinators avow that reentry orientation is important for assisting participants. The sessions may help to pacify issues that could have led to lawsuits. Participants have a forum to air negative experiences. Then resolution may come without further, legal action. Additionally, reentry orientation can counteract a participants' reverse culture shock. They may be struggling to reacclimate with a static home environment that has not evolved with them through overseas experiences.

Also, postprogram assignments and educationally rich activities bring a more enriching program experience to students and faculty and augment the overall quality of the program. After a short-term study abroad program, I have interested students, faculty participants, and program leaders write short, educational scripts or lessons. Those scripts, along with images from abroad that correspond to the lesson, are given to members of our institution's television recording studio. The participants go into the studio and record five-minute video lessons that appear on our cable television station and the Study Abroad/International Education webpage.

These video lessons are meant to benefit the community. Our college professors will use these short video lessons, accessed online, to supplement class instruction. The videos also serve to inform and engage anyone who desires study abroad; they are "warmed up to the idea" when viewing the testimony from others' past learning experiences. Admittedly, these video lessons are also great promotional pieces for advocating study abroad at my institution.

Coordinator Desiree imparts additional postprogram activities that augment the short-term study aboard experience: "Posttrip, each participant is tasked with sharing what they learned through their individual research with students, faculty, staff, and community members. Individuals are able to choose to share their experience by creating posters, PowerPoint presentations, or a media exhibit." This is a great follow up to a program.

I use postprogram capstone projects and a formal collegewide event to further enrich the participants' study abroad experience. More specifically, prior to and during study abroad, my students do research and journaling. The information gathered helps them to develop a postprogram capstone project. The preapproved project tends to directly relate to their discipline and/or professional goals. Similarly, faculty members conduct research during the study abroad experience for professional development used to internationalize their course curriculum.

It is awesome when the two fuse. For example, in order to garner far-reaching samples for the pH balance of numerous water sources in Iceland, a chemistry professor had students assist in data collection while abroad. The students were given test strips and needed to record findings that would not only be included in the professor's overall data but also would assist with their own project approaches.

With a collegewide event, students and faculty come together once again to showcase findings, completed projects, and professional development that resulted from the study abroad experience. Usually, this comes in the form of fifteen-minute PowerPoint presentations. During this collegewide event, institutional members, family, friends, and the community share in the experience. I highly recommend this approach for positive closure to short-term study abroad programs (although long-term study abroad students also take part in the event) to increase overall program engagement, quality, and satisfaction.

11. Program Procedures

Coordinators surmise that study abroad programs that fail to mirror educational objectives and philosophies promoted by the home institution are more susceptible to shortcomings.

Coordinator Felix suggests that "every college or university [has] a certain philosophy of instruction, and it [is] helpful for study abroad programs to be consistent with those policies." He recommends to "provide each participant a handbook that details individual study abroad programs offered at the institution . . . [using] the same language provided in the college's handbooks, [and] mirroring the institution's educational goals and philosophies."

Concurrently, Coordinator Poppy boasts "the materials constructed for [my] study abroad [programs are] influenced by documents that contain the educational goals and philosophy of the institution." She asserts that "the implemented procedures of individual study abroad programs must have similar objectives as the institution's policies on education."

Steps for Students to Obtain Long Term Study Abroad and Transfer Credits

To ensure that educational goals of the institution are met for long-term study abroad programs, students need to work through a number of college officials. Far too often students hold the misconception that a semester abroad will delay their graduation. One thought is the overseas courses will fail to transfer back to the home institution. Another concern is the foreign institution may lack the necessary course offerings in their discipline that would not allow for degree completion in the timeframe outlined by the home institution. None of the aforementioned concerns should be a problem with study abroad. This is the case at my own institution.

Here is how the transfer of foreign course credits works at my institution. First, an academic advisor needs to map out the proper class schedule for the student while abroad so that needless courses are not taken. If a student desires to take one or two academically based courses outside of their discipline, it is their choice. I require a student to initially complete an Application for Semester or Year-Long Study Abroad (see Appendix M). A spot remains on the application for the academic advisor to sign, ensuring that both student and advisor are satisfied with the course selections.

Second, as the collegewide coordinator of our study abroad office, I interview the student to understand his or her rational for the selected foreign program and classes. I consider the practicality of these choices while making sure that the academic goals set by my office and the institution will be fulfilled. Then I sign my approval.

Last, a transcript evaluator from the Registrar's Office reviews the courses for reasons similar to my own and that of the academic advisor. Students at other colleges and universities may be required to use outside agencies to provide course evaluations if their registrar does not provide this service.

However, we desire to simplify this process for the student, so a transcript evaluator from our Registrar's Office makes the course equivalency determinations. There is a spot on the application that requires a signature from the Registrar's Office for study abroad to be approved. At this point, course equivalents that will transfer from abroad are agreed upon; the student will have to earn a "C" grade (or its equivalent) or better in the foreign classes for transferability.

Short Term Programs Must have Academic Rigor

Short-term study abroad should also satisfy the educational objectives of the home institution. Coordinator Levi shares that short-term study abroad programs "[need] to academically and socially connect with the learning objectives of a class, and [I] only offer a short-term study program if it was part of an already existing college course."

This is the proper approach. Short-term study abroad programs should link to an existing cataloged course offering. Typically, a study abroad program serves as the culminating learning module to a course; therefore, it usually takes place at the conclusion of the class. The high-impact educational experiences of short-term study abroad bring a new reality to the reading, discussions, and themes brought forth in the classroom. Nothing in the classroom can serve as a full substitute for the hands-on interaction that the study abroad component brings.

The rigor of a short-term study abroad program is felt with daily lectures, symposiums, and/or debriefing sessions that occur with various experts. This may include foreign professors at overseas institutions, faculty leaders on the bus, clergy in churches, curators of museums, or by archeologists on prehistoric grounds, to name a few examples. It is not unlikely for a short-term program to accumulate more lecture hours than the semester-long course at the home institution.

However, coordinators will inevitably butt heads with ill-informed individuals who fail to recognize that *lectures* can take place outside of the constraints of a four-walled campus enclosure at the home institution. Museum curators, program site guides, faculty leaders, program tour guides, and foreign instructors, unfortunately, as brilliant as they may be, are not always adequately valued as educators on the college and university campus.

This mentality seems odd when considering the efficiency of distance-learning courses which provide effective instruction outside of the campus classroom. Yet, to further ensure that immense studies and work have resulted for students, attach the short-term program to an existing cataloged semester course.

Endorse with the Waiver

Academic objectives and educational goals of the institution should be emphasized in risk-averting documents and waivers of study abroad. For example, Waiver F (Appendix F) promotes academic policies while clarifying participant expectations for long-term study abroad:

I acknowledge and understand that I am responsible for maintaining a full-time course of study, taking at least fifteen semester hours of work or the equivalent in quarter hours per semester or term while participating in the Program. I understand that I must attend all classes, take all examinations, and do all assigned work.

This waiver also holds the participant accountable for maintaining necessary educational standards:

I agree to take only those courses that have been approved by the College. If I take courses that have not been approved by the College, I understand that the credits may not be transferred to the College. In the event that a change in my course of study must be made, I agree to communicate with and receive approval from the College for all changes prior to making them. I am aware that I must receive the equivalent of 1.0 grade points (2.0 for non home-institutional programs) or better in each course in order for the course to be counted toward my degree program at the College.

Risk-averting documents and waivers are instrumental in orienting study abroad partici-pants about program procedures that mirror educational objectives and the philosophy of the home institution. As a result, students can gain increased understanding for the expectations that come with study abroad.

12. Participant Medical History

Hazards and legal issues may be circumvented when the medical history of study abroad participants is fully disclosed prior to departure. Coordinator Lonna shares, "[As a means of] emergency preparedness, we collect health information about the [students in our programs], we collect employment about them, we collect emergency contact leads and numbers, and we have a lot of information about students on our programs."

Similarly, Coordinator Felix and Coordinator Poppy expect participants to disclose medi-cal conditions, medication use, and/or treatments. Coordinator Levi sees parents of partici-pants as key sources for acquiring this information: "[There is] a need for parental involve-ment and [to have the ability to] ask parents of participants to discuss any medical problems their son or daughter has." Coordinator Levi adroitly perceives that "the parents of participants often [have] better access and greater knowledge of this information than the participant."

Coordinator Pearl is assertive in her stance that "participants' medical history must be made clear, along with the proper treatments." Past negative incidents have shaped her per-spective. One such incident included a student who failed to properly administer medication for his ailment, leading to a violent episode that cut short his semester abroad.

Due to ethical concerns, Coordinator Pearl remains brief and nondescript in her account: "I've kicked a couple [participants] out over the years, than the college president would know and we'd handle it the best way we can. I can't go too much [into explaining it] for a lot of reasons. But one young man was [studying abroad] and [was] bipolar and was not dealing with his medicine. [He] was a very sweet young man. He literally needed to get out of that apartment and get home. It was not safe for him to stay there." The coordinator and college president rightly understand the need to confer when a student's program abruptly ends, and consider potential grievances that might result.

To personally interject, coordinators should make medical history disclosure mandatory for study abroad participants. A sample Health Disclosure Form (see Appendix L) is provided to help coordinators obtain this invaluable information in a sensitive manner. The form should be universally required among all study abroad participants. No participant should feel as if they are being singled out. Its completion should occur prior to departure. Attempting to figure out a medical issue that arises *while* overseas may leave that participant and program in dire straits.

Furrh v. Arizona Board of Regents as an Example

Furrh v. Arizona Board of Regents brings to focus the havoc that might result on a study abroad program when a student fails to disclose their medical history. In this case, the student Jonathan Furrh did not divulge chronic mental disorders.[21] Furrh's behavior created potential-ly serious harm.[22]

He had delusions that the other persons were "Mafioso" who were going to kill him, and on a boat trip to Ventana Island he believed he was going to be thrown to the sharks.[23] In addition, on two occasions he wielded a knife.[24] As a result, Furrh had to be physically restrained during the study abroad program.[25]

With this difficult situation abroad, Furrh's temporary detainment (and the means taken to effect it) was reasonably necessary and justified.[26] This was done in the best interest of the student and other members of the group.[27] In fact, had program leaders not detained Furrh, they would have been negligent in their duty of care for him and the other program participants who were being put in harm's way.[28]

Again, in order to protect students from potential issues of disruption and harm, coordinators must know the medical history of participants in advance of study abroad.

13. Institutional Administrators/Committees

In contrast with past years, coordinators see a greater need to address threats to students and to protect themselves from potential lawsuits (i.e., Coordinator Felix, Coordinator Levi, and Coordinator Poppy). They have created risk-assessment committees that have increased their involvement with university officials. As a result, coordinators and committee members have a shared stake in the matter, and everyone's understanding for ways to protect students and thwart potential lawsuits has improved.

Coordinator Baron, Coordinator Felix, and Coordinator Poppy each formed a risk assessment committee to examine possible risks and liabilities that accompany their individual programs. Coordinator Poppy conducts her risk management "through the university's deans' office, legal office, and faculty council," and Coordinator Felix's risk assessment team is "made up of faculty, administrators, and legal counsel that help to form an emergency response plan and guide, should an issue materialize while abroad."

To avoid risks and liabilities, Coordinator Baron presents program itineraries to his risk assessment committee: "A travel and risk group looks at legal issues we may encounter from an itinerary standpoint." More details on the advantages of having a committee and other groups dedicated to emergency responses come with best practice #17, Emergency Response Plan.

Coordinators search out dialogue with other college department members and groups that directly work with institutional students. For example, Coordinator Felix confers with the Director of International Student Services in order to gain a better understanding for the academic and civic status of international students who desire study abroad:

> The Director of International Student Services' office focuses on international students' needs and is the immigration person for us. All people who come into the college with immigration or exchange issues, our Director of International Students will take care of it. Her department has better records on prior academics and needs of international students. When trying to figure out what visa or passport information is necessary to allow these students to study abroad, I talk to the director of international services.

Similar to other coordinators, Coordinator Eve formed a risk management committee. Her committee is a diverse one "of college officials made up of faculty, the registrar, the director of international programs, the study abroad coordinator, members of student services, and financial aid officials." She adds that "the committee assists with issues relative to study abroad credit transfer, scholarships, tuition waivers, programs risks, and issues of liability."

Although the members of the committee come from outside departments, their interests and job responsibilities interconnect with those of coordinators. Therefore, coordinators should take this affiliation a step further and invite committee members to accompany them to professional conferences. If it is a large national organization holding a conference there should be plenty of workshops to interest everyone. As a result, hopefully this will further congeal your relationship and make the group's philosophical approach to risk management congruent.

Thackurdeen v. Duke University Shows the Need to Use a Risk-Management Committee

Once coordinators have risk-management committees in place, they need to determine how to effectively use them when issues arise abroad. This became a clear point of concern with *Thackurdeen v. Duke University*. The grieving parents who filed the suit believe improper measures contributed to their son's death in Costa Rica.[29]

During the study abroad crisis, Duke University had an International Travel Oversight Committee (ITOC) in place.[30] The ITOC was formed to establish a universal policy regarding international policy, specifically where and how travel could proceed under the auspices of Duke University.[31] The committee considered who should be served and what level of risk was appropriate.[32]

Some of the self-proclaimed responsibilities of the ITOC were "to establish methods of tracking travel (compliance with policy, emergency assistance, etc.)" and "to determine how emergency assistance would be provided."[33]

Duke University officials noted that risk management was a responsibility shared between multiple parties at the university: its risk management office, the ITOC, the general counsel, the Office of Global Strategy & Program, its human resources department, its public relations department, and any other departments, units, and programs in charge.[34]

This is all great in theory, but how did the committee come together in practice to deal with the study abroad tragedy described in *Thackurdeen v. Duke University*? Hopefully this is what a court can determine. The Thackurdeens have major grievances with Duke University officials' approach to risk management during Ravi Thackurdeen's program.

In the lawsuit, university officials are faulted for being uninformed about the potential dangers of the area by allowing students to swim at Playa Tortuga,[35] and for exposing students to unnecessary risks.[36]

In addition, the complaint chastises the conduct of program leaders, which included the failure to inform the parents of Ravi's drowning and to "mislead and conceal Ravi's drowning from [them]; [also noted was a] failure to provide adequate search teams, supplies, and resources to locate Ravi's body promptly, leading to his body not being located or pulled out of water for over 36 hours after his death, [and] . . . careless handling and transportation of Ravi's dead body after it was eventually located."[37]

Again, these are serious charges put forth. During the crisis, hopefully Duke's International Travel Oversight Committee attempted to address the matters. In addition, hopefully a court can provide clarity on these issues so that Duke University and other institutions may gain improved insight with how to best utilize the risk-management teams and committees that they have in place.

14. Passport, Cash, and Protection of Other Valuables

Instructing participants about passport protection to avert loss or theft is essential. In fact, Coordinator Pearl sees passport protection as a top priority: "The biggest thing is [students protecting] their passport. And so I talk to students a lot about their passports, how to keep them safe, and when to carry them and not to. There are just many issues that living in this country you do not think about on a day-to-day basis. [Students] take for granted a tour will take care of [them], and it should. But I [also] want [students to be] savvier than that."

I fully agree that protection of passports, as well as other valuables, needs *special attention* to avoid theft during study abroad. Therefore, diagrams on Protecting Valuables (Figures 8.1 to 8.5) are provided to show how to sufficiently conceal valuables, including the passport, cash, and important documents, on your person.

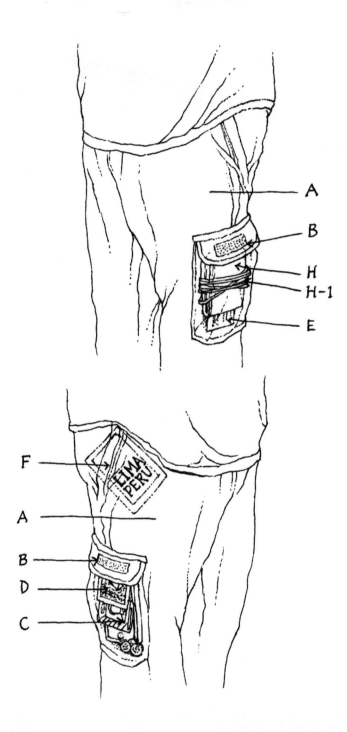

Figure 8.1.   Protecting Valuables

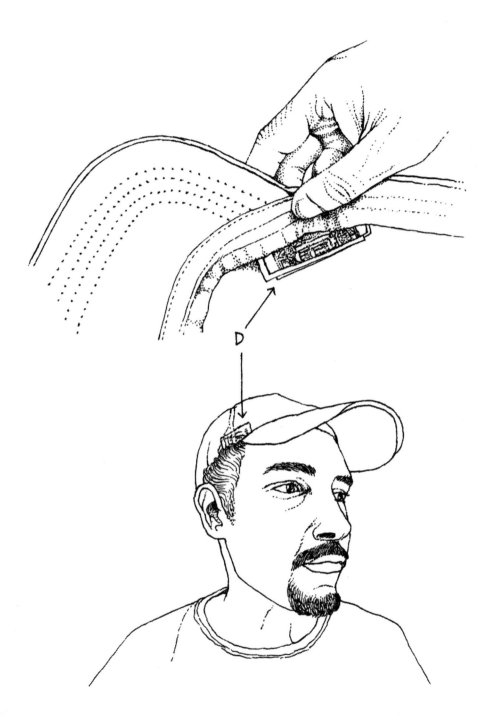

D

Figure 8.2.   Protecting Valuables (con't)

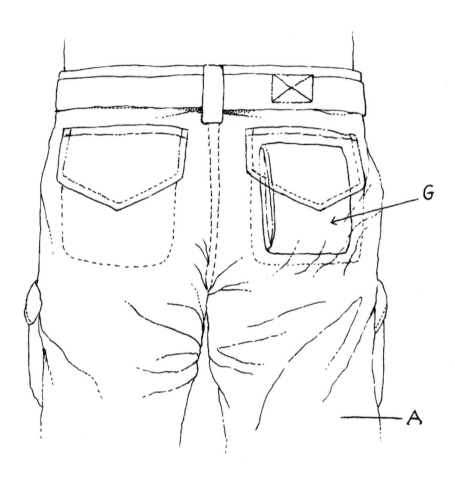

Figure 8.3.   Protecting Valuables (con't)

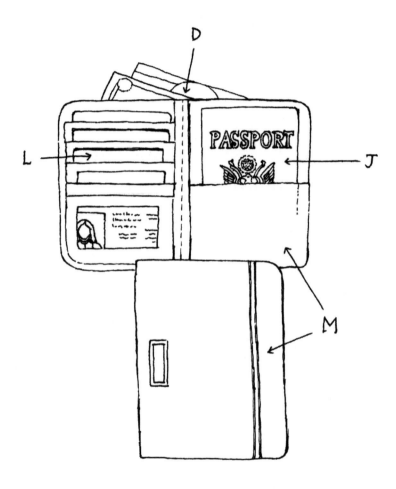

Figure 8.4.   Protecting Valuables (con't)

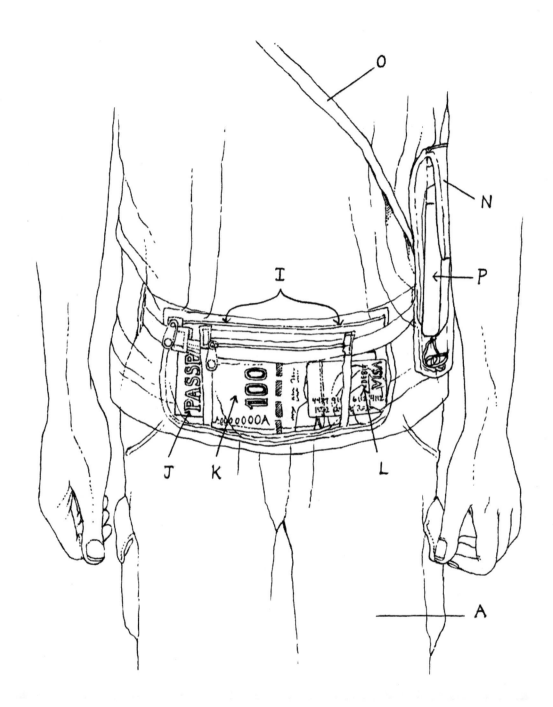

Figure 8.5. Protecting Valuables (con't)

This is what the diagrams offer. Lines with arrows point to items that are to be concealed. Letters in the diagrams refer to different valuables and items carried. As shown, cargo pants (A) are helpful for travel. They allow for storage of various items close to your body. Plus, a pickpocket must contend with choosing from as many as six pockets, as opposed to two, to target. Choose cargo pants that have velcro flaps (B) over the pockets. A pickpocket's hands cannot easily slide into an open pocket with a flap in place that needs lifting. The sound that velcro makes when the flap is lifted will alarm you to the unlawfully entry.

The location of certain pockets with cargo pants make pickpocketing more difficult for the thief. Thigh-level pants pockets are more difficult to pickpocket than waist-level pockets. So semivaluable items such as a passport photocopy (C), a small amount of spending cash (D), and the business card of the accommodation (E) where you are staying should be stored in thigh-level pockets. The items you are willing to part with should be stored in hip-level pockets.

A pickpocket may attempt to distract you by bumping into you as they reach for items in hip-level pockets. The same pockets are targeted with another pickpocket technique in which one thief gets your attention (by asking you a question) while the other slides behind you for the steal—again, at the hip level.

Unfortunately, this does not hold true for children pickpockets who can easily reach thigh-level pockets. This is why only semivaluable items, at best, are stored in cargo pants pockets. However, small spending cash can also be rolled up and placed in the inside of a hat (D) where neither an adult or child pickpocket can reach. But remember to take out the cash when you put your hat down.

This is a poor solution if you have a tendency to lose hats. It became a running joke when one of our program leaders wanted to wear a native Fedora hat while in Cuba yet would mistakenly leave his new purchase behind and buy another in a new location. Fedora after Fedora was left—in a restaurant, church, museum, and hotel as we traveled from one side of the country to the other. If he had used the system of stuffing cash in his hat, there would have been a lot of bills left behind.

The small amount of spending money that you carry in a thigh-level pocket should be local currency only. Do not pull out dollar bills. Once you do so, you have just weakened your ability to barter at an open market, a handicraft shop, or local business. A special price for you, the wealthy American, will result.

Again, the least valuable items that you do not mind parting with, such as an area map (F) and a decoy wallet (G), should be stored at hip level. If you decide to carry a practical wallet (H), which I do not recommend since a money belt (I) can hold and conceal those items, tie a few rubber bands (H-1) around the wallet and keep it in a thigh-high pocket. The rubber bands provide resistance should a pickpocket attempt to lift it from your pants pocket.

The reason for having a decoy wallet is obvious enough. The bulge in your pocket is meant for pickpockets to target and get nothing in return for their work except a few fake credit cards and game board money. If you would like to leave a personal note for the thief, it is up to you. I prefer a written note that is instructive, as opposed to insulting. Call me naïve, but a poetic stanza or scripture verse may give the sort of unexpected positive message that makes them question what they did, rather than fanning the flames by seriously maligning them. Leave it to the program leaders to help get retribution for your loss.

Your most valuable items, passport (J), bulk cash (K), and credit cards (L), should be kept in a money belt (I). The money belt fits snugly around your waist, concealed under your pants waist and shirt. However, the money belt does not allow easy access to the passport, which is needed during travel in airports. So the times that the passport is not being stored in a money belt, it should be carried in a thigh-level pocket.

RFID-Blocking Wallets and Carrying Cases

For added protection of the passport and credit cards, to deter identity theft, the items can be stored in a Radio Frequency Identification (RFID)-blocking passport wallet (M). This wallet protects electronic data stored in the passport and credit card microchip. The microchip, or RFID chip, is embedded on the U.S. passport and most credit cards. Just as an airport security scanner can penetrate through clothing and storage items, an identity thief with an RFID reader can read data from your exposed microchip. The RFID-blocking wallet is impenetrable and protects access to microchips. Royce is a company that sells RFID-blocking wallets for about $50. [38]

Details on electronic identity theft issues, and ways to protect from them while abroad, are noted in chapter 6, Increasing Concerns with Cyberthreats, Identity Theft, and Terrorist Acts.

Consideration of Purses, Cameras, and Backpacks

A purse (N) should be a small carrier for semivaluable items. Again, the money belt should be used for more valuable items. The purse should be connected by a *strong* strap (O) that lies across the chest, bandolier style. In addition, the purse itself should rest against your side, as high up as possible; the closer it rests under the armpit, the better with deterring theft. Never hang the purse strap over a single shoulder where it can easily be pulled off the shoulder.

The same goes for a camera (P). It should be stored in a small case that has a sturdy strap, worn in the same manner as the purse. When you need to use the camera, take it out of the case, but keep the strap and case fastened on your shoulder as a reminder that your camera has a place in which it needs to return. Once done using the camera, immediately put it back in the case. Never place the camera down. Thus, the steps to avoid theft are simply to take the camera out of the case, use it, and immediately place it back in the case. It never departs from having immediate contact with you.

Backpacks are convenient for travel for sure. However, they do not provide great safety from theft. It is located on, well, your back, where you have a poor angle to watch over it. Little hands can get in and out of partially opened zipper pockets and flaps. Therefore, I recommend, as shown by the illustration, keeping anything that is of worth closer to the body in specified pockets and in a money belt. The backpack is useful for storing basic day-to-day travel items such as a swimsuit, towel, toiletries, light snacks, bottled water, insect repellent, sunblock, disinfectant, bandages, and hand sanitizer.

Safeguarding against electronic and technological identity theft is just as important as physical protection of valuables. Make sure that you carefully read chapter 6, particularly the section on Identity Theft through Wi-Fi, Registration Kiosks, ATMs, and Cellular Networks.

Issue of a New U.S. Passport That Is Lost or Stolen Abroad

If a U.S. passport is misplaced or stolen abroad, having a passport-sized picture and a photo-copy of the passport's picture page will aid the process in getting a new one quickly issued (coordinators need to specify for participants to take them abroad). The participant and pro-gram leader(s) should bring these items to the nearest U.S. embassy or consulate. Officials will request that a DS-11 form be completed, and they will take your passport-sized picture and charge a fee of about $135 for a replacement passport.

Participant upon Participant Theft Abroad

Theft abroad is also perpetrated by one study abroad participant upon another. The program coordinator needs to carefully vet all participants, yet clearly it is not possible to distinguish all of the potential character flaws of a future participant through predeparture interviews or orientation. So study abroad participants have a shared responsibility in not being victimized.

As a participant, if you have decided to room with another person during your time overseas, be sure that a long and trustful relationship has already been established with your roommate. Although it is never recommended, you should feel confident that you could leave your valuables out in the open and unattended without being disturbed by your roommate.

Coordinators agree that the victimization of a participant by another is common with study abroad. For example, Coordinator Levi recalls a sad situation of forgery that occurred with a program. "The student forged some checks from a roommate and got into some serious problems regarding that. And it needed to be addressed immediately when it was discovered. The advisor contacted me right away, and as a result I was prepared to bring the student home. I had to contact parents, and I had to arrange for restitution of funds for the checks that had been cashed."

Coordinator Levi recounts better-than-expected results from the potentially disastrous situation. "That was taken care of, and everything worked out well actually. [This] worked for the students, and the best situation worked out for everyone. I didn't have to bring the student home; the student completed the time they were there, and did well on their grades. But they were a little short on funds when they went and helped themselves to someone else's."

The kind of punishment that a coordinator gives to a participant who has committed theft should be considered on a case-by-case basis. Some coordinators would argue that in the case involving Coordinator Levi's program, insufficient penalty followed since the dishonest student was allowed to finish the program and earn credits.

His closing point, "but they were a little short on funds when they went and helped themselves to someone else's," may also be seen as too dismissive in dealing with the infraction. I would have been more compelled to end that student's study abroad program early. Again, each coordinator needs to independently weigh these situations .

Regardless of the final decision made by Coordinator Levi, there has to be a policy in place "with teeth" that allows for them to penalize participants who bring risks to other group members. A more complete analysis of this topic comes with best practice #22, Empowerment of Program Leaders.

As previously noted, loss or theft of passports frequently occur with study abroad. Well aware of this, Coordinator Trevor makes sure to know "the locations of American embassies in the area where they intend to travel." He relates familiarity with assisting participants who have lost their passports:

> [If] we have a student who lost a passport, that means that [a supervisor is] going at least for a few hours to the U.S. embassy. Of course we take precautions with that; I tell students to make Xerox copies of their passport, bring an extra picture, and so on. So when they go to the embassy, it's not a difficult task. Of course if you went [to the embassy] with nothing or a driver's license [you may not be helped].

Prior to leaving abroad, I have participants make two photocopies of the picture page of their passport. One copy is brought abroad because its information provides enough detail to fill out a DS-11 form with the U.S. embassy or consulate to get a replacement passport, if needed.

The second copy remains with the security office on the home campus. So even if the photocopy that was brought abroad cannot be located, I can contact the security office, twenty-four hours a day, including holidays, to get the information I need.

On a separate but important note, the security office should have a copy of every participant's passport as an emergency precaution. If a sudden emergency arose while a group is
abroad and the program leaders could not be reached, a member of our emergency response
team could still access any individual's information. Emergency contact information and a
health disclosure form for each participant are also kept with the security office.

Coordinator Felix discloses an intelligent approach to further safeguard passports. He
"registers participants with the American Embassy . . . [and] during orientation sessions and
programs instructs participants on techniques that keep a passport physically safe from theft."
Again, the figure 8, Protecting Valuables, is provided to show how participants may protect
valuables, including their passports, from pickpockets.

What to Do When There Is No Nearby American Embassy or U.S. Consulate Abroad

Even when a U.S. embassy does not exist in a foreign country to visit, a similar American
presence may be available. This should be known prior to heading overseas.

For example, there was no available U.S. embassy to work with during past programs to
Cuba. The American embassy in Havana only reopened well into 2015. Prior to that time, you
had to work with the Cuban Interests Section. It was also the sector that helped process
documents to gain access into Cuba, and served as the contact point should an emergency arise
while in Cuba.

On a whole, coordinators recognize the importance of having foreknowledge of U.S.
embassy and consulate locations overseas and knowing what materials should be presented to
officials when passports are lost or stolen.

15. U.S. State Department Warnings

Coordinators recognize that U.S. State Department warnings and alerts for American travelers
are a valuable resource. Coordinator Arianna, Coordinator Baron, Coordinator Braxton, Coor-
dinator Desiree, Coordinator Eve, Coordinator Felix, Coordinator Levi, Coordinator Pearl,
Coordinator Tabitha, and Coordinator Trevor will not send participants to an overseas location
that has a U.S. State Department warning, and a vehement Coordinator Felix "censures any
[institutions] that attempt programs in locations with State Department warnings."

Still, the U.S. State Department's listings should not serve as the sole factor for determining whether a study abroad program should be offered in the region. Coordinator Trevor
properly contends that "the coordinator and institutional officials must ultimately rule whether
a region is safe or not." To back his point, he recalls a cancelled program to Italy. There was
no U.S. State Department warning attached to the country, but due to terrorist violence in a
neighboring country, study abroad to Italy was postponed:

> [We consider] what the State Department declares . . . Italy was not declared off limits. But our
> [school] president decided, "I cannot in good conscience allow this trip to happen. What if some-
> thing happens?" Also, other college officials felt it was unsafe to travel there. Even though no
> travel warning had come out on Italy, a neighboring area seemed unsafe. So the college was
> responsible for reimbursing the students at the tune of $45,000.

I agree that copious research by coordinators, coupled with U.S. State Department listings,
should determine if a program is viable. The halting of Coordinator Trevor's Italy program
was costly, but not as costly as running a program that he knew to be dangerous.

As was referenced with best practice #5, Reputable Travel Companies/Agencies, a planned
activity with my Costa Rica program was terminated due to sudden news that a theft and

killing of foreign hikers had taken place at the site. I gained this information from my partnering travel company, not the U.S. State Department. Do not replace proper vetting with information gathered from a single source, including the U.S. State Department.

Interestingly, just because an institution abides by U.S. State Department warnings does not mean that the coordinator will impede a student from studying in that warned country. For example, Coordinator Baron acknowledges, "We do send students to countries that have some [terrorist] risks and think it is important to have a safer itinerary [when we do]." With a safer, more insulated program approach, he believes potential hazards in the region can be avoided.

Coordinator Poppy tends to follow U.S. State Department warnings but finds that an inflexible policy that automatically follows the lead of the U.S. State Department could limit positive study abroad experiences:

> I was examining the travel warning policy of a university and trying to come up with a way to create greater flexibility with that travel warning policy. The travel warning policy is [that] if there is a travel warning, students do not go. And if they're on a program with a travel warning placed, they will be withdrawn. No questions. [It is a] very good policy, but one that can be problematic. Especially when you have graduate students come back who might to be there for further reasons that have background and ability to function with that type of environment safely.

She closes with these considerations:

> So the question that was confronting the university is "How do we change a policy, and do it in a way that it is going to cover us in terms of liability?" [It can] put the university almost in direct opposition to the Department of State. In legal terms the question may come up, "Why did you let the students study in a region where the Department of State said 'no'? What proof did you and the university [have] that was better than that of the State Department?"

Coordinator Lonna and Coordinator Poppy are willing to take on this posed concern. Both do not block students from studying abroad in places that have U.S. State Department warnings. Yet they require participants to sign an agreement in which the participant acknowledges awareness of the U.S. State Department warning, and decided not to heed it, releasing the institution from all responsibility of liability should an unfortunate occurrence result. Coordinator Poppy admits, "[I] allowed a student to study abroad in Kenya, Africa, while there was a State Department warning for the region. Again, the participant had to sign the previously described document to do so."

However, Coordinator Lonna and Coordinator Poppy cannot have it both ways (are their legal counsel offices on board with this?). They should not give students the path to study at an at-risk program location then attempt to fully disassociate themselves when students take it. Come clean and approve the program for study or don't. A signed agreement that would supposedly disconnect you from that flagged region is null once you have sanctioned study in it; and certainly you have sanctioned study in the region if you have advanced warning of the student's intent and taken the foreign institution's course equivalents just as you would for any approved program.

Consider chapters 2 through 5—the courts are becoming less tolerant of nonaccountable language provided through waivers and risk-averting documents. As a coordinator, trust your research, experience, and judgment, then make a *full commitment* to support a program. Otherwise, do not offer it. When you're fully committed to a program, so, too, will be your efforts to protect participants.

Allow caution to be the main measure used for running programs, even if it limits your offerings. Cancelled programs are a disappointing part of the job for coordinators. Ethiopia,

Jordan, Morocco, and Tibet are some locations where I had organized programs that had to be cancelled due to sudden, unexpected hazards that arose prior to departure. Every time a program gets cancelled, it is upsetting, both to organizers and participants. Yet with the infrequency with which this occurs, along with the amazing satisfaction that successful programs bring, such setbacks seem minor when considering the larger picture.

Let me emphasize that the U.S. State Department webpage is an important resource for providing information on potential safety risks abroad and should always be consulted. Its information should accompany other sources of information to inform students of regional risks and be presented at predeparture orientation sessions. Coordinator Pearl "emphasizes in predeparture orientation sessions for participants to carefully read the State Department webpage."

This is well advised, but not enough. You cannot leave to chance that some participants may not bother to carefully read the U.S. State Department site on their own. The coordinator needs to have formal discussions about the published information, back it with other reports about the location (including those from the partnering travel agency members), and carefully consider whether to move forward with the program.

CHAPTER SUMMARY

The perspectives and experiences of study abroad experts give fruitful results for best practices with study abroad to deflect potential risks and liabilities. To maintain proper safety standards for students, coordinators must do constant research on foreign laws and have apt cultural awareness for regions with study abroad programs.

To further avoid unnecessary risks abroad, coordinators should implement a selection process that only allows socially mature, academically inclined participants who take on the perspective of an ambassador. The students should have a positive rapport with employees of the home institution as well. A selection committee should have a diverse group of members, including mature students.

Coordinators determine that legal counsel should carefully review risk-averting documents. Even if the relationship between the study abroad coordinator and legal counsel is strained at times due to philosophical differences, sustained communication and commitment to student safety must be at the forefront of decision making.

Negative issues involving returning participants from study abroad may be addressed, and at times resolved, without further legal action when a reentry orientation or exit interview takes place. The reentry orientation also serves to aid participants who are attempting to become reacclimated with their home environment.

Coordinators determine that study abroad programs that fail to mirror the educational objectives and philosophies promoted by the home institution are more susceptible to shortcomings. Foreign classes must be academically and socially linked to the learning objectives of campus courses.

Acquiring a complete medical history of study abroad participants, in advance of departure, helps with averting potential problems abroad. Emergency contact information for a student should be secured in case a parent or close acquaintance needs to be contacted if a medical emergency arises.

Having a clear understanding that there is strength in numbers, coordinators have increased their communication with institutional officials in an attempt to better comprehend how hazards and legal issues may be thwarted. A team made up of faculty, administrators, and legal counsel is recommended for risk assessment and risk management.

Passports are often misplaced or stolen while abroad. Therefore, participants must be instructed on proper passport protection. Theft of valuables is often committed by one participant upon another, so each participant should be carefully vetted by the coordinator prior to being accepted into a program. The participant shares in this responsibility. To deter theft, participants need to carefully select their roommate; a trustworthy relationship should be established in advance of travel.

The U.S. State Department serves to be a major resource for safety alerts and warnings for Americans who plan to go abroad. However, coordinators must still do research on their own to adequately determine whether a location is safe to conduct study abroad.

Let's move on to chapter 9, which will conclude the best practices voiced by experts and backed by court cases and risk-averting documents.

NOTES

1. *Bloss v. Univ. of Minn. Bd. of Regents*, 590 N.W.2d 661, 663 (Minn. Ct. App. 1999).
2. *Id.*
3. *Id.*
4. *Id.*
5. *Id.*
6. *Id.* at 666.
7. Slattery Complaint at 2, 4, *Slattery v. Antioch Educ. Abroad*, No. 2:09-cv-00828 (S.D. Ohio 2009).
8. *Id.* at 1–2.
9. *Id.* at 1.
10. *Id.* at 2.
11. *Id.* at 2–3.
12. *Id.* at 4.
13. *Id.*
14. *Slattery v. Antioch Education Abroad et al.*: Docket Alarm, Inc. (2012–2015). Retrieved fromhttps://www.docketalarm.com/cases/Ohio_Southern_District_Court/3--10-cv-00010/Slattery_v._Antioch_Education_Abroad_et_al/.
15. Complaint at 5, *Thackurdeen v. Duke Univ.*, No. 14-cv-6311 (Aug. 8, 2014 S.D.N.Y.).
16. *Id.* at 5–6.
17. *Id.* at 10.
18. *Id.* at 12–14.
19. *Id.* at 13 (citing specific warnings from the U.S. Department of State and *USA Today*).
20. *Id.* at 5.
21. 676 P.2d 1141, 1142 (Ariz. Ct. App. 1983).
22. *Id.*
23. *Id.*
24. *Id.*
25. *Id.* at 1144.
26. *Id.*
27. *Id.*
28. *Id.*
29. Complaint at 1, 10–11, *Thackurdeen v. Duke Univ.*, No. 14-cv-6311 (Aug. 8, 2014 S.D.N.Y.).
30. *Id.* at 8–9.
31. *Id.* at 9.
32. *Id.*
33. *Id.*
34. *Id.*
35. *Id.* at 14.
36. *Id.*
37. *Id.* at 17.
38. Inc. 5000. (2014). Royce leather collection. Retrieved from http://www.royceleathergifts.com/UI/RFID204-5-ROYCE-LEATHER-DEBOSSED-RFID-BLOCKING-PASSPORT-JACKET.aspx?ptype=3&pid=342.

Chapter Nine

The Experts' Advice: Best Practices #16–23

This chapter completes the twenty-three most critical, best practices to reduce risks and liabilities with study abroad. Again, they result from expert opinions and are backed by legal trends and current risk-averting documents. These include:

- Coordinator-to-Student Ratio
- Emergency Response Plan
- Participants with Disabilities and the Americans with Disabilities Act
- Waivers and Their Construction
- Code of Conduct and Policy
- Foreign Housing Assignments
- Empowerment of Program Leaders
- Trial and Error

CLOSING "BEST PRACTICES" FOR AVOIDING RISKS AND LIABILITIES IN STUDY ABROAD

16. Coordinator-to-Student Ratio

Coordinators call for a healthy ratio of supervisors to students on overseas programs. For instance, Coordinator Trevor "make[s] sure that two chaperones [are] present for every study abroad program, and limit the number of student participants to twenty per program supervisor." For his annual London program, his wife, or a faculty member, serves as a chaperone with him:

> Well, actually I only take twenty [participants on a program]. . . . Two [supervisors], [sometimes] my wife and I, have done very well. And my wife who is a mother [serves the students well when they] are away from home. Again, [students] are away for two weeks. They are fending for themselves—food, shelter, and they're doing their laundry. And I've had kids who are homesick, which is natural. I've had kids that have had tummy aches, [and wondered] "Where is my mommy?" My wife is really good at that.

He continues to relate the assistance his wife provides, as well as the expected help that will come with a new program leader:

And she has tended to them well . . . and she's been on this [London program] probably seven or eight times at least. She would make a chili dinner toward the end; by that time the kids have just about run out of money . . . But this year I'm taking a colleague who is an American historian. And he's never been out of the United States . . . Well, he's been to the Bahamas . . . He's really looking forward to this too. But he knows that if something happens to a student, he takes care of them while I take the group to wherever.

Concerns are raised with Coordinator Trevor's method to study abroad leadership. While a supporting component—his wife in this case—is a good addition to a program, this approach is not ideal.

Coordinator Trevor opens up his program and institution to potential consequences because a family member, friend, or spouse does not qualify as an official program leader, unless they are a full-time employee of the institution. A short-term program usually takes on the focus of an academic discipline or two. That co-leader needs to be an expert in the discipline and should already have visited the overseas region.

Even if a spouse is a full-time employee, instructs in the discipline connected to the program, and has been to the foreign location, their serving as a co-leader may still be viewed as a conflict of interest. If inattention to the group results from having a family member, friend, or spouse present, you could be perceived as negligent.

There is an additional concern with Coordinator Trevor's approach. He notes, "But this year I'm taking a colleague who is an American historian. And he's never been out of the United States . . . Well he's been to the Bahamas." Actually, this may be a downgrade from having his wife serve as a co-leader. She has experience co-leading multiple programs to London, whereas the new co-leader has never been out of the country, except for the Bahamas.

Again, it is most ideal for all program leaders to have past experience within a program region. However, if one does not, at the very least, that co-leader should have firsthand knowledge of the area. Coordinators and their institutions should not have lingering questions attached to a study abroad program from the start that include: Is the discipline of the overseas program the same as the supervisor's expertise at the college? Did the supervisor teach the semester course that merges with the overseas program? Hopefully a "yes" answer can always follow each.

A ten to one ratio of students to program leader is recommended for study abroad programs, and a program should never run with less than two leaders. Coordinator Eve and Coordinator Felix also arrange for two program leaders to be present with every twenty participants. Similarly, Coordinator Levi avows "there must be two tour leaders on a program to avoid risks [and] this [is] a policy instilled in [my] study abroad programs."

The chapter 2 section, Leaving No Participant Alone for an Extended Period and a Proper Student/Leader Ratio also provides rationale for utilizing a proper ratio of leaders to participants. In short, with short-term programs, there needs to be a leader available to remain behind if a sick, injured, culturally shocked, or passport-lost participant needs assistance. Meanwhile, the additional program leader, or leaders, may continue to lead the rest of the group.

Evinced by the Courts

Courts support study abroad programs that have a healthy ratio of program leaders to students. This is underscored with *King v. Board of Control of Eastern Michigan University*, *Fay v. Thiel College*, and *Thackurdeen v. Duke University*.

King v. Board of Control of Eastern Michigan University

There were two program organizers for Eastern Michigan University's South Africa program, but only one led the group while abroad.[1] Under no circumstance should a single supervisor lead a short-term program.

Perhaps with an additional program leader, Dr. Okafor would have been given guidance, or gained nerve to address the hostile environment that ensued in South Africa. The case is considered with greater detail in chapter 5.

A brief recap of *King v. Board of Control of Eastern Michigan University* is the Eastern Michigan University program leader was present and neglected to correct male students' address of female students as "bitches," "hoes," "wideloads," and "sluts," or the male students' soliciting of South African women for sex from the tour bus, or resolving a threat made by one student to "slit [the] throat" of another.[2] As a result, seven students left the program more than a week before its scheduled conclusion.[3]

Fay v. Thiel College

Even when a program has a sufficient ratio of program supervisors to participants, coordinators must be able to determine how to properly distribute supervision among participants. *Fay v. Thiel College* brings this concern to the forefront. There were three program leaders in place for the Peru program, and all three left student Amy Fay alone in a foreign clinic for several days as they continued the program with other participants.[4] During that time, Fay was sexually assaulted and subjected to the unnecessary surgical removal of her appendix.[5]

The court asserted that the college could be held liable for Fay's injuries merely with a finding that "(1) 'abandoning' [Fay] in the Peruvian medical clinic was likely to create a situation whereby the male Peruvian doctors could take sexual advantage of a young American female, and (2) the male Peruvian doctors might avail themselves of the opportunity to commit such a tort and/or crime."[6] It is doubtful that the issue of abandonment would have surfaced if a program leader remained behind with Fay at the clinic. With three program leaders in place, having one remain with Fay seemed doable. Chapters 2 and 5 go further in depth with the case.

Thackurdeen v. Duke University

Again, coordinators and their institutions need to produce study abroad programs that have a healthy supervisor/student ratio. Yet if program supervisors give poor care to students, that ratio serves to be useless. This issue is at the forefront with *Thackurdeen v. Duke University*.

The lawsuit points out that Duke University's Organization of Tropical Studies (OTS) program brochures convey that a "low student-to-faculty ratio [exists so that] professors will provide [students] with close personal attention."[7]

Program leaders brought Ravi Thackurdeen and the other students to Playa Tortuga beach.[8] While there, Thackurdeen was caught in a rip current and drowned.[9]

The suit claims that students were told that it was safe to swim in the waters and were given the sole instruction to swim parallel to the shore if they were caught in a rip current.[10] Whether Thackurdeen received proper attention from supervisors was put to question.

If brought to trial, a court can determine the number of program leaders who were present during the tragic event. Hopefully, an appropriate ratio of supervisors to students existed. In addition, a court should determine if program leaders gave proper care to Thackurdeen and students at the beach. Again, even if a healthy supervisor/student ratio existed at the beach and supervisors were negligent, the ratio is negligible.

17. Emergency Response Plan

Various coordinators emphasize the need to have an emergency response plan in place while abroad. As a part of that plan, emergency evacuation is necessary for sudden risks that might arise including terrorist attacks, breakout of epidemics, natural disasters, and serious injuries.

Coordinator Trevor recalls a student who was nearly killed due to a series of coordinated terrorist bombings in central London that targeted civilians. City trains and a double-decker bus were destroyed in the attacks; his student happened to be on the double-decker bus. He describes, "[An] incident abroad occurred when a student was in London at the time of [terrorist] bombings. He was actually on the top part of a Double Decker [bus] in which the bomb went off. The first three rows were totally destroyed. He was in the fourth row. His ears continued to ring a long time after this, so incidents do occur."

This student was fortunate to narrowly escape serious injury, even death. Increasing threats of terrorism have plagued study abroad. Coordinator Pearl concurs. "I do think terrorism is becoming a problem." This is a bit of an understatement. The threat of terrorism for American students is significant, and therefore, merited attention in a chapter—chapter 6, Increasing Concerns with Cyberthreats, Identity Theft, and Terrorist Acts.

The support of an emergency response group or committee must be in place at the home campus should an overseas emergency arise. Coordinator Poppy appropriately describes the group—"an on-campus committee [looks] at emergency response here at [the college]. [Study abroad officials] work with that committee to [form] an emergency response plan [in] the event of an emergency that [is] all outlined for the faculty [who intend to lead study abroad] in handbooks so they know that before they go [abroad]."

A plan and accompanying handbook augments safety for participants. Designated committee members must also be prepared to carry out emergency plans. Even if their communication is lost or blocked from participants abroad, a committee leader, or leaders, should be gauging the group's activities according to the daily itinerary. With this information, committee members can know if an emergency plan needs to be enacted without being contacted by program leaders abroad.

Essential background information and contacts for all study abroad participants should be left with the campus security office; therefore, the committee leader can always access vital information about participants. This is also helpful should a sudden, inexplicable medical emergency occur with a participant abroad. A family member may be contacted to discover if the participant has a preexisting medical issue that brought on the malady.

Just as study abroad leaders must be alert with potential threats abroad, so must the emergency response members. Again, with consideration to terrorist threats, the U.S. State Department does not list every terrorist threat. Few if any safe havens exist for American travelers. This is what Coordinator Trevor came to realize due to terrorist bombings that disrupted his student's program in London.

In addition, terrorism comes in many forms, not just violent acts committed by fringe groups. Kidnapping and human trafficking pose legitimate threats for Americans abroad. Again, details on the topic are provided in chapter 6, Increasing Concerns with Cyberthreats, Identity Theft, and Terrorist Acts.

Emergency response plans are integral to shielding participants from foreign disease outbreaks. This is why Coordinator Lonna formed a committee to create an emergency response plan and to produce a handbook to assist faculty-led programs:

> In light of all the Avian flu stuff, we had a campus committee looking at emergency response here at [the college]. [Study abroad officials] worked with that committee to [form] an emergency

response plan [in] the event of an emergency that [is] all outlined for faculty [leaders] in hand-books so they know that before they go. . . . They will be responsible, God forbid, [if] something were to happen in a country where they were with students.

Likewise, Coordinator Pearl has an emergency evacuation plan in place to safeguard students from sudden epidemics abroad.

I am also realizing if we are have a pandemic or there was something horrendous going on in the world, how am I going to get my students out of there? I register them with the American embassy [and] I know where the air force bases are because they will evacuate Americans for free [and] get them out of there. If [participants] have to stay there, I actually have an agreement with my partners [abroad] that they have special insurance for [participants] if they are not allowed to come back.

Coordinator Pearl adeptly brings forth three groups to assist with an emergency response plan—the U.S. embassy, American air force bases, and the partnering travel agency. Program leaders should certainly know the location of the closest U.S. embassy, or a similar branch to it, should they need quick safety in a foreign country. Therefore, registering with the U.S. State Department is an important step for risk management.

Here is how to register with the U.S. State Department and American embassies. You should directly go through the U.S. Department of State, which works with consular officers in American embassies around the world.[11] The U.S. Department of State webpage allows individuals to register with the Smart Traveler Enrollment Program (STEP).[12] STEP has replaced dated programs such as Travel Registration or Registration with Embassies.[13] Once registered with STEP, country-specific information, travel alerts and warnings, fact sheets, and emergency messages are provided to the participant.[14]

In addition, the free service helps with recovering lost or stolen passports, and aids with the evacuation of U.S. citizens in emergency situations.[15] This is a great service that should be utilized. Students should bring abroad a photocopy of the pictured page of their passport, as well as a passport-sized photo; this will expedite the process with getting a new passport if the original comes up missing.

Coordinator Pearl makes a good point, of which coordinators may not be aware—the U.S. Air Force will assist with emergency evacuation. It is just a matter of there being a base near the overseas location.

Coordinators must also be in frequent contact with the partnering travel agency members in order to remain abreast of potential threats prior to or during overseas travel. If a threat arises while abroad, any respectable travel agency will assist with arranging safe departure through the airlines. Again, the U.S. embassy, the U.S. Air Force, and regional police may also assist with emergency situations and evacuations.

Additionally, coordinators acknowledge that the sudden onset of a natural disaster is a common hazard with study abroad. Therefore, there should be an emergency committee and plan prepared to assist. Coordinator Tabitha "researches emergency evacuation options due to concern for natural disasters."

My own experience confirms that natural disasters can be a common problem with study abroad. For example, one of my students dealt with calamity resulting from a major earthquake while studying for a semester in New Zealand. Fortunately, the student was uninjured. However, his campus was so damaged by the natural disaster that it was deemed unsafe for use. My student was given the option to come home or continue with his studies at a separate, distant college that had remained intact from the earthquake. He chose to remain in New Zealand to finish his studies.

The partnering institution and I had an emergency response plan in place that allowed for the student to transfer to the other institution some fifty miles away. There, the student was able to complete his semester and coursework. During our postprogram meeting my student spoke with pride in having persevered over trials brought from the quake, and success with adjusting to *two* college environments in a foreign land. In the end, he believed this trial made him more resolute in completing his education. I think he was absolutely correct. He successfully graduated from our institution the semester after his return from New Zealand.

As previously noted, U.S. embassies and U.S. Air Force bases assist with emergency evacuation. But you still need to get to these locations to be evacuated, which may not be practical for a student who is alone overseas. Student participants, for long term or short term study abroad, should have evacuation insurance as part of their medical plan, prior to departure. Coordinators need to make this a requirement. Serious accidents and injuries sustained by participants in isolated regions may also require medevac by helicopter to get quick treatment at proper medical facilities.

University of Florida

Courts also affirm that hazards and lawsuits may result if study abroad participants fail to procure evacuation insurance coverage. For example, a lawsuit against the University of Florida apprised university officials of the pitfalls that come with students not having emergency evacuation insurance in place.

A student was severely burned when a kerosene lamp exploded while participating in the University of Florida's Bolivia program.[16] Its officials had not required medical insurance with emergency evacuation, and the university chartered a plane to bring her back to the United States at the cost of $50,000.[17]

In consequence, the associate director of educational exchange at the University of Florida reassessed this policy; the result was a new policy, also noted in their waiver, necessitating participants to purchase evacuation medical insurance.[18]

Build Into Your Waiver

Among sample waivers used by coordinators, only Waiver C (Appendix C) mentioned the need for study abroad participants to acquire emergency evacuation insurance. It specifically states that "health, accident and emergency evacuation insurance coverage is required of all participants in College study abroad programs." This type of inclusion should appear in waivers as a reminder for students to obtain this, and to further solidify a policy that all institutions should have. It is also best to make the policy clear and present in orientation materials and other risk-averting documents beyond the waiver.

Thackurdeen v. Duke University Reveals the Need for an Emergency Response Plan

Thackurdeen v. Duke University considers the importance of having an emergency plan in place when conducting study abroad. The lawsuit discloses that Duke University student Ravi Thackurdeen drowned in Playa Tortuga on the afternoon of April 29, 2012; his body was not located or pulled out of the water until thirty-six hours later.[19] In part, the lawsuit charges the university with being negligent in creating and implementing an emergency plan in response to dangers and the resulting tragedy at Playa Tortuga.[20]

To prove this, the suit details ways that the university failed to properly act during the emergency and thereafter. Ravi and a fellow student were wading in shallow water when they got caught in a rip current that pulled them out to sea.[21] A tourist swam out and was able to save the classmate's life.[22] However, Ravi was pulled over three hundred yards away from the shore and treaded water for over thirty minutes while waiting for help.[23]

According to the suit, in response to the emergency, university officials failed to assist Ravi after he was caught in the rip current and yelled out for help, and did not rescue him from drowning in Playa Tortuga.[24]

The lawsuit also charges the university with an improper emergency response plan to recover Ravi. When the Thackurdeen parents arrived in Costa Rica to the beach where Ravi was last seen, the family joined the Red Cross and the coast guard in the search for Ravi.[25] According to the suit, Duke and the Organization of Tropical Studies (OTS) agreed to provide the search team with supplies, such as water and flashlights, but the supplies never came.[26]

The lawsuit notes that the lack of supplies caused the search team to disband at nighttime, with only the head of the Red Cross team staying behind with the Thackurdeens to continue the search.[27] Since they did not have any flashlights, the Thackurdeens could only use the moonlight and the headlights from the cars to continue the search throughout the night.[28]

In addition, the suit conveys that the very next day, on April 30, 2012, while Ravi's dead body was still missing in the ocean, Duke and OTS took their students out to celebrate the last day of the program in Costa Rica.[29] The next day, Ravi's body was located by a local fisherman at approximately 5:30 a.m. on May 1, 2012.[30]

More so, the lawsuit faults the university's lack of emergency plan and procedures for transporting students in the case of an emergency (or in this case, death). The suit details "even after this tragic death, Duke and OTS failed to take appropriate care of Ravi. Ravi's body was transported on the back of an open truck in 90 degree weather for approximately four and a half hours for the autopsy, with no ice or other attempts to preserve the body."[31] This left Ravi's body in a worse state.

A court trial had not taken place prior to the publishing of this book. However, the concern with having a proper emergency response plan in place is clearly an issue outlined in the lawsuit.

18. Participants with Disabilities and the Americans with Disabilities Act

Coordinators are immensely challenged by the task of expertly serving the needs of students with disabilities who go overseas. Chapter 3's section, Disability Support and Its Implications with Medical Liability, gives increased insight into the matter. Concerns include limited study abroad promotion geared toward this group and inconsistent protections provided by courts for these students. In addition, the section gives coordinators resources for advising these students, and offers a "top 10" list of "best practices" that may be implemented to serve students with disabilities who study abroad.

Coordinators admit having difficulty with creating solutions that allow for inclusion of students with disabilities in study abroad. The coordinators believe that increased risks for students, the program, and institution may result from their participation. Though his experience is limited, Coordinator Levi puts a lot of thought into how to serve students with disabilities while keeping program costs affordable:

> I've never had to send a student abroad with a disability. Many countries do not have disability support services, and even if they are provided by the host college, it becomes enormously expensive to send someone abroad. If someone is deaf, what if a school doesn't have signers? Then you have to send a signer abroad and it becomes extraordinarily expensive for the college involved.

He further surmises, "So [coordinators] have to find a way to make things available for disability students, and there are some countries that do provide services. But you need to know which ones they are. When students [come] to me with disabilities, I [have] to ask our host organizations what schools provide for deaf or blind or disability support. Then that way I can send the disability student abroad."

I would point to the Resources for Coordinators to Aid Students with Disabilities section of chapter 3 as a starting point for Coordinator Levi to gain increased awareness for serving students with disabilities.

Coordinator Poppy places the needs of students with disabilities at the forefront of her program coordination, and suitably consults outside handbooks for solutions:

> [Study abroad coordinators] have to be looking at how the university itself actually addresses disability issues. And you can have universities that take very different approaches. Some universities in terms of [being] Americans with Disabilities Act (ADA) compliant adhere to beyond a compliance philosophy, which means that not only are they actively encouraging students with disabilities to participate in things, but they are actually making it possible for them to do it beyond the letter of the law.

She continues to aptly note that "Mobility International is an advocacy group that has spent a lot of time looking at the issues of ADA compliance. And they've put together a handbook that is almost two hundred and fifty pages long which basically looks at study abroad issues. So it's an excellent resource."

Overall, coordinators feel a profound desire to serve the needs of students with disabilities, and to honor the Americans with Disabilities Act. At the same time, they feel anxieties—in order to effectively serve these students, their program costs will have to skyrocket, and risks and liabilities could increase.

Courts Consider Students with Disabilities Studying Abroad

Furrh v. Arizona Board of Regents, *Bird v. Lewis & Clark College*, and *Arizona State University* give perspective on how coordinators may properly assist students with disabilities who take part in study abroad.

Furrh v. Arizona Board of Regents

Furrh v. Arizona Board of Regents instructively shows how coordinators appropriately contained a potentially dangerous situation abroad with a mentally ill participant. It was done with respect and care for the participant.

A court cited thirty-four separate findings to explain the bizarre emergency created by University of Arizona student Jonathan Furrh's conduct while studying abroad in Mexico.[32] In brief, on several occasions, including after dark, Furrh ran away from the group, once to the village of Bahia de los Angeles, fifteen miles away.[33] The site where the study group had its permanent camp was in a remote area, and the surrounding desert and mountains were dangerous.[34] Both rattlesnakes and cholla cactus presented serious problems.[35]

Aside from presenting danger to himself, he posed a potential threat to group members. On the way from the village to camp, Furrh was taken by a delusion that he was in the custody of the Mafia and that [members of the group] were going to kill him.[36] Furrh thereupon attempted to jump from the moving vehicle and had to be physically restrained.[37] In the ensuing struggle, Furrh obtained a knife, which the other members of the party present at the time reasonably believed he intended or might have used on them.[38]

During this time, and at other necessary times, members of the party acted reasonably and properly in attempting to restrain him.[39] While he was so restrained he was in the company of Dr. Keith Pierce, who attempted to make sure that Furrh was not unduly uncomfortable, that he was fed, and that his needs were attended to.[40] During this period Furrh showed no fear or irrational belief that he was in the custody of anyone wishing him harm.[41]

The case is a lesson in showing that suitable treatment should come with an emotionally and cognitively ailing student. The program leaders' course of action brought safety to the ill student as well as to other participants.

Legal Officials Give Conflicting Messages on Extraterritorial Status of the Rehabilitation Act and Americans with Disabilities Act

Two key pieces of legislation, Section 504 of the Rehabilitation Act (1973) and the Americans with Disabilities Act, serve to protect people with disabilities. Section 504 gives civil rights protection to people with disabilities,[42] and the Americans with Disabilities Act (ADA) prohibits discrimination against people with disabilities in employment, transportation, public accommodation, communications, and governmental activities.[43]

In addition, the Department of Education's Office for Civil Rights (OCR) enforces Section 504 and the ADA as they relate to disability accommodations for college and university students.[44]

Legal officials have sent conflicting messages concerning whether the same duty of care shown to individuals with disabilities on campus may be expected with study abroad. Therefore, extraterritorial application of Section 504 and the ADA remains unsettled in U.S. courts. To be clear, extraterritorial application relates to whether federal disability discrimination laws are applicable to overseas programs.

Bird v. Lewis & Clark College

With *Bird v. Lewis & Clark College*, a federal district court in Oregon held that Section 504 and the ADA *do* apply to a study abroad program.[45] Student Arwen Bird used a wheelchair to participate in Lewis & Clark College's own sponsored study abroad program in Australia.[46] For the majority of the activities, the college accommodated her disability; at times she had to be carried.[47]

At the conclusion of the program, Bird sued the college for being in violation of Section 504 and ADA claims.[48] Bird's claim is that while staying in Australia, the college discriminated against her on the basis of disability by failing to provide her with wheelchair access.[49]

The district court emphasized that Bird was an American student participating in an American university's overseas program, taught by American faculty.[50] In addition, the court cautioned that if Section 504 and the ADA did not apply to study abroad programs, "students in overseas programs would become the proverbial 'floating sanctuaries from authority' not unlike stateless vessels on the high seas."[51]

On appeal, the Ninth Circuit did not address the district court's ruling on extraterritoriality, yet nonetheless denied the plaintiff's Section 504 and ADA claims, finding that Lewis & Clark's program, "when viewed in its entirety, [was] readily accessible to and usable by individuals with disabilities."[52]

Noteworthy is the fact that while the court denied the student's federal discrimination claims, the court determined that the college had a fiduciary relationship with the student under state law because the college assured the student that it would accommodate her disability and indicated that adequate facilities would be available for most of the outdoor trips.[53]

Also, the court found that the student had reason to trust the college's guarantees since the college had accommodated the student on the home campus. [54]

The rulings in *Bird v. Lewis & Clark College* connote that the same duty of care and rights afforded to students with disabilities under U.S. law should also take place overseas, and that those rights will be protected in a court of law. However, other court rulings are not consistent with *Bird v. Lewis & Clark College*.

Arizona State University

Law officials are not consistent with granting equal protection to students with disabilities while abroad as given at the home campus. This has been made clear with one Department of Education's Office for Civil Rights (OCR), which has openly made its position known that the ADA and Section 504 *do not* apply to overseas programs. [55]

A case with Arizona State University has fueled this controversy. A deaf student asked university officials to provide a sign language interpreter for him while he studied abroad at an Irish university. [56] The university rejected the request, and the student filed a complaint with OCR. [57]

In reply, OCR determined that "Section 504 and Title II protections *do not* extend extraterritorially . . . [n]or does either statute otherwise prohibit discrimination on the basis of disability in overseas programs." [58]

However, in contrast to this decision, OCR area offices determined that under certain factual scenarios, Section 504 and the ADA *do* apply to study abroad programs. [59] Those cases involved Husson College, College of St. Scholastica, and St. Louis University. [60]

Consequently, there is no clear indication as to whether students with disabilities will receive extraterritorial application of Section 504 and the Americans with Disabilities Act by law officials. However, coordinators must continue to make the greatest efforts to comply with Section 504 and ADA standards with study abroad programs in order to best accommodate students with disabilities.

19. Waivers and Their Construction

Coordinators have given a range of responses from "ineffective" to "extremely effective" to describe how well waivers serve to protect against risks and liabilities with study abroad. Coordinator Poppy argues, "the waiver in itself does not do anything," while Coordinator Levi believes "the waiver . . . allows for the minimization of risks."

The Issue of Overgeneralized Wording in Waivers

Long-winded, lengthy risk-averting documents are frequently used with study abroad programs. Coordinator Pearl accurately relates "that a judge might throw out a waiver in a case if it were wordy, deeming it ineffective." Sometimes the waiver serves as the institution's main line of defense. So when a judge dismisses it, the college no longer "has a leg to stand on." This is another reason for providing thorough orientation sessions to accompany waivers. But let's continue to focus on overgeneralized wording in waivers and its impact.

The Risk of a Waiver Not Being Read

There is the increased potential for students to skim, or not fully read through, a waiver that is repetitive and wordy. Coordinator Pearl is aware, and notes that "if a student signed a waiver, but did not read it, then the waiver was pointless."

The Issue of a Laundry-List-of-the-Blameless Approach to the Waiver

Lengthy waivers often provide a great laundry list of named individuals and groups who will not be held accountable if study abroad issues occur. Too much of this kind of language may serve to weaken the effectiveness of the waiver. Words may be better spent informing students of potential dangers and specifying expected conduct for the program. Coordinator Pearl is similarly critical:

> [Waivers] that I've been noticing now have everything in there and include any airlines or bus services. Anything [or anyone that coordinators] hire or use, whether it is public or private transportation, is mentioned in [the waiver stating] they are not responsible. So it's expanded to include almost everything but the grandmother that they are not going to be accountable for. . . . Some of these are two or three pages.

Again, wording in longer waivers that contain a sizable list of unaccountable parties may be better spent yielding practical risks and safeguards connected to the program location.

Program Specificity Is Desirable in Waiver Descriptions

Coordinator Levi also relates dissatisfaction with his current "institutional waiver [that] uses language that [is] outdated and long-winded, making it lack some effectiveness." He is critical of legal counsel, which assists him with waiver construction:

> [What] we use is a four- to five-page document that was developed by me with legal counsel from the college and it was reviewed every year, and brought up to date. And there were times I felt things needed to be reworded to be more appropriate to the time we were in the moment. And since the world is changing so much we need to do some changing with the waiver form to address problems we have and have no control over.

His point that "since the world is changing so much we need to do some changing with the waiver form" is telling. Recent and increasing concerns have arisen with study abroad, such as cyberattacks, identity theft, and terrorist threats. This is detailed in chapter 6, Increasing Concerns with Cyber Threats, Identity Theft and Terrorist Acts. Therefore, threats germane to study abroad, *along with* statements about regional-specific risks, need to be included in waivers.

The Healthy Tension between Coordinators and Legal Counsel

When it comes to waiver construction, a natural opposition between coordinators and legal counsel has been widespread and long standing. Yet this is a *healthy* tension. In general, coordinators desire more program-specific, nonrepetitive language to produce a short, succinct waiver. Legal counsel tends to want documents to be legally sound, without potentially leaving out official language; often, that official language is repetitive and adds length to a waiver.

Each side pushes for the most articulate document to protect participants and the institution. If equilibrium occurs, likely the most suitable document results. The Malveaux Sample Recommended Waiver is provided to give coordinators and legal counsel an exemplary waiver to work from. They should alter it as needed to fit their own institution's needs.

The feelings of Coordinator Levi underscore this tension: "I have complained to legal counsel about having [participants] read all that, and absorb all that, because I have seen forms only a page long. But they refused to change it based on the fact that even though it is repetitive, they feel it is important for a student to be signing a document they are sure the student has been reminded about what is [expected conduct]."

Yet he should continue to push for succinct language that addresses individual program risks and requirements. Again, overgeneralized, wordy expression in risk-averting documents has not served study abroad programs and institutions well with recent court trends. Two cases immediately come to mind—*Fay v. Thiel College* and *Paneno v. Centres*.

Overgeneralized Waivers according to Fay v. Thiel College and Paneno v. Centres

The court in *Fay v. Thiel College* rejected the medical consent form as a means of protection for Thiel College. "The consent form [did] not spell out, with the greatest of particularity and by express stipulation, the intention of the parties to release Thiel College from any liability stemming from any medical decisions that one or more of the faculty supervisors made on behalf of, or in conjunction with, a student while participating in the Thiel-sponsored study abroad trip to Peru . . . [and] is *not* . . . a waiver of liability."[61] The risk-averting document was not only vague in expression but also was not recognized as a waiver (even though college officials believed it to be).

Then of course with *Paneno v. Centres*, a seemingly irritated judge felt that the provider, CAPA, gave vague wording in their waiver as a means to avoid accountability,[62] and the judge chided CAPA for using "trickery."[63]

Westmont College as a Case Study

For coordinators who are eager to dismiss waivers as unessential, I would caution them to consider litigation that was aimed at Westmont College. The college was left vulnerable to liability when there was no waiver in place for the study abroad program.[64] Incidentally, a Westmont College student who participated in a program with the Coalition for Christian Colleges and Universities in Costa Rica was bitten by a mosquito and contracted leishmaniasis, which causes disfigurement.[65]

The student sued the college and the coalition, charging they had not adequately warned her of the risks.[66] The lawsuit was settled out of court, prior to trial.[67] Up until that lawsuit, the Coalition for Christian Colleges and Universities (and Westmont College) had never required such a release; the court ruled in favor of the student.[68] After the lawsuit, the institution altered its policy and now uses waivers.[69]

Clarity and Consistency Lacking with Currently Used Waivers

Of all the sample waivers currently used by coordinators, only Sample Waiver F (see Appendix F) includes a statement on "terrorist activities" as a risk. Yet in the same waiver, there is no mention of potential disease transmission as a potential hazard with study abroad. Balance and consistency is lacking with these sample waivers, and with many waivers on a whole in study abroad. If you are not going to identify the common risks with study abroad, at least address the risks specific to that program's region.

The Malveaux Sample Recommended Waiver (see Appendix I) is designed to assist coordinators with waiver construction. It includes a statement on the potential threat of terrorist attacks and disease transmission, among other concerns, that may come with study abroad:

I understand that I am not required by Perilpure College (the College) to participate in this particular program. I further understand that there are certain inherent risks associated with any travel abroad and with the participation in a program of this type. These inherent risks may include, but are not limited to, terrorist threats and political unrest, a lack of access to health care, potential disease native to the area, sexual assault and other crimes, dangers associated with public or private transportation, safety of the road systems and other means of transportation.

Again, general waivers and risk-averting documents should be amended in order to give description of the unique risks, customs, and laws for a program region. This also holds true for the Malveaux Sample Recommended Waiver; in its current form, it is general in description. Certainly it takes more work to tailor fit a waiver for each program, but the succinct details will bring improved safeguards to participants. In turn, this will potentially offset legal issues for the institution.

20. Code of Conduct and Policy

Coordinators affirm that study abroad hazards and liability issues diminish when policies and code of conduct from the institution's handbook are included in study abroad materials. Coordinator Trevor, for example, uses his college's code of conduct to regulate behavior abroad:

> Our study abroad program is mirrored by student conduct [at the college]. If you become a problem child in my class, I can have you removed. If you become a problem child in London, England, I can send you on a plane, and you will pay for it. I can send you back home. That's the classroom—London, England, is the classroom. So the student handbook and code of conduct we mirror in London.

Moreover, to assure that students adhere to the set code of conduct, Coordinator Eve requires each student to say the college's honor pledge prior to and during study abroad. "Our students also take an honor pledge when they come to the college. And it's social as well as academic. So, we always say the honor pledge holds while you are abroad as well as being here. [They repeat that honor pledge abroad]. We generally don't have problems."

This gesture may seem minor, but if it encourages participants to respect the proper code of conduct, it is quite useful. Having participants witness each another making the pledge will likely help to solidify it.

Other coordinators believe a signed pledge is an effective approach for enforcing the institution's code of conduct. For example, consider Coordinator Desiree's approach to clarifying expected student conduct: "We have a written participant code of conduct agreement form that is discussed at the initial orientation meeting. Participants sign the document and are provided with a copy of it. The document outlines behavioral expectations and the consequences of violating them."

Again, coordinators advocate for the college code of conduct and policy to be merged into study abroad programs. Coordinator Felix maintains that "every college or university has a certain philosophy of instruction that can be found in its institutional handbook, and it [is] helpful for study abroad programs to consistently follow such policies."

Likewise, to ensure this approach, Coordinator Poppy recommends:

> [Coordinators get] a policy handbook, a manual, and [other] information that sort of governs the university's philosophy and approach, [and then make] study abroad a part of that. That is something I've designed to share with students and to share with parents as well. [This] is reinforced in [study abroad] orientation materials and in predeparture materials, and that it should be something that echoes the forms [coordinators] want to be writing.

She continues to provide suggestions on ways to merge college policies into study abroad programs:

> For example, our study abroad handbook will say . . . that it comes right out of the NAFSA guidelines that study abroad safety, [security,] and well-being is a shared responsibility . . . [It] is reiterated in the Study Abroad Conditions of Participation form which really sets the expectations for a student. And in some ways becomes a contract between the student and the university and the expectations for their behavior when they are abroad. That at the very beginning says [participants] are responsible for [their] own actions and decisions, and echoes that shared responsibility that is in the handbook.

Risk-averting documents in themselves are useful with informing students about expected conduct that mirrors institutional policies. Sample Waiver H (see Appendix H), Study Abroad Participant Conduct Agreement, especially serves this purpose. At the same time, coordinators should confer with legal counsel to see if the document is a compatible fit with their own institutional policies.

Policy for student conduct is habitually made clear in waivers. However, expectations for program leaders are not always emphasized. Court cases and lawsuits in chapter 5, The Tragedy of Supervisory Neglect in Study Abroad, show that program leaders will be held accountable for their actions abroad.

This *shared* responsibility means that clear expectations of the program leader's approach are outlined for participants. Risk-averting documents should reflect this shared responsibility. This concern is also addressed in the Clear Delineation of Roles and Responsibilities with Program Leaders in Waivers section in chapter 5.

Courts Expect College Policy and Code of Conduct to Be Echoed in Study Abroad Programs

Bloss v. The University of Minnesota Board of Regents illustrates that courts favor study abroad programs that clearly echo the expected code of conduct and policies set by the home institution and its affiliates. Study abroad orientation materials and handbooks that reiterate language in the institutional code of conduct and policy handbook serve to reduce potential risks and liabilities. This point is confirmed with *Bloss v. The University of Minnesota Board of Regents* and *King v. Board of Control of Eastern Michigan University*.

Bloss v. The University of Minnesota Board of Regents

During her study abroad with the University of Minnesota's cultural immersion program in Cuernavaca, Mexico, student Adrienne Bloss alleges that while traveling to meet friends for a social evening she was raped at knifepoint by a taxi driver.[70]

Bloss sued the University of Minnesota for negligence due to failure to secure housing closer to the Cemanahuac campus, imprudence in not providing transportation to and from the campus, and inattention to impart warnings about various serious risks, including the use of taxicabs in Cuernavaca.[71]

The favorable decision that was awarded to the university was due in large part to having related the standards of conduct expected of participants who partake in the program.[72] Orientation materials gave warning about dangerous behavior for the region.[73]

The warnings included specific admonitions that it was dangerous for women to go out alone at night, they should call for a taxi at night rather than hail a taxi on the street, and that women should never sit in the front seat of taxis.[74] These warnings specifically addressed the circumstances under which the student sustained her injuries.[75]

The misfortune that fell upon the student Bloss is extremely sad. Yet good that can come from *Bloss v. The University of Minnesota Board of Regents* is that it demonstrates that college policy and code of conduct should be echoed in study abroad program materials. It did not serve to Bloss's advantage, but the hope is that by restating institutional policy and code of conduct in study abroad materials, most students will be more enlightened with how to remain safe. Plus, courts are likely to hold a more favorable outlook for institutions that distinctly outline policies and procedures for study abroad students.

King v. Board of Control of Eastern Michigan University

In contrast, *King v. Board of Control of Eastern Michigan University* is a case in point that perils and legal issues can result when a supervisor ignores an institution's set policies. Codes of conduct and policy must not only apply to students but also to program leaders. The faculty supervisor shirked school policy by allowing a hostile environment to ensue in South Africa where male students sexually harassed female students without censure.[76] The hostile environment that arose is fully detailed in chapter 5, but here are some brief, pertinent facts.

The Eastern Michigan University (EMU) program leader was present and failed to act during times when male students referred to female students as "bitches," "hoes," "wide-loads," and "sluts," when male students solicited South African women for sex from the tour bus, and when a student complained that another student threatened to "slit his throat."[77] The program concluded with seven students leaving the program more than a week before its scheduled conclusion.[78]

In consequence, the court directly pointed out where the university's policies and code of conduct were not followed.[79] The university has a set campus policy that allows students a secure instructional environment; when this code is violated, faculty instructors are supposed to diffuse the disruption.[80]

Practices for the study abroad program should also hold true to federal policy.[81] Plaintiffs were persons in the United States when denied equal access to EMU's resources, created by EMU's failure to address and stop the actions of disruptive participants.[82] When the female students were disallowed institutional resources and were discriminated on the basis of sex, although initiated abroad, the program was always under the control of EMU in every respect, rather than under the control of any foreign educational facility.[83]

Last, the court maintained that the faculty supervisor was in violation of the university's set policy, and as an agent working on behalf of the university, the university was also in violation of its own set policies.[84] Coordinators put programs and their institutions at risk by not integrating institutional policy while abroad. The faculty leader should have followed policies and code of conduct that were outlined in institutional handbooks, mission statements, and other educational materials.

Reiterate Policies and Expected Conduct within Waivers

All of the current sample waivers outline expected conduct, roles, and responsibilities for participants while abroad.

Waiver E (Appendix E) provides a statement for the participant to acknowledge this:

> I understand that each foreign country has its own laws and standards of acceptable conduct, including dress, manners, morals, politics, drug use, and behavior. I recognize the behavior that violates those laws or standards could harm the College's relations with those countries and the institution therein, as well as my own health and safety. I will become informed of, and will abide

by, all such laws and standards for each country to or through which I will travel during the Activity.

Additionally, waivers offer ways to help minimize risks and liabilities in higher-education study abroad by encouraging prudent conduct among participants. Waiver E (Appendix E) takes this approach: "I also agree that I will (a) not buy, sell, or use illegal drugs any time, (b) not engage in abusive use of alcohol, (c) participate in all classes and scheduled activities unless ill, and (d) abide by dress and cultural codes suitable in the countries visited."

Risk-averting documents and waivers can serve as excellent tools to further echo institutional policies and code of conduct also reflected in study abroad materials and orientation. This may serve to further inform study abroad participants of expected behaviors, and in turn serve to aid risk prevention while overseas.

21. Foreign Housing Assignments

Careful review of brochures that describe foreign housing and residence hall regulations is essential according to coordinators. In fact, Coordinator Pearl conveys that "a residence administrator from our home institution works in the housing unit abroad [which] is provided for [our] study abroad students." This is a luxury for most institutions. The ability to have a home college administrator present at each foreign program location is not only a rarity but often unrealistic due to limited resources. More feasible steps that can be taken are considered in this section.

Clearly, coordinators should orient participants about their housing arrangements prior to departing. As Coordinator Poppy remarks, "Information on housing should be in study abroad participants' predeparture materials."

Coordinator Eve had a student who dealt with a homestay issue that is not rare with study abroad. Apparently, the student was sexually harassed by a host family member while engaging in the college's study abroad program in Mexico. As Coordinator Eve recalls:

> One of the students claimed that the son of the host family in which she was living invited her to the top of the roof to look at the sunset. She claimed he made an advance on her, and so she called home all upset and her mother called me. So we called the [foreign] school; we told her she had to contact the [foreign] school—take care of it and report it and all. She did, and the [foreign] school investigated it. We were constantly back and forth [by phone] with [officials of] the [foreign] school, with the student, with the parents, and so forth.

To her credit, Coordinator Eve quickly secured the potentially dangerous situation:

> And the student [was] immediately [taken] from that family and [the foreign school] put her with a different family. But she was freaked out and decided she was coming home. So [our college] made arrangements, and paid the supplemental difference in airfare to exchange her ticket. And [it] didn't go anywhere beyond that [in the form of a lawsuit].

She concludes, "It was a pretty bad situation with parents and grandparents involved. It seemed to take care of itself with her coming home. We offered to pay the ticket for her to come home. I could see no sense in saying she had to stay [even after] she was in a different house."

Securing safe housing for students is certainly achievable by coordinators. It just means that they must be extra vigilant with vetting foreign program providers who assign housing for students. Research the provider's past history with garnering secure housing. Make sure that they have successfully done so for numerous years. In addition, check to see that the foreign provider has gained a responsible, enduring relationship with community members. To ensure this, Coordinator Desiree works "with an educational group based in the country."

Personally visit the study abroad housing accommodations furnished by your existing provider. As Coordinator Eve suggests, risk and liability issues are deterred when study abroad coordinators "closely scrutinize housing assignments issued by foreign providers for their participants." If this is not possible, keep close dialogue with the foreign administrator in charge of housing.

Courts Also Consider the Issue of Secure Accommodations for Study Abroad Students

Courts have had to scrutinize proper duty of care for study abroad participants resulting from living arrangements procured by coordinators and their institutions. Correlating cases include *Paneno v. Centres*, *Bloss v. The University of Minnesota Board of Regents*, and *Earlham v. Eisenberg*.

Paneno v. Centres

Student Rocky Paneno lived in an apartment in Florence with roommates while participating in a Pasadena Community College (PCC)–sponsored study abroad program.[85] PCC provided the accommodations for Paneno through the partnering travel agency, Centres for Academic Programmes Abroad (CAPA).[86]

Paneno and a friend were on the apartment's balcony; Paneno leaned against the balcony railing and a portion of it gave way.[87] He fell six stories and sustained serious injuries, including paralysis, as a result.[88] Paneno sued CAPA, which made the housing arrangements, and the court ruled in his favor.[89]

This case underscores the point that coordinators should closely examine housing assignments issued by foreign providers for students. When this is not possible, coordinators must keep close dialogue with the foreign administrator in charge of housing.

Bloss v. The University of Minnesota Board of Regents

Bloss v. The University of Minnesota Board of Regents also marks a case that examined proper accommodations procured for a study abroad student. Student Adrienne Bloss, while participating in the University of Minnesota's cultural immersion program in Cuernavaca, Mexico, traveled to meet friends for a social evening and was raped at knifepoint by a taxi driver.[90]

Bloss was housed with a host family that lived approximately 2.5 miles from Cemanahuac, thirty minutes by bus or ten minutes by car.[91] She took the bus to and from school and to attend social and cultural events.[92] In her lawsuit, Bloss held the university at fault for failing to secure housing closer to the Cemanahuac campus.[93]

Bloss v. The University of Minnesota Board of Regents substantiates that coordinators must weigh safety risks in a region and decide what kinds of transportation are suitable for students to use. In addition, the case weighs the potential need for student housing to be in close proximity to the foreign institution.

Earlham v. Eisenberg

It can be learned from *Earlham v. Eisenberg* that coordinators should directly communicate with a student's designated homestay family, both prior to and during study abroad. The partnering company should be able to assist with this communication.

Student Erika Eisenberg alleged she was sexually harassed and raped while participating in Earlham College's program in Japan.[94] She claimed that her host father, the head of the family to which the college assigned her in Tokyo, was the perpetrator of the assault.[95] Eisenberg filed a suit, seeking $3 million from Earlham and other organizations that ran the program.[96] The parties settled the case for an undisclosed amount and on confidential terms.[97]

Earlham v. Eisenberg confirms that ongoing communication between the coordinator and the host family is essential to ensure that safe accommodations are in place for the student. In addition, the coordinator should frequently check in with the study abroad student to know his or her level of satisfaction with the homestay experience.

22. Empowerment of Program Leaders

A lack of decisive management can cause a study abroad program to quickly spiral out of control. Also, participants' respect for the foreign environment and co-participants can diminish. The structure of the program may also be lost as participants come late or miss appointed times to depart for venues. This kind of environment can infuriate participants who want to see venues in a timely fashion. Demands for partial or full program reimbursement may follow, perhaps in the form of litigation.

Therefore, coordinators have to be willing to wield authority to maintain program integrity when an unhealthy learning environment surfaces. Program code of conduct forms and risk-averting documents should allow program leaders the authority to discipline as needed.

For example, if you recall in best practice #20, Code of Conduct and Policy, Coordinator Trevor effectively uses the college code of conduct to empower him to discipline disruptive students abroad: "Our study abroad program is mirrored by student conduct here [at the college]. If you become a problem child in my class, I can have you removed. If you become a problem child in London, England, I can send you on a plane, and you will pay for it. I can send you back home."

In addition, the chapter 5 section, Strong Faculty Leaders Are the Best Defense, provides insight about leading with competence during study abroad programs. Students appreciate an orderly study abroad program that delivers the quality that is expected. They paid for a program and anticipate experiencing everything in the outlined itinerary. That itinerary serves to be a contractual promise to them, which coordinators must deliver.

Court Approval to Use Authority in Study Abroad

King v. Board of Control of Eastern Michigan University and *Furrh v. Arizona Board of Regents* are sample cases that shed light on appropriate use of authority by study abroad program leaders. Courts appear to support coordinators who use their power to improve the quality of programs.

King v. Board of Control of Eastern Michigan University illustrates that a study abroad program can greatly deteriorate when a leader fails to use their authority to fix a hostile, educationally inept environment.

Also important is that legal documents, such as waivers, should be written in a way that helps to empower program leaders. Court proceedings have shown that waivers can assist with providing coordinators and their institutions power to enforce rules and policies.

With *King v. Board of Control of Eastern Michigan University*, a federal district court for the eastern district of Michigan noted that the program leader's indifference to correcting a hostile environment of sexual harassment on a program to South Africa brought trauma to female participants.[98] The court also found that because the students were constantly under the care of Eastern Michigan University, the program leader had the power to correct the disorderly conduct.[99]

The program leader was present during times when male students referred to female students as "bitches," "hoes," "wideloads," "sluts," and so forth, and did nothing.[100] He was also present when male students allegedly solicited South African women for sex from the tour bus, yet did nothing.[101] As a result, the court declared the program leader and university to be negligent in failing to use their authority to correct the hostile environment, and ruled in favor of the plaintiffs.[102]

"Use your power to secure a safe environment, or you will be penalized," is the message that the court clearly sent.

Furrh v. Arizona Board of Regents

Furrh v. Arizona Board of Regents reveals a program in which leaders had to use their authority to physically detain a study abroad student who brought danger to himself and the group while in Mexico. The court established that program leaders have the authority to take action when a participant poses a threat to themselves and others.

Unknown to anyone involved, student participant Jonathan Furrh had a chronic mental and emotional disorder and had been under the care of a psychiatrist for several years.[103] This mental illness was exacerbated by the experience of the trip to the point where Furrh was a threat to the safety of himself and other members of the group.[104]

He had delusions that the other persons were "Mafioso" that were going to kill him; on a boat trip to Ventana Island, he believed he was going to be thrown to the sharks, and on two occasions he had a knife.[105]

Because program leaders believed there was the realistic possibility that Furrh, through various acts, may bring serious injury or death to himself or others, at times he had to be restrained.[106] After the completion of the program, Furrh sued the university, claiming that program leaders assaulted him and unlawfully restrained him.[107]

The court found the restraint used was reasonable under the circumstances, and no undue force or restraint was used.[108] While he was so restrained he was in the company of Dr. Keith Pierce, who attempted to make sure that Furrh was not unduly uncomfortable, that he was fed, and that his needs were attended to.[109]

The court authorized "where a person is a danger to himself or others because of his mental condition, that it is lawful to restrain him so long as necessary until other lawful measures can be followed."[110] Furrh's temporary detainment (and the means taken to effect it) was necessary and justified and in the best interest of the student and other members of the group.[111]

In consequence, program leaders must take steps to secure the safety of study abroad participants, in a reasonable manner, without having to fear retribution. This authority should be supported with language in risk-averting documents.

Risk-Averting Documents Should Empower Program Leaders

All of the sample waivers currently utilized by coordinators contain language authorizing program leaders to reprimand noncompliant participants. For example, Waiver C (Appendix C) asserts that dismissal from a program may result from behavior deemed unfit by the college:

The College or its agent(s) reserve(s) the right to dismiss any participant from a program for reasons of unacceptable personal behavior and/or unsatisfactory academic participation. Such dismissal will be without refund, and return transportation to the point of origin will be at the dismissed participant's expense. In addition, participants dismissed from the program will be denied access to any accommodations arranged by the College.

It is a credit to coordinators and legal counsel to recognize this need for the waiver. Clearly, program safety improves when a program leader penalizes or removes a participant who brings danger to themselves or other participants. In this case, the waiver also helps to provide the legal foundation for program leaders to enact their authority without fear of liability.

23. Trial and Error

Coordinators agree that in order to improve study abroad programs, they should be creative and allow themselves some room for mistakes. For instance, Coordinator Trevor notes that "the best practices for conducting a study abroad program, and to gain knowledge of risks or possible liability issues that may harm programs, [come] from trial and error." He avows that "study abroad [is] a unique educational approach that [is] less formulaic than campus approaches."

He insists that "coordinators [need] to be willing to work through trial and error . . . [and] the best-quality, most cost-efficient approach to conducting [my] annual program to London results from trial and error . . . [I learn] the best recipe for incorporating various individual companies to assist." Coordinator Trevor details how this approach is used with his London program:

> [For a best practice with study abroad] I hate to say "trial and error," but I'm going to say "trial and error." Like a lot of people I've used companies. Now I do [much of the program arrangements] myself. I do the travel arrangements, [yet] I go to a travel agent that gets the flights for me because I don't want to sit on the phone for x number of hours with British Airways.

Coordinator Trevor continues:

> But I found this [separate] company that leases the flats [and] I found the company that leases buses, so I get a good rate there. [For London] I get [the] tube passes, and I can get them here in the [United] States. [Also] I get British Heritage passes that get us into a lot of sites we want to see. Again, this is all cutting the price down . . . [One] could not do two weeks in London and do what we do for the price that we are doing it.

"Trial and error" has assisted with program building for Coordinator Trevor; in addition, a "trial and error" approach may give coordinators valuable experience to better protect program participants from potential hazards abroad. As Coordinator Felix points out, "The best study abroad coordinators [are] those who made mistakes in the past and learned from them."

At the same time, "trial and error" should not be mistaken for imprudence. Experience comes from knowing what works and what does not. Unpredictable factors are a part of study abroad, and leaders need to be able to be quick thinkers and planners who are malleable to the situation at hand.

If you lack familiarity with the environment, it is best to leave arrangements to professional travel companies and their contracted guides. While abroad, it is not the time to carelessly experiment. For example, an experimental program activity described by Coordinator Pearl, though well intentioned, could have turned out to be costly:

[While in Egypt I] had arranged for a ride on donkeys with participants along a river. [The group was] going on donkeys to a site away from the river . . . in a different path. [I] got concerned [and asked for the local guide] to follow the set path. [Angered, he] made [us] get off [the donkeys], and [left the group] in a town. [We] didn't know where [we] were, and walked and [eventually] found our way [back to familiar territory]. And why would the [foreign guide] do that? It doesn't sound good. It is odd. So I think [I] was lucky.

Again, "trial and error" that is used indiscriminately while abroad is inadvisable. However, "trial and error" through trusting, professional partners may actually serve to improve a set program. Two of my own program experiences immediately come to mind to support this— one to Peru and the other to Senegal and The Gambia.

While leading a short-term program group in Peru, I was faced with an unexpected, disruptive issue. Reserved for the program was an archaeological dig site for students to visit. When we arrived to the site, it was closed and no entry was allowed. This was a premier venue for our program, and suddenly it was lost due to unexpected renovations and hazards at the site.

If we continued with the planned program itinerary, a major hole would have remained (no pun intended with the lost dig). A quick alternative plan needed to be formed. People are usually happy when they are fed, so an early lunch was arranged for the group. This allowed me about an hour to get on the phone with the partnering tour company, weigh new options, and get a comparable activity speedily secured.

Apparently, there was a more recently discovered archeologically rich area that was only two towns away. We had our new site.

It turned out that this area was less traversed. Students were able to engage in more hands-on excavation than the originally planned site. In addition, the ebullience of the site's archaeologist was clear as he shared the newly acquired treasures that were being unearthed. His energy drew out the curiosity of students, and served to intensify the learning experience in that classroom without walls.

The program change worked in my favor. "Trial and error" has shown me that when one program activity falls apart, automatically skipping to the next might not be the best practice.

The same argument can be made for a program I conducted in Senegal and The Gambia. The developed program itinerary called for the group to take a ferry from Senegal to The Gambia, and continue with a number of venues that day in The Gambia. We planned our schedule around the expected time of arrival of the ferry. The ferry arrived, but we were not allowed to board. Due to politics (the proper bribe did not occur), we were not to receive a ride for a number of hours.

Over the course of this time, and while our guide negotiated with ferry operators, meaningful dialogue was struck between us and local Senegalese and Gambian citizens. We discovered that many of the young men were on the docks looking for odd jobs in an attempt to raise enough money to reattend high school. They were not permitted to stay in school because they had not purchased the required uniforms and books. Public education is not free for many. Earlier in the program, our group had visited the high school that some of them had attended.

My co-leaders and I decided to put "trial and error" to the test. We had been waiting for nearly two hours to get a ferry ride and did not know how much longer we would be delayed. So we used this opportunity to return to the high school that was within walking distance, confirm which students had been recently removed, and assisted with reregistering them. Dialogue with the school principal, basic paperwork, and a small pledge served to get those Senegalese students through to graduation. Lifelong friendships and service came from this act of "trial and error." This unexpected activity turned out to be a highlight of the program.

CHAPTER SUMMARY

A healthy ratio of supervisors to students is essential for every study abroad program to ensure the greatest safety for participants. Leaders of a program must be qualified for the task, serving as full employees of the college, with experience traveling to the program location. At least one program leader should be an instructor of the semester course that merges with the short-term study abroad program; co-leaders should be experts in the disciplines that mirror the program focus.

The element of unpredictability within study abroad brings unique risks, which include terrorist threats, natural disasters, and epidemics. Well aware of this, coordinators believe that emergency backup plans must always be in place. Some preemptive steps to aid student safety is requiring medical evacuation insurance for participants, registering students with a U.S. embassy, and having advanced knowledge of American military bases abroad.

Coordinators admit feeling trepidation when having to serve students with disabilities; some fear that exorbitant program costs could result from making special accommodations. Coordinators believe in the Americans with Disabilities Act compliance while abroad, and hope to meet the challenges that come with serving students with disabilities.

Also, coordinators have split opinions about the effectiveness of waivers for deterring risks and liabilities with study abroad. Yet they agree that legal counsel should carefully review these documents, and that coherent, instructive language must be used when constructing them. Current waivers that use broad, long-winded language pose a threat because participants may not read or understand the content. As a result, outlined expectations and risks may remain unclear to overseas participants.

In addition, expectations outlined in an institution's handbook on policies and proper code of conduct should also be reflected in study abroad materials that are provided to participants. Coordinators should carefully review brochures that detail foreign housing assignments and residence hall regulations prior to sending students abroad.

In order to improve the quality of study abroad programs, coordinators should accept the fact that they will make mistakes with program creation and execution. If backed by prudence, "trial and error" is an approach that may be used to bolster existing programs and increase practical knowledge for future programs.

NOTES

1. *King v. Bd. of Control of E. Mich. Univ.*, 221 F.Supp.2d 783, 784 (E.D. Mich. 2002).
2. *Id.* at 786.
3. *Id.*
4. 55 Pa. D. & C.4th 353, 355 (Com. Pl. 2001) (leaving the student alone with an unaffiliated Lutheran missionary to serve as her translator).
5. *Id.* at 356.
6. *Id.* at 367.
7. Complaint at 9, *Thackurdeen v. Duke Univ.*, No. 14-cv-6311 (Aug. 8, 2014 S.D.N.Y.).
8. *Id.* at 5.
9. *Id.* at 6.
10. *Id.* at 5.
11. U.S. Department of State—Bureau of Consular Affairs. (2015). U.S. passports & international travel. Retrieved from http://travel.state.gov/content/passports/english/country/guatemala.html.
12. *Id.*
13. *Id.*
14. *Id.*
15. *Id.*
16. Rubin, A. M. (1996, May 10). Making it safer to study abroad. *Chronicle of Higher Education*, p. A49.

17. Kast, R. (1997). In loco parentis and the "reasonable person." *International Educator 7*, 1. Rubin, A. M. (1996, May 10).

18. Rubin, A. M. (1996, May 10).

19. Complaint at 6, *Thackurdeen v. Duke Univ.*, No. 14-cv-6311 (Aug. 8, 2014 S.D.N.Y.).

20. *Id.* at 15.

21. *Id.* at 6.

22. *Id.* at 5.

23. *Id.*

24. *Id.* at 15–16.

25. *Id.* at 6.

26. *Id.* at 6–7.

27. *Id.* at 7.

28. *Id.*

29. *Id.*

30. *Id.*

31. *Id.*

32. *Furrh v. Ariz. Bd. of Regents*, 676 P.2d 1141, 1142 (Ariz. Ct. App. 1983).

33. *Id.*

34. *Id.*

35. *Id.*

36. *Id.* at 1143.

37. *Id.*

38. *Id.*

39. *Id.*

40. *Id.*

41. *Id.*

42. U.S. Department of Health and Human Services: Office for Civil Rights. (2006). Fact sheet: Your rights under Section 504 of the Rehabilitation Act. Washington, DC:
    U.S. Department of Health and Human Services. Retrieved from
    http://www.hhs.gov/ocr/civilrights/resources/factsheets/504.pdf.

43. U.S. Department of Labor. (2015). Disability resources: Americans with Disabilities Act. Washington, DC: U.S. Department of Labor. Retrieved from
    http://www.dol.gov/dol/topic/disability/ada.htm.

44. NACUANOTES. (2012, April 26). Federal disability laws: Do they translate to study abroad programs? Retrieved from http://www.calstate.edu/gc/documents/NACUANOTES10.pdf.

45. 303 F.3d 1015, 1020-21 n.1 (9th Cir. 2002).

46. *Id.* at 1017.

47. *Id.* at 1018.

48. *Id.* at 1019.

49. *Id.*

50. NACUANOTES. (2012, April 26), p. 16.

51. NACUANOTES. (2012, April 26), p. 17.

52. NACUANOTES. (2012, April 26), p. 18.

53. NACUANOTES. (2012, April 26), p. 19.

54. NACUANOTES. (2012, April 26), p. 20.

55. NACUANOTES. (2012, April 26), p. 23.

56. NACUANOTES. (2012, April 26), p. 24.

57. *Ariz. St. Univ.*, 22 N.D.L.R. 239, 239 (2001).

58. *Id.*

59. NACUANOTES. (2012, April 26), p. 26.

60. NACUANOTES. (2012, April 26), pp. 26–30.

61. *Fay v. Thiel Coll.*, 55 Pa. D. & C.4th 353, 369 (Pa. Com. Pl. 2001).

62. *Paneno v. Centres for Acad. Programmes Abroad, Ltd.*, 13 Cal. Rptr. 3d 759, 766 (Cal. Ct. App. 2004) (noting the use of the term *CAPA*, rather than *CAPA-UK* or *CAPA-USA*).

63. *Id.*

64. Rubin, A. M. (1996, May 10).

65. *Id.*

66. *Id.*

67. *Id.*

68. *Id.*

69. *Id.*

70. *Bloss v. Univ. of Minn. Bd. of Regents*, 590 N.W.2d 661, 662 (Minn. Ct. App. 1999).

71. *Id.* at 663.

72. *Id.* at 666.

73. *Id.*

74. *Id.*

75. *Id.*

76. *See King v. Bd. of Control of E. Mich. Univ.*, 221 F.Supp.2d 783, 786 (E.D. Mich. 2002).

77. *Id.*

78. *Id.* at 785–86 n.1.

79. *Id.* at 790–91.

80. *Id.* at 791.

81. *Id.*

82. *Id.*

83. *Id.*

84. *Id.*

85. *Paneno v. Centres for Acad. Programmes Abroad, Ltd.*, 13 Cal. Rptr. 3d 759, 762 (Cal. Ct. App. 2004).

86. *Id.* (pointing out that CAPA subsequently contracted with Mitwohnzentrale to arrange the apartment accommodations).

87. *Id.* at 763.

88. *Id.*

89. *Id.* at 763, 766.

90. *Bloss v. Univ. of Minn. Bd. of Regents*, 590 N.W.2d 661, 662 (Minn. Ct. App. 1999).

91. *Id.*

92. *Id.*

93. *Id.* at 663.

94. Guernsey, L. (1997, April 11). A lawsuit raises difficult questions about liability and study-abroad programs. *Chronicle of Higher Education 43*, 31, p. A37, A39.

95. *Id.*

96. *Id.*

97. *Id.*

98. *See* 221 F.Supp.2d 783, 784 (E.D. Mich. 2002) (describing the hostile environment and sexual harassment that students were subjected to while abroad).

99. *Id.* at 791.

100. *Id.* at 786.

101. *Id.*

102. *Id.*

103. *Furrh v. Ariz. Bd. of Regents*, 676 P.2d 1141, 1142 (Ariz. Ct. App. 1983).

104. *Id.*

105. *Id.* at 1143.

106. *Id.*

107. *Id.* at 1142.

108. *Id.* at 1143, 1146.

109. *Id.* at 1143.

110. *Id.* at 1146.

111. *Id.* at 1144–46.

Chapter Ten

Final Thoughts and Encouragement

During the creation of, and with the completion of this book, I came to a major realization. This insight emerged from critical literature, court proceedings, lawsuits, and legal documents. It manifests through risk-averting documents and waivers. And most strikingly, it shines through the insights of interviewed study abroad experts. *Even with inherent challenges, study abroad stands strong.* Overall safety for students, efficiency of study abroad offices, and security for the institutions that house them is solid.

I have gained a profound respect for those in the field: within study abroad, international education, global studies, and relative departments. It has been a privilege to have the opportunity to closely engage with my colleagues for this book. Clear to me is the pride and passion that they share in the most engrossing, highly impactful work imaginable—study abroad.

My colleagues are the best people for the job because they do it to serve the student, the community, and the world. They are not motivated by immense monetary compensation or institutional accolades (good thing). It is what *others gain* from their work that motivates them to be the best. The production of this book confirms that study abroad participants, overall, are in good hands.

However, if these people were perfect, there would not have been a need to write this book. And even if they were, study abroad in itself is far from risk-free. You all have come to fully know that intrinsic risks come with study abroad. Students cannot be completely insulated from the environmental hazards of another country. Just like home, they are vulnerable to risks the minute they walk out of their doors. Most Americans are reasonably aware of the potential dangers that surround them at home. I strive to give them similar awareness with study abroad dangers, whether it is future participants, coordinators, or generally intrigued individuals.

As I stated from the start, it is not possible for all risks to students, nor potential liabilities for institutions, to be disclosed in a single work. However, by passing on knowledge of the most common risk factors in what I coin as the "LARGEST 3" (Liabilities And Risks in Global Education and Study-Travel's (1) medical risks, (2) sexual assault, and (3) supervisory neglect), study abroad participants and institutional members are put at a great advantage. You have learned what makes up the vast majority of study abroad tragedies and subsequent lawsuits. Armed with this information, along with knowledge of best practices to avoid threats, you can develop protective strategies to safeguard yourself while abroad.

The sobering fact is that new and continued tragedies surface with study abroad, along with subsequent lawsuits; this is inevitable as study abroad participation grows. Even as this book neared completion, new calamities came about, including that of a University of Iowa student who allegedly died from falling off a bridge in Italy, and a George Washington University student who allegedly drowned to death in South Africa. This study could continue to no end as new cases surface again and again. But it has to come to closure at some point. I am comfortable concluding with knowing that essential tools have been provided to assist with averting risks and liabilities.

Indeed, intrinsic risks with study abroad are not going to suddenly cease to exist. But knowing what you are getting into, and having plans to protect yourself from hazards, should be the ultimate goal. Once again, this is the point of the book—to improve students' opportunities for safe studies overseas, and to assist coordinators' administration of these programs to help ensure it.

I encourage my colleagues to continue with their strong work ethic, and the duty of care that they have provided students. While I praise my colleagues for the work they have done, I also see room for improvement.

With the production of this book, clearly there was a bit of reticence among coordinators to disclose information about their programs, or to openly share risk-management documents. I do not believe this response is due to fear of disclosure in this book but is "across the board." This lack of transparency serves to weaken study abroad. Unnecessary concerns about judgment could limit the effectiveness of study abroad program delivery, and put people at unnecessary risk.

My advice to coordinators is to not be afraid to ask for help—from fellow coordinators, legal counsel, faculty counsel, other campus departments, and members of your risk management team (and form a team if you don't have one in place). You don't have to "go at it alone." Utilize the professional organizations that you have at your disposal, both at the state and national level. Participate in workshops and confer with colleagues at professional conferences to learn about current approaches and strategies for managing study abroad.

While there appears to be considerable literature available about educational benefits of study abroad, there seems to be a shortage of literature on risks, and certainly liabilities and repair, with study abroad. I hope this book helps to fill this gap in an illuminating way. I hope through my unveiling of court cases and lawsuits, I was able to give a clear, fair, and compassionate voice to sufferers and their family members of study abroad tragedies. Many times I was moved by their struggles and pursuit for closure; these individuals served as a major inspiration for this book.

Certainly an overarching motivation for this book came from my desire to protect students, programs, and institutions. As I noted, study abroad growth will continue, but risks and liabilities do not have to expand with it. If you take on study abroad knowing its risks and approach it safely, you should be able to confidently navigate through your educational venture knowing that you did not jump into it blindly. For those of you entering study abroad for the first time, as well as those who participate in it time and time again, I leave you with firm encouragement to always "look before leaping."

Appendix A

Sample Waiver A

RELEASE

NAME:
Last First Middle
ADDRESS:

The undersigned person hereby requests permission to participate in field trips, class trips, live projects, extracurricular events, and/or any activity(ies) sponsored by _____ College or in which the College has any involvement or participation and affirms:

(i) I recognize and am aware that participation in any of these activities could result in physical and/or mental injury including death; and,

(ii) I am in proper physical condition to participate in these activities. Further, I recognize and am aware that there are risks of physical and/or mental injury and death that might result from accidents, negligence, or the intentional acts of others occurring during travel to and from said activities, whether by transportation provided by _____ College or by private vehicle or otherwise or at any time and by any other means.

In consideration of _____ College and any of its personnel in any capacity allowing me to participate in any such activities based on my request and affirmations, and other good and valuable considerations, the receipt and sufficiency of which are hereby acknowledged, I hereby waive, release, and agree to hold harmless _____ College, its instructors, personnel, employees, agents, successors, or assigns acting in whatever capacity, all sponsors and organizers of any such activities and all other persons and entities involved in the preparation for, conduct, and/or control of any said events in any capacity or role whatsoever of and from any and all actions, claims, demands, costs, loss of services, expenses, compensation, and all consequential and/or punitive damages on account of any and all injuries, illness, or other damages, including death, which may result directly or indirectly from my participation in or attendance at or observation of any such activities.

This RELEASE has been read by me, and I understand its contents and that it shall be binding on me, my heirs, personal representatives, executors, successors, and assigns. I further certify and affirm that as of the signing of this Release, I am eighteen (18) years of age or older.

IN TESTIMONY WHEREOF, I have set my hand and adopted as my seal the typewritten word "SEAL" appearing beside my name, this the day of , .

(SEAL)
Signature
Witness

INSTRUCTIONS THAT APPLY WHEN A STUDENT IS TO SIGN THIS RELEASE:
The student must sign above if the student is eighteen years of age or older. If the student is under the age of eighteen, then the student does not sign but the parent(s) or guardian(s) sign on the next page.

PARENT RELEASE
I/We hereby certify and affirm that the above student is under the age of eighteen (18), that I/we are his parent(s) or legal guardian(s), that I/we hereby execute this Release on his or her behalf and on behalf of myself/ourselves and his or her and my/our respective heirs, personal representatives, executors, successors, and assigns so as to fully release all persons and claims as set forth in detail above in the body of this Release.

If this Release is signed by only one parent or guardian, he or she certifies that he or she is signing this Release on behalf of, as the agent of and with the permission of the other parent or any other guardian or guardians and any other person or person who may have any claim whatsoever in connection with any injuries, illness, or other damages, including death, to the above-named student and fully binds such other person or persons and their heirs, personal representatives, executors, successors, and assigns to this Release.

The undersigned(s) certify that I/we have read this Release and understand its content and that it is binding on the above-named student, on me/us, and on the student's and my/our heirs, personal representatives, executors, successors, and assigns.
IN TESTIMONY WHEREOF, I/we have set my/our hand and adopted as my/our seal the typewritten word "SEAL" appearing beside my/our name(s), this the day of , .

(SEAL)
Signature of Parent or Guardian
(SEAL)
Signature of Parent or Guardian

Witness

Appendix B

Sample Waiver B

WAIVER OF RESPONSIBILITY
STUDY ABROAD PROGRAM
UNIVERSITY OF _____

_____	_____
Applicant's Full Name	Program Name, Semester Attending
_____	_____
Parent or Legal Guardian	_____
(If Applicant is under age 18)	Permanent Mailing Address

The undersigned, being the above-named Applicant, or, if such Applicant is under the age of eighteen (18) years, the parent or legal guardian of such Applicant, in consideration of acceptance of Applicant for participation in the above-named Study Abroad Program (the "Program") by the University of _____ (the "University") does hereby agree that:

1. Before signing this Waiver, Applicant has read the materials provided by University that describe the Program, the Applicant's responsibilities while participating in the Program, and the potential health, safety, and other risks associated with Applicant's participation in the Program. Applicant has taken the opportunity to ask any questions he or she may have about the Program, and the responsibilities and risks involved.

2. Applicant agrees to attend predeparture programs, orientation programs, and other meetings that the University may conduct regarding the Program.

3. The duration, itinerary, or other details of the Program may be canceled, curtailed, altered, or modified without prior notice or obligation to Applicant, except that in the event of cancellation, refund shall be made of all monies paid by or on behalf of Applicant to the University for participation in the Program, excluding the nonrefundable application fee. If the Program is curtailed, refund shall be made of an appropriate share of such monies paid to the University, said sum to be determined by the University in its sole discretion.

4. Applicant shall abide by all laws of the country or countries visited, including but not limited to laws governing the use of alcohol and drugs. If Applicant chooses to use alcohol, as allowed by law, Applicant agrees to do so responsibly and at his or her sole risk. Applicant agrees to comply with all rules, regulations, and standards of conduct, including but not limited to violations of the Code of Academic Integrity (www.---/conduct.html) and the Code of Student Conduct (www.---/conduct.html) fixed by the University, their agents, and employees who, in the event of violation, reserve the right to limit or terminate Applicant's participation in the Program. If Applicant's participation in the Program is terminated, return to Applicant's home shall be at Applicant's sole expense.

5. Applicant releases fully and finally from any and all liability and claims, and covenants not to sue or cause to be sued in any judicial or administrative forum, the State of _____, the University, and their officers, agents, and employees with respect to any and all matters relating to or arising from Applicant's participation in the Program. It is understood that the University shall in no way be deemed responsible for the operation or management of any means of transportation, public or private, or facilities used or by the Program.

6. Refund of monies paid to the University by or for Applicant for participation in the Program, excluding the nonrefundable application fee and deposit, shall be made upon withdrawal from the Program only in the event that Applicant gives written notice to the University of his or her withdrawal at least four weeks prior to the date of departure for the program.

7. The Applicant warrants that he or she has been examined by a qualified physician of his or her choice; that such physician was in possession of all pertinent facts concerning Applicant and the Program; and that such physician has reported that the Applicant is in good health, may travel as required, and is free from any physical or mental ailment or disability requiring medical, surgical, or other care or treatment that might endanger the health or safety of the Applicant or those with whom the Applicant may come in contact. APPLICANT WARRANTS THAT HE OR SHE IS CURRENTLY ENROLLED IN A HEALTH INSURANCE PROGRAM THAT PROVIDES COVERAGE FOR EXPENSES INCURRED WHILE PARTICIPATING IN THIS PROGRAM.

8. This Waiver shall not be modified except by another agreement in writing signed by the Applicant.

9. The Applicant acknowledges that prior to signing this Waiver, he or she has read this Waiver, has full understanding of its terms and conditions, and voluntarily executes it with the understanding that the University shall rely on the statements and warranties herein contained.

10. The terms of this Waiver shall be governed by the laws of the State.

_____

Signature
Date:
(Must be signed by parent or legal guardian if Applicant is under 18 years of age.)

Appendix C

Sample Waiver C

_____ COLLEGE
INTERNATIONAL EDUCATION
Study Abroad Programs
and
Study-Travel Tours (International and Domestic)
INSURANCE COVERAGE FORM for OVERSEAS ACADEMIC PROGRAMS

Participant (Type or Print)

Program:
Location Abroad:

Health, accident, and emergency evacuation insurance coverage is required of all participants in College study abroad programs. The College strongly advises a policy that is designed specifically for study abroad. Such a policy could minimally include basic medical, accidental death, and dismemberment coverage. If the participant plans to travel before the program starts or after it concludes, and the participant's policy does not cover these periods, short-term coverage should be arranged with a private company so that insurance protection will be adequate for the entire period away from home.

This is to certify that I will be covered by a health, accident, and emergency evacuation insurance policy for the duration of my stay abroad as a participant in the above-named program. This insurance is provided through:

Policy Number:
Issued by the _____ Insurance Company.

I have checked out with the company to be sure that I will be adequately covered while abroad and that payment of claims can be made abroad. I have paid any additional premium required for overseas coverage.

The College reserves the option to cancel at any time any program of travel for just cause as the College may determine in its sole discretion to protect the participants and the College.

It is recommended that participants of the travel program purchase cancellation insurance and medical evacuation insurance to protect their investment in the travel program. Coverage may be available through your insurance company. Brochures for this coverage are available from the College International Education Study Travel Program office or travel agent.

Participant's Signature
Date:

As a condition of acceptance of any application, each applicant must agree to and sign the CONDITIONS OF PARTICIPATION as set forth below.

_____ COLLEGE
INTERNATIONAL EDUCATION
Study Abroad Programs
and
Study Travel Tours (International and Domestic)

PARTICIPANT NAME:

PROGRAM LOCATION (city, country):

PROGRAM DATES:

As with all academic programs, certain conditions must be adhered to in order to preserve program integrity. As a necessary precaution to protect _____ College, those conditions are listed above. We ask that you read them carefully, and indicate with your signature that you understand them fully and will comply with them. If you are a participant under the age of eighteen, your parent or guardian's signature is also needed.

CONDITIONS OF PARTICIPATION

Participation

Participants must maintain an adequate standard of academic work in the program, and behave responsibly both in their living situation and on group excursions. The participant agrees to participate fully in all portions of the program and further agrees that any deviation from the program design must be requested in advance and in writing by the participant, and must be approved by both the program director and the program instructor. This includes any intention by the participant to spend any night away from the program site and/or to leave the country in which the program is based.

Academic Credit

Unless arrangements are made (in advance and under the guidelines provided by the International Education Office) to enroll in the course through the Continuing Education program, the participant acknowledges that she/he is taking the course for academic credit or audit. Letter grades will be awarded upon completion of the course. Please see the ____ College catalog for the College's policy on course withdrawal.

Policy

The participant agrees to read and abide by the conditions listed in the travel brochure and/or any other materials provided by the Office of International Education at _____ College.

Host Regulations

The participant agrees to abide by all the rules and regulations as set out by the host institution and/or host country, and by all the laws pertaining to his/her participant status. The participant also acknowledges and understands that should he/she develop legal problems with any foreign nationals or the government of the host country, the participant will attend to the matter personally, with his or her own personal funds. The College is not responsible for providing any assistance to the participants under such circumstances.

While in the host country, for their own safety, all participants must refrain from all political activity. Participants in overseas programs may not participate in such political activities as: joining a political party, a union, or a demonstration; distributing political materials; picketing.

Breaches of the local laws of the host community or country are referred to and handled by the appropriate law enforcement authorities.

Medical Treatment

The participant accepts sole responsibility for securing all necessary immunizations prior to departure. The participant agrees to fully describe any health and physical or psychological problems or conditions that she/he may have on the application form. In the event of illness or injury to the participant, the undersigned authorizes any official representative of the College or the overseas host institution to secure medical treatment on the participant's behalf, including surgery and the administration of an anesthetic. Further, the undersigned and/or the participant fully accept all financial responsibility for such treatment. The participant is required to be covered by a health insurance policy for foreign countries visited.

Payment Details

The participant (and his/her parent/guardian, if said participant is a financial dependent) is aware of the nature and the cost of the problem, and will guarantee that all financial obligations will be met by the deadline(s) specified in the travel brochure or host institution payment schedule. Please note that the College will not authorize any deferral of payment(s) based on financial aid disbursements.

Dismissal from the Program

The College or its agent(s) reserve(s) the right to dismiss any participant from a program for reasons of unacceptable personal behavior and/or unsatisfactory academic participation. Such dismissal will be without refund, and return transportation to the point of origin will be at the dismissed participant's expense. In addition, participants dismissed from the program will be denied access to any accommodations arranged by the College.

Appendix D

Sample Waiver D

UNIVERSITY
INTERSESSION PROGRAM ABROAD
STUDENT ASSUMPTION OF RISK AND RELEASE
To Be Reviewed and Signed by the Student Participant

I, _____, am a student at _____
University, in the Division of _____. I am participating in the Intersession Program Abroad in _____ during _____.

I understand that I am not required by _____ University (the University) to participate in this particular program. I further understand that there are certain inherent risks associated with any travel abroad and with the participation in a program of this type. These inherent risks may include, but are not limited to, a lack of access to health care, crime, dangers associated with public or private transportation, safety of the road systems, and other means of transportation. I am voluntarily accepting the risks associated with participating in this program and agree to cooperate with and abide by the guidelines established by the University. I further acknowledge that neither the University nor any of its employees, agents, or students can absolutely guarantee my safety in every situation.

I represent that I am covered for the duration of the study abroad program and throughout my absence from the United States by a policy of comprehensive health and accident insurance that provides coverage for illness or injuries I sustain or experience while abroad. I release the University from any responsibility and liability for my injuries, illness, medical bills, charges, or similar expenses.

In the event of sickness or injury, I authorize the University program instructor or primary contact at the host institution to secure whatever treatment is deemed necessary, including admission to a hospital, the administration of anesthetic, the transfusion of blood, or surgery. Furthermore, I provide the University with permission to inform parents/guardians and the University employees with a legitimate need to know in the event of sickness or injury.

I agree to release and hold harmless the University, its employees, and agents from any and all liability and damages or losses I may suffer to my person or my property or both, which arise out of or occur during my participation in the intersession study abroad program, except if the danger or losses are caused by the gross negligence or willful misconduct of University employees.

I agree that this Assumption of Risk and Release Form is to be construed in accordance with the laws of the State of _____, and that if any portion of this agreement is held invalid by a competent court of jurisdiction, the remainder of the agreement shall continue in full force and effect.

I acknowledge that I have read this entire document, and, that in exchange for the University's agreement to my participation in this program, I agree to its terms.

_____

Name (Please print)

_____

Signature

_____

Date

Appendix E

Sample Waiver E

**RELEASE OF LIABILITY, WAIVER,
DISCHARGE, AND COVENANT NOT TO SUE
COLLEGE OF _____
INTERNATIONAL STUDIES PROGRAM
THIS IS A RELEASE OF LEGAL RIGHTS
READ AND UNDERSTAND BEFORE SIGNING**

Name of Student: _____

Activity: _____

I, _____ will be participating
in cross-cultural study abroad in _____ (the
  "Activity") for the period of [INSERT DATES OF ACTIVITY]. I hereby agree as follows:

1. I understand that participation in the Activity involves risk not found in study at the College of _____ (the "College"). These include risks involved in traveling to and within and returning from one or more foreign counties; foreign political, legal, social, and economic conditions; different stand of design, safety, and maintenance of buildings, public places, and conveniences.
2. I understand that each foreign country has its own laws and standards of acceptable conduct, including dress, manners, morals, politics, drug use, and behavior. I recognize the behavior that violates those laws or standards could harm the College's relations with those countries and the institution therein, as well as my own health and safety. I will become informed of, and will abide by, all such laws and standards for each country to or through which I will travel during the Activity.
3. I will comply with all rules and regulations issued by the College or any coordinating institution. It is within the sole discretion of the College, through its identified representative (the "Representative"), to determine that my behavior violates any such rules and regulations and warrants my termination from the Activity. I agree that the College has a right to enforce the rules and regulations, through the Representative, in its sole

discretion, and that it will impose sanctions, up to and including termination of my participation in the Activity, for violating the rules and regulations for any behavior detrimental to or incompatible with the interests, harmony, and welfare of the College, the Activity, or the other participants in the Activity. I recognize that due to the circumstances of foreign study programs, procedures for notice, hearing, and appeal applicable to the student rights at the College do not apply. If I am asked to terminate my participation, I consent to being sent home at my own expense with no refund of fees. I also agree that I will (a) not buy, sell, or use illegal drugs any time, (b) not engage in abusive use of alcohol, (c) participate in all classes and scheduled activities unless ill, and (d) abide by dress and cultural codes suitable in the countries visited.

4. The College, in its sole discretion, determines that circumstances within a foreign country may require cancellation of the Activity within the country. The College will provide me with as much advance notice as possible of its intention to cancel all or a portion of the Activity. I also understand the College, an overseas institution, or a foreign government may prematurely terminate all or a portion of the Activity.

5. In consideration of being permitted to participate in the Activity, I do release, waive, forever discharge, and covenant not to sue the College, the Board of Trustees of the College, the officers, officials, employees, or agents of the College (the "Releasees") from and against any and all liability from any harm, injury, damage, claims, demands, action, causes of action, costs, including reasonable attorneys' fees, and expenses of any nature that I may have or that may thereafter accrue to me, arising out of or related to any loss, damage, or injury, including but not limited to suffering and death, that may be sustained by me or by any property belonging to me that there caused by the negligence or carelessness of the Releasees, or otherwise, while I am engaged in the Activity, or in transit to or from the premises where the Activity or any adjunct to the Activity, occurs or is being conducted.

6. I understand and agree that the Releasees are hereby granted permission to authorize emergency medical treatment to me, if necessary, and that Releasees assume no responsibility for any injury or damage that might arise out of or in connection with such authorized medical treatment.

7. I am aware that travel insurance may be available through [INSERT THE NAME OF THE TRAVEL AGENT] (the "Travel Agent"). If available, the Travel Agent will inform me of the specific terms and coverage of any such insurance.

8. It is my express intent that, with respect to the Releasees, this Release shall bind the members of my family and my spouse, if I am alive, and my family, estate, heirs, administrators, personal representatives, or assigns, if I am deceased. I further agree to save and hold harmless, indemnify, and defend Releasees from any claim by my family, or me arising out of my participation in the Activity.

9. I agree that the Releasees are not representatives or agents for the Travel Agent, transportation carriers, hotels, and other suppliers of services connected with the Activity, and the Releasee are not responsible for the actions of these entities.

10. In signing the Release, I acknowledge and represent that I have fully read this Release and that I understand what it means and that I sign this Release as my act and deed. No oral presentations, statements, or inducements, apart from the foregoing written statement, have been made. I further represent that there are no health-related reasons or problems that preclude or restrict my participation in all or part of this Activity, and that I have currently in effect health insurance as required by the College to provide for any medical costs that may be attendant as a result of my participation in the Activity.

11. I further agree that this Release shall be construed in accordance with laws of the State of _____. If any term or provision of this Release shall be held illegal, unenforceable, or in conflict with any law governing this Release, the validity of the remaining portion shall not be affected thereby.

12. I hereby represent that I am at least eighteen years of age as of the date of this Release, or if I am younger than eighteen years my legal guardian has read and signed (or will read and sign prior to the Activity) this Release in the space designated below. I am fully competent to sign this Agreement, and I have executed this Release for full, adequate, and complete consideration fully intending for me and for my family, estate, heirs, administrators, personal representatives or assigns to be bound by the same.

This Release shall be effective on the date it has been signed by me, and if applicable, my legal Guardian.

DATE: _____
Student/Participant _____

I: (a) am the parent or legal guardian of the above participant/student; (b) have read the foregoing Release (including such parts as may subject me to personal financial responsibility); (c) am and will be legally responsible for the obligations and acts of the student/participant as described in this Release; and (d) agree for myself and for the student/participant to be bound by its terms.

DATE: _____
Parent/Guardian _____

Appendix F

Sample Waiver F

_____ **COLLEGE**
ACCEPTANCE, RELEASE, WAIVER, AND INDEMNIFICATION AGREEMENT
FOR INTERNATIONAL PROGRAMS

I, (*print name*), _____, am a student at ____ College (the "College") and have decided to study abroad for the (*semester/year/summer*) _____ at (name of the program) _____ (the "Program").

I understand that I am not required to participate in the Program, that my participation is wholly voluntary, and that it is my responsibility to select a program of study abroad. In consideration of the opportunity to participate in the Program, the receipt and sufficiency of which is hereby acknowledged, I agree as follows:

1. Assumption of Risk and Release of Claims. I understand and agree that there are certain dangers, hazards, and risks inherent in international travel and activities included in the Program, including but not limited to risks of injury, permanent disability or death, property damage, and severe social or economic loss, which may result from, among other things, the actions, failure to act or negligence of myself or others, weather conditions, conditions of equipment used, differing standards of design, safety, and maintenance of buildings, public spaces and transportation, language barriers, strikes, natural disasters, civil unrest or hostilities, terrorists activities or acts of war, varying quality of available medical treatment and differing health, safety, legal, cultural, and religious beliefs and conditions. I further understand that the above risks are also associated with any activities I undertake that are not associated with the Program, such as independent travel during vacation periods, periods of time extending beyond the termination of the Program, or other periods in which I am not participating in Program activities. I understand that the College cannot and does not assume responsibility for any personal injury, loss of life, property, damage, or other loss arising from my participation in the Program or in activities incident thereto. Accordingly, I voluntarily and without reservation agree, on behalf of my family, heirs, and personal representative(s), to assume all risk for any such personal injury, loss of life, property damage, or other loss and on behalf of myself, my heirs, and my estate, RELEASE and HOLD HARMLESS and INDEM-

NIFY the College and its directors, officers, employees from and against any present or future liability, claims, demands, and causes of actions arising out of or related to any personal injury, loss of life, property damage, or other loss sustained during my participation in the Program or in activities incident to the Program.

Service Providers. I understand that the College does not represent or act as an agent for the transportation carriers, hotels, and other suppliers of services connected with the Program. I further understand and agree that the College, its director, officers, employees, and agents are not responsible or liable for (i) any injury, damage, loss, accident, delay, or other irregularity that may be cause or contributed to by the defect of any vehicle or the negligence or default by any company or person engaged in providing or performing services in connection with the Program, or (ii) any disruption of travel arrangements or any additional expense that may be incurred as a result thereof.

Standards of Conduct. I agree to abide by the individual and group standards appropriate to the cultural setting of the Program, including the laws and standards of conduct of the host country, and to comply with any rules and regulations regarding student behavior promulgated by the College and/or the host of the Program, whether or not such rules and regulations, or are judged to be injurious to the Program, seriously offensive to the host culture, and/or damaging to the College's reputation, I acknowledge that the College may, in its sole discretion, impose sanctions up to and including my expulsion from the Program. If my enrollment in the Program is terminated, I consent to being returned to the United States at my own expense and without any refund of tuition or fees.

Academic Responsibilities. I acknowledge and understand that I am responsible for maintaining a full-time course of study, taking at least fifteen semester hours of work or the equivalent in quarter hours per semester or term while participating in the Program. I understand that I must attend all classes, take all examinations, and do all assigned work. I agree to take only those courses that have been approved by the College. If I take courses that have not been approved by the College, I understand that the credits may not be transferred to the College. In the event that a change in my course of study must be made, I agree to communicate with and receive approval from the College for all changes prior to making them. I am aware that I must receive the equivalent of 1.0 grade points (2.0 for non-College programs) or better in each course in order for the course to be counted toward my degree program at the College. I am fully aware and understand that the registration of course generally takes place overseas. I acknowledge and understand that if I do not successfully enroll in and complete the courses offered through the Program that I need to progress in my degree program at the College, I may not graduate on time. I agree that it is my responsibility to satisfy all prerequisite courses for my program of study at the College and abroad.

Name _____ Date Received _____

I have read and understand this agreement and the contents of all written documents regarding the Program that I have chosen.

Insurance Carrier:
Policy Number:

Printed Student Name:

Student Signature:
    Date:

Parent or Guardian Signature (*if student under 18 years of age*):

Study Abroad Advisor:
Date:

Appendix G

Sample Waiver G

STUDENT/PARENT LIABILITY FORM
The University of _____
Office of Study Abroad

Name of Participant
Program

In conducting study abroad programs, the University makes every effort to protect the welfare and safety of the participants. The official representative of the University at the study abroad site will make such rules and regulations for the conduct of the participants as will reasonably safeguard the health, well-being, and safety of all such participants. Recognizing, however, that participation in the program is voluntary and that there are certain inherent risks that the participant must assume, the participant understands that neither the University, nor any cooperating institution, assumes any responsibility for damage to or loss of property, personal illness or injury, or death while a participant is in the program. While the University will assist in providing information on health care and insurance, it is the individual student's responsibility to ascertain that he/she has adequate health and accident coverage, valid during his/her stay abroad. Proof of such coverage must be attached to this document. A form will be provided by the Office of Study Abroad. (Please see specific program instructions regarding insurance.)

Should a participant be placed in a position in which, because of his/her incapacity to act, the question arises as to who may act on the participant's behalf or as his or her parents', guardians', or spouse's agent, the representative abroad shall be duly appointed attorney-in-fact for such student and for such parent, guardian, or spouse.

The University strongly discourages students owning or operating vehicles while participating in study abroad programs. Traffic congestion and different traffic laws and regulations, civil and criminal, can make driving motor vehicles in foreign countries extremely hazardous. Insurance requirements, or other financial responsibility laws, vary from country to country. If, however, a participant is determined to operate a motor vehicle while abroad, he or she recognizes that the University assumes no financial responsibility for legal aid, or for the care of the participant should he/she be involved in an accident while operating a motor vehicle.

Opportunities for individual travel are plentiful, and the University does not wish to discourage participants from taking advantage of them. The University, however, undertakes no responsibility for the participant when he/she is traveling during the course of the study abroad period.

Each participant is required to sign the following statement as an indication that the above conditions and limitations are understood and accepted.

I hereby release the University and any cooperating institution and their officers and agents from any and all claims and causes of action for damage to or loss of property, medical or hospital care, personal illness or injury, or death arising out of any travel or activity conducted by or under the control of the University or cooperating institution.

Participant's Signature:

An American student abroad is expected to be able to cope with day-to-day occurrences, but occasionally events arise that are of an emergency or legal nature. Therefore, we request that one copy of this form, signed by the student and by the student's parent(s) or guardian (if the student is unmarried) or by the student and the student's spouse (if the student is married) and duly notarized, be returned to the University by the date indicated on your acceptance letter.

On occasion, emergencies arise which require medical care, hospitalization, or surgery for a student participant. So that such treatment can be administered without delay, we ask that each participant sign the following statement authorizing the University representative abroad to secure, at the expense of the participant, any treatment deemed necessary.

In the event of injury or illness to the undersigned, I hereby authorize the representative of the University, at my expense, to secure necessary treatment, including the administration of an anesthetic and surgery, and such medication as may be prescribed. It is further agreed that, if my condition so requires, I may be returned to the United States, at my expense.

Participant's Signature:

State of:

County of:

Subscribed and sworn to before me, a Notary Public within and for the County and State above set out this day of ____, 20__.

Notary:

My commission expires:

Signature of Parent(s)/Guardian/Spouse:

State of

County of

Subscribed and sworn to before me, a Notary Public within and for the County and State above set out this day of ____, 20__.

Appendix H

Sample Waiver H

Study Abroad Participant Conduct Agreement

While you are abroad, you will be viewed as an unofficial ambassador of the United States in general, and _____ College in particular. You should therefore conduct yourself in a manner that befits that position, and reflects well upon the College and yourself. Standards of conduct help to ensure satisfaction with the study abroad experience. In registering to study abroad, you agree to abide by the behavior expectations outlined in this document.

General Conduct Policy

_____ College study abroad participants must adhere to the College's Student Conduct Code, specific program rules, and the laws of their host country. The College's Student Conduct Code can be found at: (webpage address)

Program Rules & Requirements

Coordinators are responsible for supervision, welfare, and behavior of participants during official program classes, travel, excursions, and events. They oversee the participant's room and board arrangements as well for the duration of the trip. They monitor each participant's conduct in relation to _____ College and other applicable rules, regulations, and standards of conduct and the laws of the host country. This supervision extends to housing requirements and reassignments, if the latter is necessary.

Participants are expected to cooperate with staff and accept responsibility for adult standards of behavior. Program coordinators have developed the following rules and requirements for study abroad participants:

1. Full Participation

Participants are expected to participate fully in the program classes, travel, excursions, and events. Failure to attend such activities and complete required assignments and tasks are grounds for dismissal.

2. *Attendance*

Participants are expected to be on time for all appointments, classes, trips, and activities. Personal activities such as buying water, snacks, and getting ATM withdrawals should be completed prior to the meeting time/trip departure time so that participants and instructors do not have to wait.

Due to safety and security issues, leaving a participant behind creates problems in certain circumstances; however, if the trip originates from the program's housing this may not be an issue. In that case, late arriving students may find that they have "missed the bus." Participants are responsible for arranging and paying for any transportation necessary to "catch up" to the group when that happens.

Coordinators can utilize the same disciplinary measures on site as they would on campus for students who miss events or who are habitually late.

3. *Rude, Aggressive, & Offensive Behavior*

_____ College will not tolerate rude, aggressive, or offensive behavior, or verbal abuse toward program coordinators, host families, other program participants, or program staff. Participants who do not maintain acceptable standards of behavior may be removed from the program.

4. *Lodging Accommodations Abroad*

Lodging may be in hotels, homestays, or a combination of the two. Participants will be assigned two in a room/homestay. Considerations for privacy and modesty are made by separating sexes. Opposite sex participants may not share rooms unless they are a married couple traveling together. Late night and overnight guests are not permitted in your hotel room or homestay under any circumstances. Violation of the lodging accommodations policy may result in removal from the program.

5. *Alcohol & Drugs*

A) Alcohol Use:

Prior to your departure, familiarize yourself with both the laws in your host country regarding alcohol and drug use AND the rules of the study abroad program.

The legal drinking age within the United States, twenty-one years of age, will be adhered to during the study abroad program. Participants under the age of twenty-one are not permitted to drink alcohol.

While you may be allowed to consume alcohol under the laws of your host country, be aware that any alcohol-related incident abroad will be treated by the College just as it would be here on campus. Cultural norms also differ among countries. If you have any questions about alcohol use in the host country, please consult your program coordinators. For participants that are of legal drinking age in the United States: Participants need to understand that the inability to handle alcohol and public drunkenness are unacceptable in any program destination. The legal consequences of public drunkenness in your host country may also be more severe than in the United States (public fines, jail time).

B) Drug Use:

Avoid any involvement with drugs and other illegal substances. _____ College study abroad participants are expressly forbidden from using drugs, regardless of whether drugs are legal in the host country. In addition, many countries have more severe punishments regarding drugs than those in America, and while abroad, you are subject to the punitive measures of your host country.

Should you be arrested on drug charges, there is nothing the College, the U.S. government, nor the U.S. embassy can do to exempt you from your host country's legal process. Bail provisions as we know them in the United States are rare in many other countries, and pretrial detention without bail is not uncommon. The principle of "innocent until proven guilty" is not a tenet of legal systems abroad.

Please see the U.S. State Department's Tips for Traveling Abroad: Special Warning about Drug Offenses Abroad at: http://travel.state.gov/travel/tips for further details.

Abuse of alcohol and use of illegal drugs and prescription drugs not prescribed to the participant are grounds for dismissal and return home at your own expense.

Failure to comply with conduct rules and requirements may result in disciplinary action. In cases of misconduct, a participant may be warned, placed on probation, academically withdrawn, or dismissed from the program as the circumstances warrant. The College reserves the right to dismiss any participant from its program for reasons of unacceptable behavior. Program coordinators reserve the right to dismiss participants at any time during the duration of the program for academic or disciplinary reasons.

In cases in which participants are dismissed from the program:

• There will be no refund to the participant.
• Dismissed participants will not be allowed to remain in program facilities (such as housing).
• Dismissed participants will not be allowed to participate in any group activities.
• Dismissed participants will be responsible for arranging and paying for their travel back to the United States.
• Dismissal from the program may also result in academic or financial consequences upon return to the College, which are solely the participant's responsibility, including the repayment of any scholarships that were awarded by the college.

Statement of Consent

I agree to adhere to all _____ College Study Abroad Rules and Regulations in regard to participant conduct during the program. I have read and received a copy of the _____ College Participant Code of Conduct. I understand that failure to comply with the College's rules and regulations can result in disciplinary action that may include: probation, academic withdrawal, and/or dismissal from the program. If such an event occurs, I agree to abide by the academic and economic sanctions that will follow.

Participant Name: _____
Participant Signature: _____ Date: _____
Witness Signature: _____ Date: _____

Appendix I

Malveaux Sample Recommended Waiver for Minimizing Risks and Liability in Study Abroad

Perilpure College
WAIVER OF RESPONSIBILITY
STUDY ABROAD AND GLOBAL STUDIES PROGRAM

I understand that I am not required by Perilpure College (the College) to participate in this particular program. I further understand that there are certain inherent risks associated with any travel abroad and with the participation in a program of this type. These inherent risks may include, but are not limited to, terrorist threats and political unrest, a lack of access to health care, potential disease native to the area, sexual assault and other crimes, dangers associated with public or private transportation, safety of the road systems and other means of transportation. These inherent risks may lead to serious injury, or even death. I am voluntarily accepting the risks associated with participating in this program and agree to cooperate with and abide by the guidelines established by the College, particularly with orientation sessions, orientation materials, and any other educational materials that warn of risks and provide guidelines on acceptable cultural behavior and understanding of foreign laws. I further acknowledge that neither the College nor any of its employees, agents, or students can absolutely guarantee my safety in every situation.

I represent that I am covered for the duration of the study abroad program and throughout by absence from the United States by a policy of comprehensive health and accident insurance with an evacuation policy that provides coverage for illness or injuries I sustain or experience while abroad. I release the College from responsibility and liability for my injuries, illness, medical bills, charges, or similar expenses.

In the event of sickness or injury, I authorize the College program instructor or primary contact at the host institution to secure whatever treatment is deemed necessary, including admission to a hospital, the administration of anesthetic, and the transfusion of blood or surgery. Furthermore, I provide the College with permission to inform parents/guardians and the College employees with a legitimate need to know in the event of sickness or injury.

I agree to release and hold harmless the College, its employees, and agents from liability and damages or losses I may suffer to my person or my property or both, which arise out of or occur during my participation in the intersession study abroad program, except if the danger or losses are caused by the gross negligence or willful misconduct of program supervisors or any other College employees.

I agree that this Waiver of Responsibility Form is to be construed in accordance with the laws of the State of _____, and that if any portion of this agreement is held invalid by a competent court of jurisdiction, the remainder of the agreement shall continue in full force and effect.

I acknowledge that I have read this entire document and that in exchange for the College's agreement to my participation in this program, I agree to its terms.

_____

Full Name of Participant (Print)
Date:

_____

Signature of Participant
Date:

_____

Signature of Parent/Guardian (if participant is under 18)*
Date:

Appendix J

Internship Agreement

INTERNSHIP AFFILIATION AGREEMENT
By and Between
_____ **UNIVERSITY BOARD OF TRUSTEES**
and

_____

This AGREEMENT is entered into this _____ DATE by and between _____ AGENCY, hereinafter referred to as **AGENCY**, and the _____ UNIVERSITY BOARD OF TRUSTEES, with its main campus located in _____, hereinafter referred to as the **UNIVERSITY**.

WHEREAS, the **UNIVERSITY** has curricula in _____, which require that enrolled students receive internship experience as a part of their professional preparation. The **UNIVERSITY** therefore wishes to enter into an agreement with the **AGENCY** whereby **UNIVERSITY** students enrolled in this curriculum may receive internship experience at the **AGENCY**. WHEREAS, the **AGENCY** has an interest in and the resources for providing such internship experience for **UNIVERSITY** students, **IT IS THEREFORE AGREED**, this Affiliation Agreement, hereinafter referred to as **AGREEMENT**, shall set forth the terms and conditions which will govern the internship experience of **UNIVERSITY** students at the **AGENCY**.

Article I: Responsibilities of the UNIVERSITY

I.01 <u>Plan and Administer</u>: Plan and administer, in consultation with the representatives of the **AGENCY**, the educational program for its students assigned to the **AGENCY**.

I.02 <u>Placement Plan</u>: Provide the **AGENCY** with its overall plan for the placement of students at the **AGENCY** at least four weeks prior to the commencement of the academic term. The plan shall include, as a minimum, the objectives of the academic plan, the number of students to be assigned, the dates and times of assignment, and the level of each student's academic preparation. The **UNIVERSITY** shall consider any modification necessary to accomplish the reasonable requirements of the **AGENCY**.

I.03 <u>Provide Names of Students</u>: Provide the names of students as soon as possible after registration for each semester, but no later than four weeks prior to the beginning of placement at the **AGENCY**.

I.04 <u>Preplacement Instruction</u>: Provide adequate preplacement instruction to each student in accordance with standards acceptable to both parties, and to present for placement only those students who have completed the preplacement instructional program to the **UNIVERSITY'S** satisfaction.

I.05 <u>Instruction of Regulations and Procedures</u>: Instruct its students submitted for placement with regard to general regulations and procedures for which the parties have agreed are necessary, including those regulations regarding:

A: Confidentiality of **AGENCY** records and information.

B: Authority of **AGENCY** staff over administrative operations.

I.06 <u>Educational Records</u>: Maintain all education records and reports relating to the educational program of its students, and to comply with all applicable statutes, rules, and regulations respecting the maintenance of and release of information from such records. The **AGENCY** shall have no responsibility regarding such records and shall refer all requests regarding such information to the **UNIVERSITY** prior to release of any such records.

I.07 <u>Health Insurance</u>: Instruct each student submitted for placement to have in force health insurance policies of a scope and with limits satisfactory to the **AGENCY**. The **UNIVERSITY** shall inform each student of the importance of maintaining in force such a policy to defray the cost of hospital and medical care that might be sustained during the period of placement. The **UNIVERSITY** shall also inform each student of the potential monetary liability the student might incur as a result of failure to maintain sufficient coverage.

Article II: Responsibilities of the AGENCY

II.01 <u>Primary Responsibility</u>: Plan and administer all aspects of internship responsibilities at facilities. The **AGENCY** has primary and ultimate responsibility for the quality of care, service, or operations, and as such, **AGENCY** staff have final responsibility, authority, and supervision over all aspects of quality of care, service, operations, and administrative operations. **UNIVERSITY** students shall at all times abide by such supervision.

II.02 <u>Supervision of Students</u>: Provide qualified supervision of students during their placement. **AGENCY** supervisory employees may, in an emergency or based upon applicable standards of operation, temporarily relieve a student from a particular assignment or require that a student leave an area or department pending a final determination of the student's future status by the parties. If such a removal occurs, the **AGENCY** agrees to promptly inform the **UNIVERSITY**.

II.03 <u>Placement of Students</u>: Cooperate with the **UNIVERSITY** in the planning and conduct of the students' placements in order that the placements may be appropriate to the **UNIVERSITY'S** educational objectives.

II.04 <u>Facilities</u>: Make available to students the use of its cafeteria, conference rooms, dressing or locker rooms, library, or any other appropriate facilities as required by the educational program. Except for charges for food consumed by the student, there should be no charge to the student for this access.

II.05 <u>Preplacement Instruction</u>: Provide the **UNIVERSITY** with all rules, regulations, procedures and information necessary for preplacement instruction no later than thirty days prior to the beginning of the internship.

II.06 <u>Release and Withdrawal of Students</u>:

a. Have the authority to refuse any student who has previously been discharged for cause, relieved of responsibilities for cause, or who would not be eligible to be employed by the **AGENCY**. The **AGENCY** shall notify the **UNIVERSITY** of its refusal to accept a student and its reasons for doing so in writing.

b. Have the authority to request the withdrawal of any student from the program for reasonable cause related to the need for maintaining an acceptable level of client services and business operations, and the **UNIVERSITY** shall immediately comply with the request. The request shall be in writing and shall state the reason for the request.

c. In the event the **UNIVERSITY** does not agree with the **AGENCY'S** refusal to accept a student or request for withdrawal, it shall provide the **AGENCY** with a written statement setting forth the reasons for any such disagreement within ten (10) working days after receipt of the written notice.

Article III: Mutual Responsibilities

III.01 <u>Refusing to Accept or Withdraw a Student</u>: In the event that either party is determined by any court or administrative agency of competent jurisdiction to have acted in an unlawful manner in refusing to accept or requesting the withdrawal of a student, the offending party shall defend, indemnify, and hold the other party harmless from any and all claims and costs arising from its unlawful act. Each party shall promptly notify the other party of any such claim, provide the other party with an opportunity to defend, and provide all reasonable assistance, except financial, in making such defense. No settlement of any such claim shall be effected without the consent of the other party.

III.02 <u>Students Serving as Employees</u>: The students assigned to this experience should be considered student interns, and may serve as employees of the **AGENCY**. As employees, they may be covered by the **AGENCY** for purposes of compensation, fringe benefits, workers' compensation, unemployment compensation, minimum wage laws, income tax withholding, social security, or any other purpose. Each student is placed with the **AGENCY** to receive a field experience as part of his or her academic curriculum; those duties performed by a student intern are performed as an employee, in fulfillment of these academic requirements and are performed under supervision. The **UNIVERSITY** shall notify each student of the contents of this paragraph.

III.03 <u>Compliance with Laws</u>: Each party agrees to comply with and to be separately responsible for compliance with all laws, including, but not limited to, employment and antidiscrimination laws, which may be applicable to their respective activities under this program. Both parties promise not to discriminate illegally in employment because of race, color, creed, religion, national origin, age, marital status, sex, height, weight, disability, veteran status, sexual orientation, or gender identity.

III.04 <u>Indemnity Provisions</u>: Each party agrees that statutory and common law theories and principles of indemnification, contribution, and equitable restitution shall govern and apply to claims, costs, actions, causes of action, losses, or expenses—including attorney fees, resulting from or caused by its actions, the actions of its employees or students, pursuant to this **AGREEMENT**.

III.05 <u>Insurance</u>: Both Parties agree to maintain Comprehensive General Liability Insurance or its equivalent that covers employees and students whenever the liability might exist. A certificate of insurance will be furnished to the other party, upon request, indicating effective coverage and liability limits.

III.06 <u>Administration</u>: The parties shall cooperate in administering this program in a manner that will tend to maximize the mutual benefit provided to the **UNIVERSITY** and **AGENCY**.

III.07 <u>Nonteaching Client</u>: No provision of this **AGREEMENT** shall prevent any client from requesting not to be a teaching client or prevent any member of the **AGENCY'S** staff from designating any client as a nonteaching client.

III.08 <u>Extension of Rights</u>: This **AGREEMENT** is intended solely for the mutual benefit of the parties hereto, and there is no intention, express or otherwise, to create any rights or interests for any party or person other than the **AGENCY** and the **UNIVERSITY**.

III.09 <u>Sole Conduct</u>: In the performance of their respective duties and obligations under this **AGREEMENT**, the **UNIVERSITY** and **AGENCY** are independent contractors, and neither is the agent, employee, or servant of the other, and each is responsible for its sole conduct.

III.10 <u>Contacts</u>: Any and all notices given under this **AGREEMENT** shall be directed to: **AGENCY: UNIVERSITY:**

_____ _____

III.11 <u>Term and Termination of Agreement</u>: This **AGREEMENT** shall terminate on the _____ day of _____. However, it may be terminated by either party upon forty-five (45) days written notice of termination, provided that the student then receiving instruction in any program shall be given an opportunity to complete the full program during that instructional period.

III.12 <u>Entire Agreement</u>: This **AGREEMENT** constitutes the entire agreement between the **AGENCY** and the **UNIVERSITY** for program specified, and all prior discussions, agreements, and understandings, whether verbal or in writing, are hereby merged into this **AGREEMENT**.

III.13 <u>Headings</u>: The headings of Articles and Sections in this document are for convenience of reference only, and are not part of this **AGREEMENT**.

III.14 <u>Changes to Agreement</u>: No amendment or modification to this **AGREEMENT**, including any amendment or modification of this paragraph, shall be effective unless in writing and signed by both parties.

IN WITNESS WHEREOF, the parties hereto have executed this **AGREEMENT** as of the day and year first above written.

UNIVERSITY: **AGENCY:**

By: By:

Name: Name:

_____

Title: Title:

_____

Dated: Dated:

_____

Appendix K

Service Learning Agreement

SERVICE LEARNING EXPERIENCE AGREEMENT
Between
_____ University Board of Trustees
and

Agency Name: _____

As the faculty member at _____ University in _____, I want to thank you for providing _____ students with service-learning opportunities at Agency: _____, hereinafter referred to as **Agency**. To assure that we are all working from the same framework, I would like to outline for you the nature of the service-learning requirements that the University places on its students and what we hope you can provide.

This agreement will be in effect from _____ until _____ and shall apply to any future students who may fulfill their service-learning requirements at the **Agency** until the agreement expires.

Responsibilities of _____ **University**:

1. Plan and administer, in consultation with the **Agency** and the student, a service-learning experience that will qualify for the intended academic experience and benefit the **Agency**.
2. Provide the **Agency** with the name(s) of student(s) to be assigned to the **Agency**.
3. Inform all students that they shall be required to abide by the rules of the **Agency**.
4. Maintain all education records and reports relating to the educational program of its students, and comply with all applicable statutes, rules, and regulations respecting the maintenance of and release of information from such records. The **Agency** shall have no responsibility regarding such records and shall refer all requests regarding such information to _____.
5. Recommend that each student have in force a health insurance policy to defray the cost of hospital or medical care that might be required during the period of the service-learning experience. _____ shall also inform each student of the potential monetary liability the student might incur as a result of failure to maintain sufficient coverage.

6. Maintain Comprehensive General Liability Insurance for all students.

Responsibilities of the **Agency**:

1. Make the final determination as to whether to accept a particular student for the service-learning experience.
2. Provide qualified supervision of each student during their service-learning experience.
3. Promptly notify the service-learning coordinator or faculty member of any inappropriate behavior on the part of the student. The **Agency** shall have the authority to request the withdrawal of any student for reasonable cause and _____ will immediately investigate and take appropriate action.
4. Provide a final evaluation of the student's work to the _____ faculty member at the end of the experience.
5. Maintain Comprehensive General Liability Insurance or its equivalent.

Signatures:

_____
Faculty Member / Date

_____
Agency / Date

_____
University / Date

Appendix L

Health Disclosure Form

Student Health Form to Study Abroad

The purpose of this form is to help health professionals to provide appropriate assistance to you should the need arise during study abroad. Mild physical or psychological disorders can become serious under the stresses of life while studying abroad. Disclosure on this form is voluntary, but if you have any past or current physical or mental health problems that might affect you during study abroad, it is important that the program be made aware of them.

The Study Abroad Office expects that, before committing to or participating in study abroad, you will evaluate your own medical history and, in consultation with your health care provider(s), determine if study abroad is appropriate for you. If you require special accommodations, make your needs known to the Study Abroad Office in a timely way. Otherwise, it may delay your participation in study abroad until reasonable accommodations or adjustments can be determined. Note that laws abroad regarding access for those with physical disabilities may differ from laws in the United States, and there is no guarantee that all individual needs and circumstances can be met.

The information that you provide below will remain confidential and will be shared with program staff, faculty, or appropriate professionals only as it relates to your health and safety. **This information does not affect your admission to the study abroad program.**

As you complete this form, please answer "N/A" if not applicable. Attach additional sheets if necessary.

STUDENT INFORMATION	
NAME	[COLLEGE] ID #
DATE OF BIRTH (MM/DD/YY)	**PROGRAM AND TERM ABROAD**

Do you have any allergies? ☐ Yes ☐ No *If yes, please explain.*	
Do you have any dietary (food) restrictions? ☐ Yes ☐ No *If yes, please explain.*	

Figure 10.1.

Appendix M

Application for Semester or Year-Long Study Abroad

_____ College Application for Semester or Year-Long Study Abroad

The Application for Semester or Year-Long Study Abroad form needs to be submitted to the Study Abroad Office no later than _____ for fall study abroad, _____ for spring study abroad, and _____ for summer session, in order to allow ample time for evaluation and program approval by an academic advisor, program coordinator, and transcript evaluator.

Instructions:

1. Complete the top portion of the form.
2. Fill out the courses to be taken at the foreign institution portion if you already have an institution in mind.
3. You will be contacted by the Study Abroad advisor on your campus.

Study Abroad Advisors:
_____ (Coordinator), _____ Campus;
_____ (Campus Advisor), _____ Campus;

Student Name: _____
(Print) Last Name First Name Middle Initial / Signature
Phone: _____
Email: _____
Student ID Number: _____
Date: _____
Semester for Study Abroad: _____
Overall Earned Credits at _____
Overall GPA (grade point average must be 2.5 or higher): _____
U.S. Host Institution: _____
Country: _____
Institution Abroad: _____
Consortium of the Institution Abroad: _____

Will you be applying for Financial Aid? _____ Yes _____No

Permission to enroll in another Institution (must be a full time student enrolled in twelve or more

semester hours)

Courses to be taken at the Foreign Institution / Equivalent to be determined

1. _____

2. _____

3. _____

4. _____

5. _____

Academic Advisor Review of Course Selections:

_____

Signature Date

Study Abroad Advisor Approval:

_____

Signature Date

Registrar (or Designee) Approval:

_____

Signature Date

References

11 ways to prevent identity theft while traveling. (2015). *IndependentTraveler.com*. Retrieved fromhttp://www. independenttraveler.com/travel-tips/travelers-ed/11-ways-to-prevent-identity-theft-while-traveling.

Ability Info. (2015). Your disability help and information site. Retrieved from. http://abilityinfo.com/.

Allan, C. C., Gooding, J. L., Jercinovic, M., & Keil, K. (1980, September 19). Altered basaltic glass: A terrestrial analog to the soil of Mars. Department of Geology and Institute of Meteoritics, University of New Mexico. Retrieved fromhttp://www.mars.asu.edu/christensen/classdocs/Allen_Alteredbas_icarus_81.pdf.

Allies Against Slavery. (2014–2015). Around the world and around the corner slavery still exists. Retrieved fromhttp://www.alliesagainstslavery.org/slavery.

Astin, A. W. (1984). Student involvement: A developmental theory for higher education. *Journal of College Student Personnel 25*, 297–308.

Astin, A. W. et al. (2002). *The American freshman: Thirty year trends.* Los Angeles: Higher Education Research Institute, University of California, Los Angeles.

Bagri, N. T., & Varma, V. (2013, June 4). American tourist gang-raped in Manali, police say. *New York Times*. Retrieved fromhttp://india.blogs.nytimes.com/2013/06/04/american-tourist-gang-raped-in-manali-police-say/.

Bates, J. (1997). *The effects of study abroad on undergraduates in an honors international program. Dissertation Abstracts International 58*, 8, 4162A. (UMI No. 2637042). Retrieved from Dissertations & Theses database.

BBC News. (2015, December 9). Paris Attacks: What Happened on the Night. Retrieved from www.bbc.com/news/ world-europe-34818994.

Boorstein, M., & Wright, S. W. (1998). Fears about safety—and lawsuits—plague study abroad programs. *Community College Week 10*, 12.

Buckley, T. J. (1997, September 12). India crash wake up call for schools and parents. *USA Today*, p. A1.

Carlson, J. S., Burn, B., Useem, J., & Yachimowicz, D. (1990). *Study abroad: The experience of American undergraduates.* New York: Greenwood Press.

Carr, J. W., & Summerfield, E. (1995). *Forms of travel: Essential documents, letters and flyers for study abroad advisors.* Pennsylvania: NAFSA Publishers.

Chen, D. (1998, January 19). 5 from Md. College sexually assaulted on Guatemala trip. *New York Times*. Retrieved fromhttp://www.nytimes.com/1998/01/19/us/5-from-md-college-sexually-assaulted-on-guatemala-trip.html.

Chickering, A., & Reisser, L. (1993). *Education and identity.* San Francisco: Jossey-Bass.

Children's TherAplay. (2010–2013). Hippotherapy. The Children's TherAplay Foundation, Inc. Retrieved fromhttp://www.childrenstheraplay.org/hippotherapy.

Clark, C. (2015, April 13). The serious cyber security threat that could hurt hotels. *Leading Meeting Professionals: Professional Convention Management Association.* Retrieved fromhttp://www.pcma.org/news/news-landing/ 2015/04/13/the-serious-cyber-security-threat-that-could-hurt-hotels -.

Dannells, M. (1997). From discipline to development: Rethinking student conduct in higher education. *ASHE-ERIC Higher Ed. Report 25*, 2.

DisabledTravelers.com. (2015). Airline travel information. Retrieved fromhttp://www.disabledtravelers.com/ airlines.htm.

Donohue, D., & Altaf, S. (2012, May). Learn by doing: Expanding international internships/work abroad opportunities for U.S. STEM students—A briefing paper from IIE's Center for Academic Mobility Research. Retrieved fromhttp://www.iie.org/Research-and-Publications/Publications-and-Reports/IIE-Bookstore/Learn-by-Doing.

Durso, Christopher. (2014, December 1). Cyber-security basics. Professional Convention Management Association. Retrieved fromhttp://www.pcmaconvene.org/departments/working-smarter/cyber-security-basics/.

Emerging Horizons. (2015). Travel information for wheelchair users and slow walkers.http://emerginghorizons.com.

Evans, R. B. (1991). "A stranger in a strange land": Responsibility and liability for students enrolled in foreign-study programs. *Journal of College and University Law 18*, 2.

Father of U.Va. student who died studying abroad files lawsuit. (2013, November 2). *Richmond Times-Dispatch.* Retrieved fromhttp://www.richmond.com/news/virginia/article_d966a9cb-da4f-5bb6-ba03-198c6bfc7cc7.html.

Federal Bureau of Investigation. (2015). Definitions of terrorism in the U.S. Code. Retrieved fromhttps://www.fbi.gov/about-us/investigate/terrorism/terrorism-definition.

Gehring, D. (1993). Understanding legal constraints on practice. In M. J. Barr & Associates (Eds.), *The handbook of student affairs administration* (pp. 274–99). San Francisco: Jossey-Bass.

Guernsey, L. (1997, April 11). A lawsuit raises difficult questions about liability and study-abroad programs. *Chronicle of Higher Education 43*, 31, p. A37, A39.

Halleck, Thomas. (2015, March 4). Mandarin Oriental hacked: Luxury hotel chain admits credit card numbers were stolen in security breach. *International Business Times.* Retrieved fromhttp://www.ibtimes.com/mandarin-oriental-hacked-luxury-hotel-chain-admits-credit-card-numbers-were-stolen-1836574.

Harris, Shane. (2015, November 2014). A 26-year-old woman is ISIS's last American hostage. *The Daily Beast.* Retrieved fromhttp://www.thedailybeast.com/articles/2014/11/16/a-26-year-old-woman-is-isis-s-last-american-hostage.html.

Hart, P., & Thomas M. A. (2005, June 9). Pitt to end pact with Semester at Sea program. *University Times: University of Pittsburgh.* Retrieved fromhttp://www.utimes.pitt.edu/?p=942.

Heller, Matthew. (2009, September 30). Woman blames study abroad program for rape in Mali. *On.Point—A new take on legal news.* Retrieved fromhttp://www.onpointnews.com/NEWS/Woman-Blames-Study-Abroad-Program-for-Rape-in-Mali.html.

Inc. 5000. (2014). Royce leather collection. Retrieved fromhttp://www.royceleathergifts.com/UI/RFID204-5-ROYCE-LEATHER-DEBOSSED-RFID-BLOCKING-PASSPORT-JACKET.aspx?ptype=3&pid=342.

Institute of International Education. (2000–2013). Open Doors data U.S. study abroad: Student profile. Retrieved fromhttp://www.iie.org/Research-and-Publications/Open-Doors/Data/US-Study-Abroad/Student-Profile/2000-13.

Institute of International Education. (2014). Press release Open Doors 2014: International students in the United States and study abroad by American students are at all-time high. Retrieved fromhttp://www.iie.org/Who-We-Are/News-and-Events/Press-Center/Press-Releases/2014/2014-11-17-Open-Doors-Data.

Institute of International Education. (2015). Press release: Study abroad by U.S. students slowed in 2008/09 with more students going to less traditional destinations. Retrieved fromhttp://www.iie.org/Who-We-Are/News-and-Events/Press-Center/Press-Releases/2010/2010-11-15-Open-Doors-US-Study-Abroad.

Kaplin, W. A., & Lee, B. A. (1997). *A legal guide for student affairs professionals.* San Francisco: Jossey-Bass.

Kaplin, W. A., & Lee, B. A. (2011). *The law of higher education.* San Francisco: Jossey-Bass.

Kast, R. (1997). In loco parentis and the "reasonable person." *International Educator 7*, 1.

Katz, E. (2007, September–October). *Education abroad: Students with disabilities studying abroad.* Retrieved fromhttp://www.nafsa.org/_/File/_/educationabroad_iesept_oct.pdf.

Krav Maga Worldwide. (2015). Self-defense. Retrieved fromhttp://www.kravmaga.com/programs/self-defense/.

Kuh, G. D., Kinzie, J., Schuh, J. H., & Whitt, E. J., & Associates. (2005). *Student success in college: Creating conditions that matter.* San Francisco: Jossey-Bass.

Kuh, G. D., Schuh, J. C., Whitt, E. J., Andreas, R. E., Lyons, J. W., Strange, C. C., Krehbiel, L. E., & MacKay, K. A. (1991). *Involving colleges: Successful approaches to fostering student learning and development outside the classroom.* San Francisco: Jossey-Bass.

LaFranchi, H. (2003, August 19). Why more students are studying abroad. *Christian Science Monitor*, p. 3.

Lawsuit filed against SMC. (2001, February 6). *St. Mary's College of Maryland: The Point News.* Retrieved fromhttp://smcm.cdmhost.com/cdm/ref/collection/SMCM/id/27667.

LegalMatch Law Library. (2014). Exculpatory Clauses. Retrieved fromhttp://www.legalmatch.com/law-library/article/exculpatory-clauses.html.

Lyngaas, Sean. (2015, April 1). Obama declares foreign cyber threats a "national emergency." *Business of Federal Technology.* Retrieved fromhttp://fcw.com/articles/2015/04/01/obama-cyber-threats.aspx.

Marklein, M. B. (2009, May 27). Students studying abroad face dangers with little oversight. *USA Today.* Retrieved fromhttp://usatoday30.usatoday.com/news/education/2009-05-27-study-abroad-main_N.htm.

Marklein, M. B. (2012, December 4). Death highlights risks of study abroad programs. *USA Today.* Retrieved from http://www.usatoday.com/story/news/nation/2012/12/03/study-abroad-safety/1742503/.

McCabe, L. (1994). The development of a global perspective during participation in semester-at-sea: A comparative global education program. *Educational Review 46*, 275–86.

McClenney, K. M. (2004). Redefining the quality in community colleges: Focusing on good educational practice. *Change 36*, 6, 16–21.

McMurtrie, B. (2002, August 2). Maryland college settles lawsuit. *Chronicle of Higher Education*, p. A37.

Medina-Lopez-Portillo, A. (2004). *College students' intercultural sensitivity development as a result of their studying abroad: A comparative description of two types of study abroad programs.* Doctoral dissertation, University of Maryland, College Park, 2004. Retrieved from ProQuest Digital Dissertations. (AAT 3137038)

Miller, A. D. (2015, August 7). Reassessing the threat from terrorism—Abroad and at home. *Wall Street Journal—Washington Wire*. Dow Jones & Company. Retrieved fromhttp://blogs.wsj.com/washwire/2015/08/07/reassessing-the-threat-from-terrorism-abroad-and-at-home/.

Mitzel, H. (1982). International education. In *Encyclopedia of educational research* (Vol. 2, pp. 945–58). New York: McGraw-Hill.

Mobility International USA. (2015). Advancing disability rights and leadership globally. Retrieved fromhttp://www.miusa.org.

Moran, L., & Ortiz, E. (2013, April 2). U.S. tourist in Brazil kidnapped, robbed and raped in front of boyfriend on bus during 6-hour nightmare: Police. *New York Daily News*. Retrieved fromhttp://www.nydailynews.com/news/crime/u-s-student-kidnapped-raped-bus-brazil-article-1.1305356.

NACUANOTES. (2012, April 26). Federal disability laws: Do they translate to study abroad programs? Retrieved fromhttp://www.calstate.edu/gc/documents/NACUANOTES10.pdf.

National Center for Education Statistics. (2014, October). Profile of undergraduate students: 2011–2012. U.S. Department of Education Institute of Education Sciences. Retrieved fromhttps://nces.ed.gov/pubsearch/pubsinfo.asp?pubid=2015167.

Nolting, J., Johnson, M., & Matherly, C. (2005). WIVA: Work abroad and international careers. In Joseph L. Brockington, William W. Hoffa, Patricia C. Martin (Eds.), *NAFSA's Guide to Education Abroad for Advisers and Administrators* (3rd Ed.). Washington, DC: NAFSA: Association of International Educators.

Onyanga-Omara, J. (2015, January 7). Timeline: Terror attacks in Europe over the years. *USA Today*. Retrieved fromhttp://www.usatoday.com/story/news/world/2015/01/07/terror-attacks-europe/21384069/.

Partlow, J. (2014, August 15). Kidnappings in Mexico surge to the highest number on record. *Washington Post*. Retrieved from https://www.washingtonpost.com/world/the_americas/kidnappings-in-mexico-surge-to-the-highest-number-on-record/2014/08/15/3f8ee2d2-1e6e-11e4-82f9-2cd6fa8da5c4_story.html.

Pascarella, E. T., & Terenzini, P. T. (2005). *How college affects students: Volume 2, a third decade of research*. San Francisco: Jossey-Bass.

Passport Health. (2015). Travel immunizations/travel health. Retrieved fromhttps://www.passporthealthusa.com.

Pazniokas, M. (1997, March 27). Woman sues college, says she was raped while studying abroad. *Hartford Courant*. Retrieved fromhttp://articles.courant.com/1997-03-27/news/9703270318_1_earlham-college-sexual-harassment-declaratory.

Pearson, D. R., & Beckham, J. C. (2005). Negligent liability issues involving colleges and students: Balancing the risks and benefits of expanded programs and heightened supervision. *Student Affairs Administrators in Higher Education (NAPSA) Journal 42*, 4, 4.

Pickert, S. M. (1992). *Preparing for a global community: Achieving an international perspective in higher education*. Washington, DC: Clearinghouse on Higher Education.

Rape case threat to colleges. (1997, May 9). *The Times Higher Education*. Retrieved fromhttps://www.timeshighereducation.com/news/rape-case-threat-to-colleges/100898.article.

Reed, T., & Stewart, S. (2013, December 26). Mexico: Tactical adaptions in virtual kidnapping. *Security Weekly*. Retrieved fromhttps://www.stratfor.com/weekly/mexico-tactical-adaptations-virtual-kidnapping.

Rhodes, G. M., & Aalberts, R. J. (1994, January/February). Liability and study abroad: "Prudent" policies and procedures are the best insurance. *Transitions Abroad*, 65–67.

Rubin, A. M. (1996, May 10). Making it safer to study abroad. *Chronicle of Higher Education*, p. A49.

Selingo, J. (2000, May 5). Florida court says colleges may be liable for off-campus injuries. *Chronicle of Higher Education*, p. A39.

Semester at Sea—A deadly program (2011). Cherese Mari Laulhere Foundation. Retrieved fromhttp://cherese.org/semester-at-sea.html.

Sherry, M. K., Mossallam, M., Mulligan, M., Hyder, A. A., & Bishai, D. (2013, December 3). Rates of intentionally caused and road crash deaths of US citizens abroad. Group.bmj.com. Retrieved fromhttp://www.jhsph.edu/research/centers-and-institutes/johns-hopkins-center-for-injury-research-and-policy/publications_resources/Deaths of US travelelers Inj Prev-2013-Sherry-injuryprev-2013-040923.pdf.

Shoichet, C., Hanna, J., & Brown, P. (2015, February 11). American ISIS hostage Kayla Mueller dead, family says. *Cable News Network (CNN)*. Retrieved fromhttp://www.cnn.com/2015/02/10/world/isis-hostage-mueller/.

Slattery v. Antioch Education Abroad et al.: Docket Alarm, Inc. (2012–2015). Retrieved fromhttps://www.docketalarm.com/cases/Ohio_Southern_District_Court/3--10-cv-00010/Slattery_v._Antioch_Education_Abroad_et_al/.

Soneson, H. M. (2009). Education abroad advising to students with disabilities. NAFSA: Association of International Educators. Retrieved fromhttp://www.nafsa.org/uploadedFiles/NAFSA_Home/Resource_Library_Assets/Publications_Library/AdvisEAstudDis.pdf.

Syracuse University Pan Am Flight 103/Lockerbie air disaster archives. (2010). Syracuse University. Retrieved fromhttp://archives.syr.edu/panam/.

Twain, Mark. (1869). *The innocents abroad or the new pilgrims' progress*. Connecticut: American Publishing Company. Retrieved from https://www.gutenberg.org/files/3176/3176-h/3176-h.htm.

UNHCR: The UN Refugee Agency. (2015). Facts and figures about refugees. *The United Nations High Commissioner for Refugees*. Retrieved fromhttp://www.unhcr.org.uk/about-us/key-facts-and-figures.html.

University of Colorado, Boulder. (2015). The Office of International Education's policy in case of political or social unrest, terrorism, and the threat of war. Retrieved fromhttp://studyabroad.colorado.edu/index.cfm?FuseAction= Abroad.ViewLink&Link_ID=7D547AD8-B6BF-5897-E81FB545DEFB9202.

U.S. Department of Education. (2015). Know your rights: Title IX prohibits sexual harassment and sexual violence where you go to school. Washington, DC: U.S. Department of Education Office for Civil Rights. Retrieved fromhttp://www2.ed.gov/about/offices/list/ocr/docs/title-ix-rights-201104.pdf.

U.S. Department of Education, National Center for Education Statistics. (2006). *Profile of undergraduates in U.S. postsecondary education institutions: 2003–04* (NCES 2006-184). Washington, DC: U.S. Department of Education. Retrieved fromhttp://nces.ed.gov/fastfacts/display.asp?id=60.

U.S. Department of Health and Human Services: Office for Civil Rights. (2006). Fact sheet: Your rights under Section 504 of the Rehabilitation Act. Washington, DC: U.S. Department of Health and Human Services. Retrieved fromhttp://www.hhs.gov/ocr/civilrights/resources/factsheets/504.pdf.

U.S. Department of Labor. (2015). Disability resources: Americans with Disabilities Act. Washington, DC: U.S. Department of Labor. Retrieved fromhttp://www.dol.gov/dol/topic/disability/ada.htm.

U.S. Department of State—Bureau of Consular Affairs. Retrieved fromhttp://travel.state.gov/content/passports/english/country/guatemala.html.

U.S. Department of State (2015). U.S. passports & international travel.

Van Der Werf, M. (2007, June 6). A wide world of risk. *Chronicle of Higher Education 53*, 30, p. A1.

Vigliotti, J., & Givens, A. (2014, September 22). I-team: Parents demand transparency from college study abroad programs after sons' deaths. Retrieved fromhttp://www.nbcnewyork.com/news/local/Study-Abroad-Program-Wrongful-Death-Regulation-Investigation-Thackurdeen-275787101.html.

Wagner, M. (2014, October 11). Americans abroad at "high risk" of ISIS kidnappings, terrorist attacks, U.S. warns. *Daily News*. Retrieved fromhttp://www.nydailynews.com/news/national/americans-high-risk-isis-kidnappings-u-s-article-1.1971063.

White House Office of the Press Secretary. (2015, February 25). FACT SHEET: Cyber threat intelligence integration center. Retrieved fromhttps://www.whitehouse.gov/the-press-office/2015/02/25/fact-sheet-cyber-threat-intelligence-integration-center.

Cases Cited

Bird v. Lewis & Clark College, 104 F. Supp. 2d 1271 (D. Or. 2000) *aff'd*, 303 F.3d 1015 (9th Cir. 2002).

Bird v. Lewis & Clark College, 303 F.3d 1015 (9th Cir. 2002).

Bloss v. University of Minnesota Board of Regents, 590 N.W.2d 661 (Minn. Ct. App. 1999).

Earlham College v. Eisenberg, No. IP97-C-0592-M/S (S.D. Ind. Sept. 10, 1998).

Fay v. Thiel College, 55 Pa. D. & C.4th 353 (Com. Pl. 2001).

Furrh v. Arizona Board of Regents, 676 P.2d 1141 (Ariz. Ct. App. 1983).

King v. Board of Control of Eastern Michigan University, 221 F. Supp. 2d 783 (E.D. Mich. 2002).

Nova Southeastern University v. Gross, 758 So. 2d 86 (Fla. 2000).

Paneno v. Centres for Academic Programmes Abroad Ltd., 13 Cal. Rptr. 3d 759 (Cal. Ct. App. 2004).

Schulman v. Institute for Seaboard Education, No. 15-11689 (S.D. Fla. Apr. 20, 2015), *aff'd per curiam*, No. 11-11689, 2015 WL 4896597, at *9 (11th Cir. Aug. 18, 2015).

Thackurdeen v. Duke University, 2014 WL 3886037 (S.D.N.Y. Aug. 8, 2014).

OTHER NOTABLE COMPLAINTS AND LAWSUITS

Arizona State Univ., No. 08-01-204, 22 NDLR 239 (Dec. 3, 2001)
India Iguana Case (1994)
Radford University in the Bahamas Program (1996)
St. Mary's College Guatemala Program (2001)
University of Florida Bolivia Program (1996)
University of Pittsburgh Semester at Sea Program in India (1997)
Westmont College Costa Rica Program (1996)

About the Author

Gregory F. Malveaux, PhD, is a professor at Montgomery College and has been a study abroad coordinator and international education director in higher education for over a decade and a half. He has traversed over sixty countries and has led student, faculty and community-based study abroad programs to Africa, Asia, Central America, South America, and Europe. His passion to be a global citizen led him to pursue overseas studies in Africa, teach ESOL throughout Southeast Asia, Chair the English and U.S. Business Department at Nation University (formally known as Yonok University) in Thailand, and serve as a study abroad specialist in American higher education. He is dedicated to cultivating lifelong service learning and safe overseas opportunities for all.